IMAGES
of America

CASS COUNTY

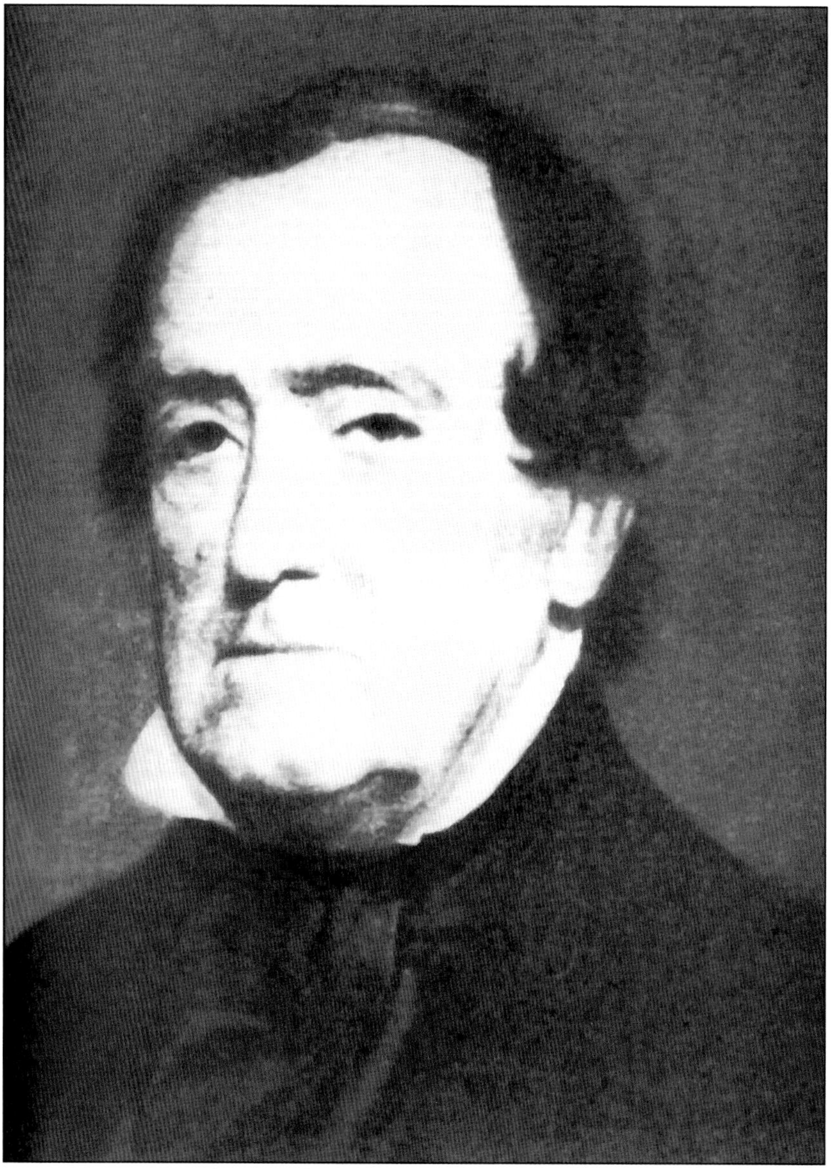

Naming states, counties, and towns after a popular or historic personage is a common practice. Cass County was named for Lewis Cass, an American lawyer and statesman. Cass had a distinguished career starting with his service in the War of 1812. He rose to the rank of brigadier general. In 1813, Cass was appointed to the post of governor of the Michigan Territory. He remained in that office until 1831, when he left to serve as secretary of war in the cabinet of Pres. Andrew Jackson. In 1845, following an assignment as ambassador to France, Cass was elected as the United States senator from Michigan. He was the Democratic nominee for president in 1848. In 1857, Cass accepted his last appointment to serve as secretary of state in the cabinet of Pres. James Buchanan. (Courtesy of the Cass County Museum in Griswold.)

On the Cover: The Spanish American War Veterans from southwest Iowa held a reunion north of Griswold in 1901. In 1905, the group merged with the national organization, the United Spanish War Veterans. (Courtesy of the Cass County Museum in Griswold.)

IMAGES
of America

CASS COUNTY

Lila Hoogeveen and Shiona Putnam

ARCADIA
PUBLISHING

ISBN 978-0-7385-8318-1

Published by Arcadia Publishing
Charleston, South Carolina

Printed in the United States of America

Library of Congress Control Number: 2011931579

For all general information, please contact Arcadia Publishing:
Telephone 843-853-2070
Fax 843-853-0044
E-mail sales@arcadiapublishing.com
For customer service and orders:
Toll-Free 1-888-313-2665

Visit us on the Internet at www.arcadiapublishing.com

This book is dedicated to the visionary men and women who helped make Cass County what it is today and to Jay and Jerry for their unwavering support and encouragement.

Contents

ACKNOWLEDGMENTS

With a plethora of photographs, letters, documents, newspaper accounts, history books, personal interviews, and family archives, it was most difficult to arrive at a decision as to what to include in the prescribed number of pages allotted. We wish to thank all those who so willingly shared their treasures and apologize for not being able to include many more. The following individuals, for a variety of reasons, were invaluable to the creation of this book: Raymond Cousins, Donna Woodward, Dana Kunze, Nadine King, Deb Herbert, Roger Steffens, Robert Camblin, Philip and Trena Chintz, Marge Sothman, Roland and Sandi Landsness, Margaret Slepsky, Richard and Pat MacCauley, Jim Carey, Kenner Baxter, Neoma Ridlen, Rosemary Broderius, Randall Baier, Maxine Christensen, Linda Sims, Linda Harms, Norma Miller, Vickie Christensen, Helen Lary, Dale Mauk, Royal Bierbaum, Don Steinbeck, Gene Sunderman, Kenny Robberts, Joy Pelzer, Verlain and Grace Rathkamp, Sherry England, Ron Schroeder, Tracy Sothman, Don Landon, Jo Ann Gerlock, Don Curry, Phyllis Stakey, Marjorie Spies Benson, Roberta Weppler, Robert Leach, and Dick Legg. Thanks also to Janet Reed and the *Griswold American*, the *Atlantic News Telegraph*, the Griswold United Methodist Church, the Atlantic Library, the Anita Library, the Cass County Museum, the Atlantic Chamber of Commerce, the Library Archives at the State Historical Society of Iowa in Des Moines, and to Ted Gerstle of Arcadia Publishing. Special thanks goes to Norma Landon, whose technical support and encouragement was invaluable and deeply appreciated, and to Kim Hoogeveen, for editing. Finally, to our husbands, Jerry and Jay, thank you for your love and encouragement and for all the spur-of-the-moment information, research, and assistance whenever requested. Unless otherwise noted, images are courtesy of the Cass County Museum.

INTRODUCTION

The Swiss educator Johann Heinrich Pestalozzi believed that learning can best be accomplished through the active use of the senses. He claimed that one should not teach with words when one can teach through seeing and doing. This book adheres to his philosophy; it focuses on making history visible through the use of vintage photographs that tell the story of an age, the story of the growth of a county, and the story of a proud and triumphant people.

The Chippewa, Ottawa, and Potawatomi Indian tribes were granted new lands in 1833 that included Cass County. It was the Potawatomi who occupied the land that is now Cass County and established their principal village, which later became known as Indiantown, at a point just west of the current town of Lewis. They named their village Mi-au-mise, meaning "the young Miami," after a favorite chief. Most of the Potawatomi left the area by 1846 after signing another treaty with the United States government; only a few stragglers were left by 1847.

Mormon refugees from Nauvoo, Illinois, found temporary refuge in the largely deserted Indian village when they arrived with their families in 1846. Barely surviving but living peacefully with the few remaining Potawatomi, about 20 Mormon families suffered through the difficult winter of 1846–1847. In the spring, they planted corn for themselves and for their stock. Several Mormon families remained at Indiantown for five or six years, and as late as 1851, they held a baptism for 15 persons in the Nishnabotna River. They set up a post office at Cold Springs, and mail was received weekly from the larger Mormon settlement at Kanesville, now known as Council Bluffs. In 1852, the last of the Mormons left Cass County to continue their trek to the Great Salt Basin.

Alfred North Whitehead writes in his *Dialogues*, "The vitality of thought is in adventure. Ideas won't keep . . . When the idea is new, its custodians have fervor, live for it, and, if need be, die for it." He could well be describing the hearty breed of men and women who settled and tamed the fertile prairies of Cass County, for they were willing to live or die in the struggle for this achievement.

These pioneers shared qualities that were integral to their success; most were visionaries, gamblers, and loners. They also possessed self-reliance, courage, and relentless optimism. Most did not set out to be the trailblazers they became; hopeful of finding prosperity, they set out to build a new life. They sought a place where the rapidly expanding restraints of government and society that restricted their individuality and freedom were not yet entrenched.

These adventurers followed the narrow, winding Indian trails searching for sites that showed the promise of two resources necessary for the successful establishment of a home in the wilderness: abundant water and timber. As one man settled, another came, and they established a practice that is still evident in Cass County today, that of extending help to a neighbor with no expectation of anything in return. The few settlers soon became many, and families banded together to establish a place of worship, a place to educate their children, and a place where they could trade and barter for needed goods and services. Business people arrived, and the need for hotels, livery stables, grocery and dry goods stores, blacksmiths, and the ubiquitous town saloon, as well as other accoutrements of a budding society, became evident.

Not every community flourished and survived. Cass County is peppered with ghost towns that now exist only via historical chronicles, like Cold Springs, Indiantown, Iranistan, Galion, Grove City, Fletchers Chapel, Hedges Grove, Edna, Newlons Grove, Reno, Turkey Grove, Whitneyville, Wakefield, Lura, Cass Center, Marker, Dewey, Gurley, McDill, Pymosa, and Lorah.

Cass County had its share of hearty individuals. Listed below are the first permanent white settlers in the 16 townships that comprise Cass County:

1. Cass: Vincent Matthew Conrad (1850) and Jeremiah Bradshaw (1851)
2. Union: Peter Hedges (1850) and Cyrus Newton (1858)
3. Benton: William Hamlin (1851) and Robert Stansbury (1853)
4. Washington: George Reeves (1851) and Thomas Coon (1852)
5. Brighton: Victor Bradshaw (1851) and Thomas Meredith (1855)
6. Pymosa: James L. Byrd (1852) and James Kincaid (1852)
7. Grove: Robert D. McGeehon (1852) and George Shannon (1852)
8. Edna: William S. Townsend (1852) and Branch Miller (1853)
9. Grant: Dr. Gershom S. Morrison (1853) and Meredith Rowland (1856)
10. Franklin: Jesse Eller (1854) and Peter Kanawyer (1854)
11. Bear Grove: Orso Baldwin (1855) and H.B. Roselle (1858)
12. Pleasant: William Baughman (1855) and Samuel Stetler (1862)
13. Noble: John Rose (1855) and Melton Smith (1857)
14. Lincoln: William Thompson (1856) and John Wogan (1856)
15. Victoria: William E. Johnson (1857) and Reverend Asa Weldon (1857)
16. Massena: Franklin H. Whitney (1858) and Eseck Whitney (1858)

Much is owed to the men and women who settled Cass County. This book strives to keep alive their stories of sacrifice and courage—ingredients that were needed to establish the life they sought. Today's residents enjoy the fruits of their early endeavors and have the opportunity to appreciate and continue the spirit with which those triumphs were achieved.

This book includes engravings from *A.T. Andreas' Illustrated Historical Atlas of the State of Iowa*, published in 1875. This unique volume has its own interesting story. Alfred T. Andreas moved from New York City to Iowa in 1857. He enlisted in the Union Army during the Civil War and quickly rose from the rank of private to that of captain and quartermaster for General Sherman. He served in that capacity during Sherman's famous March to the Sea. At the close of the war, Andreas settled in Davenport, where he married Sophia Lyter. Following the dismal failure of an ice-skating rink venture, Andreas turned his indefatigable energy to a new idea, that of producing large township maps bound into a book format. He planned to devote space to sketches of farms and biographical information on farmers and businessmen. In 1873, he set up business in Chicago at the Lakeside Building, which had been designed especially for the printing business and atlases in particular.

In 1875, he published his atlas that was the most monumental history of Iowa to that date. The exquisite steel engravings were rendered from sketches made by a group of artists sent out by Andreas to record the farms and businesses of Cass County and the state of Iowa. This book was the largest publication ever issued in one addition, absorbing 122 tons of supersized calendared paper and employing the services of 300 men for an average of 16 months.

One

In the Beginning

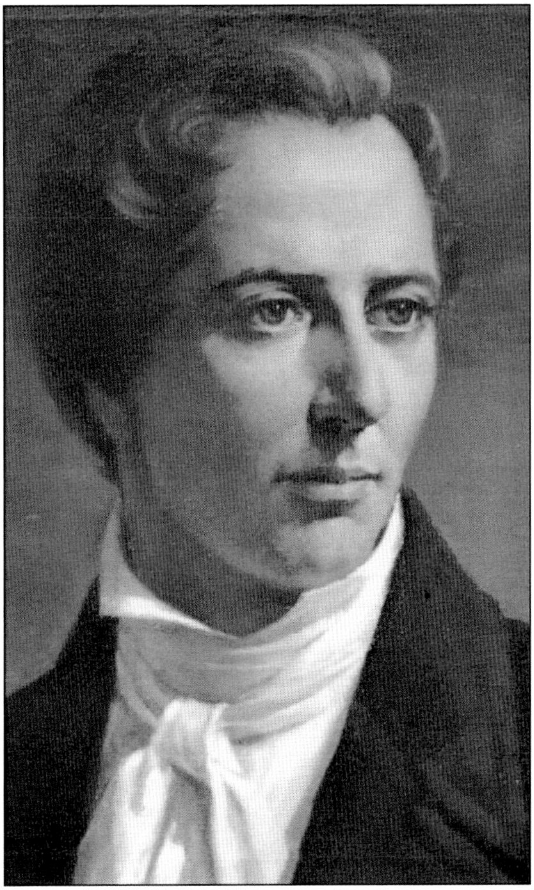

In 1830, Joseph Smith Jr. founded the Mormon Church. The Mormons met with religious persecution and were harried from New York to Nauvoo, Illinois, where they built a thriving city. Some of their religious practices and their obvious prosperity gave offense to some people. Smith, mayor of Nauvoo, ordered the destruction of a newspaper hostile to his sect; this action brought about his arrest. He was jailed at Carthage, Illinois. While there, an angry mob stormed the jail, and Smith was killed.

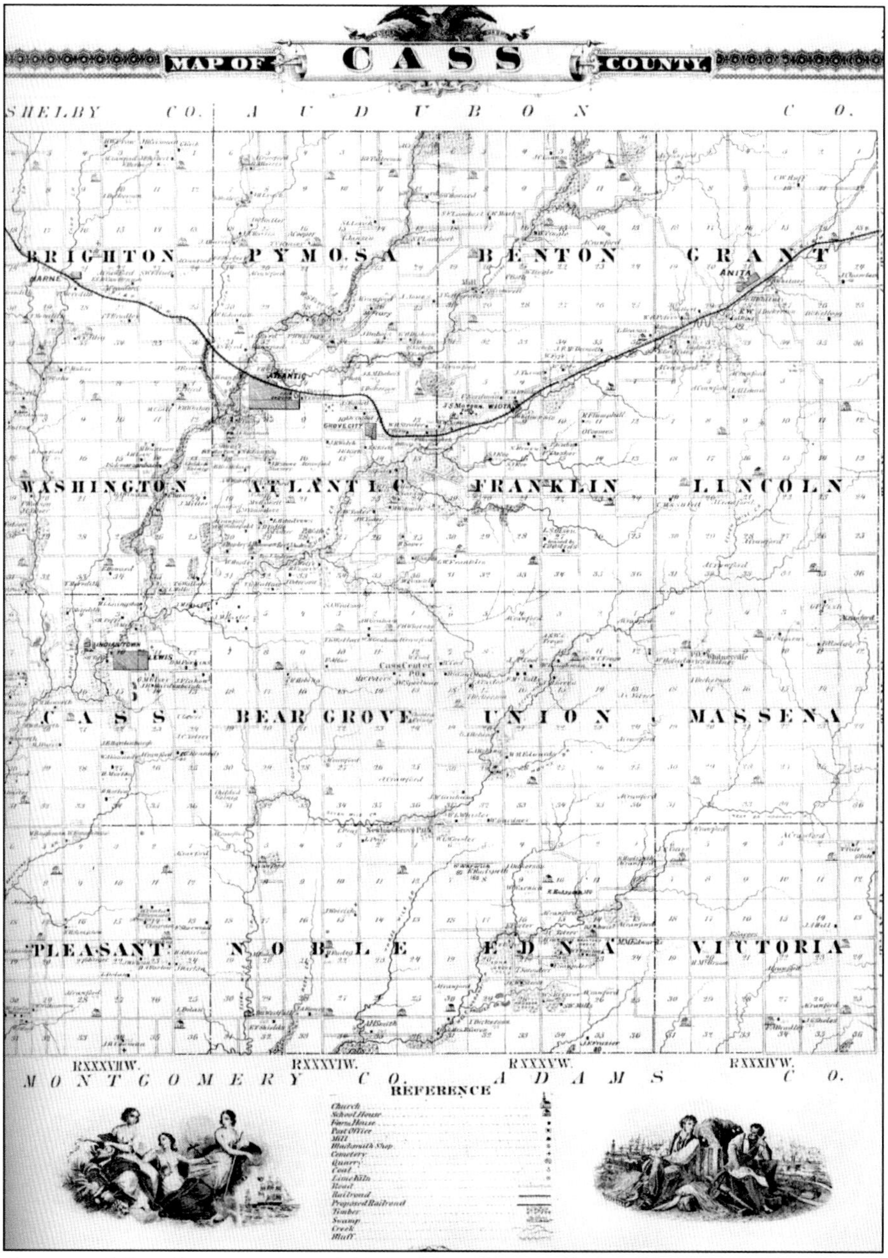

This plat map of Cass County is from A.T. Andreas' *Illustrated Historical Atlas of the State of Iowa*. When the atlas was published, Andreas said, "We send forth our work into the busy centers of trade and commerce; into the workshops of the industrial classes; into the counting houses of merchants and manufacturers; into the county offices, schools, academies, and colleges; and into thousands of families in the young, prosperous, and enlightened Commonwealth of Iowa, confidently believing that it will be received as the most complete and valuable compendium of state information." According to information from William J. Petersen of the Office of Superintendent, State Historical Society of Iowa, "Over the years the Andreas volume has been consulted more frequently than any other book in the rich collection of almost 100,000 volumes in the State Historical Society of Iowa Library."

Mahaska was a handsome warrior chief of the Ioway. In 1824, he went to Washington, DC, to meet the "Great White Father," Pres. James Monroe. Rantchewaime, his seventh and favorite wife, accompanied him, and Easterners found her to be beautiful and intelligent. Artist C.B. King painted these portraits. Mahaska promised to live in peace and signed a treaty to that effect. In 1825, after returning to Iowa from Washington, DC, Rantchewaime was thrown from her horse and died instantly. She was greatly loved, and her death caused great sorrow among her people.

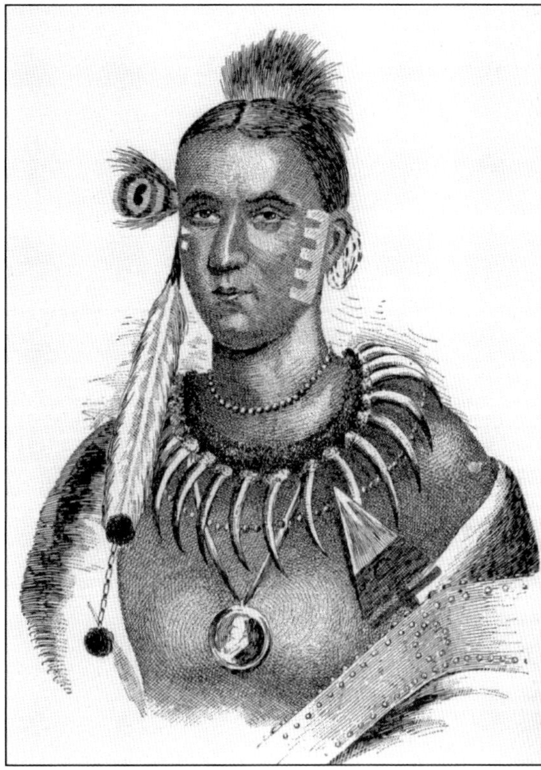

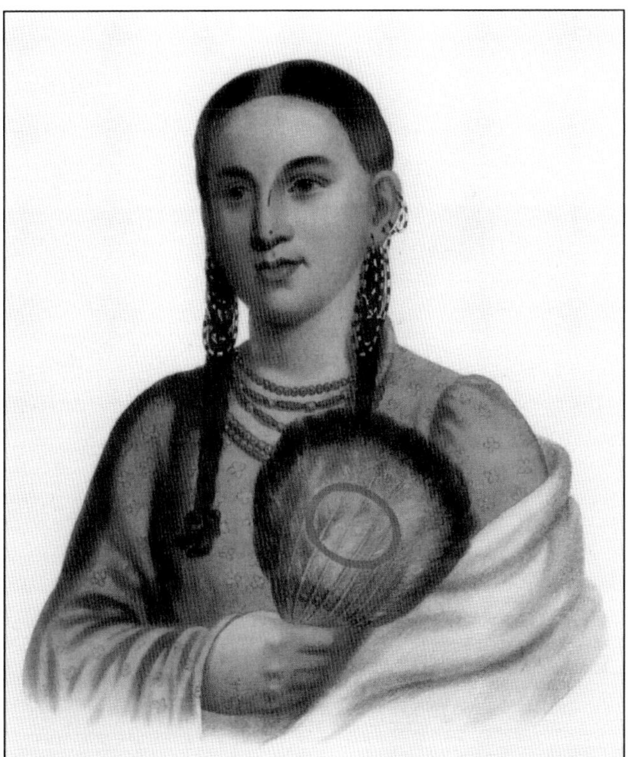

In 1833, when braves from Mahaska's tribe broke the peace treaty, Gen. William Clark, of the Lewis and Clark Expedition fame, sent officers to arrest the offenders. Mahaska knew his braves had broken the peace treaty, and he accompanied his men to Fort Leavenworth, where they were imprisoned. The braves were very angry and told Mahaska that men were not meant to live behind bars and warned him they would kill him for allowing the soldiers to imprison them. They did escape and carried out that vow. They found Mahaska sleeping in his camp beside the Nodaway River in Cass County and treacherously killed him. The Ioways moved westward, but their name was given to the land they left behind, Iowa.

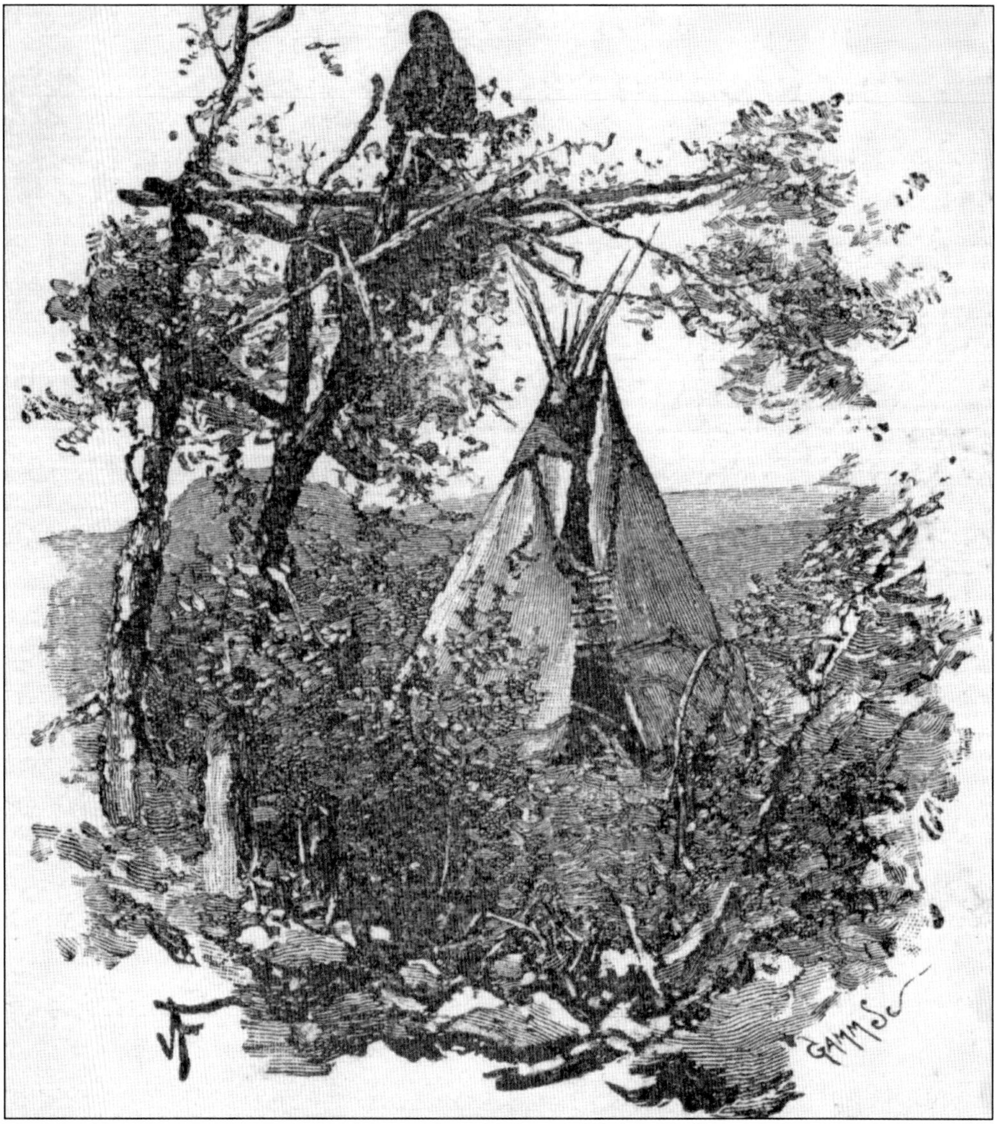

The Indian tribe most closely associated with Cass County is the Potawatomi. By way of treaty signed in 1833, some came to live along the East Nishnabotna near what is now the town of Lewis. They named their village Mi-au-mise. The village had about 100 wigwams by the time the Mormons came through on their trek to Utah in 1846. The Mormons found the Potawatomi friendly and helpful. In 1848, the Potawatomi left the area after agreeing to this removal by treaty.

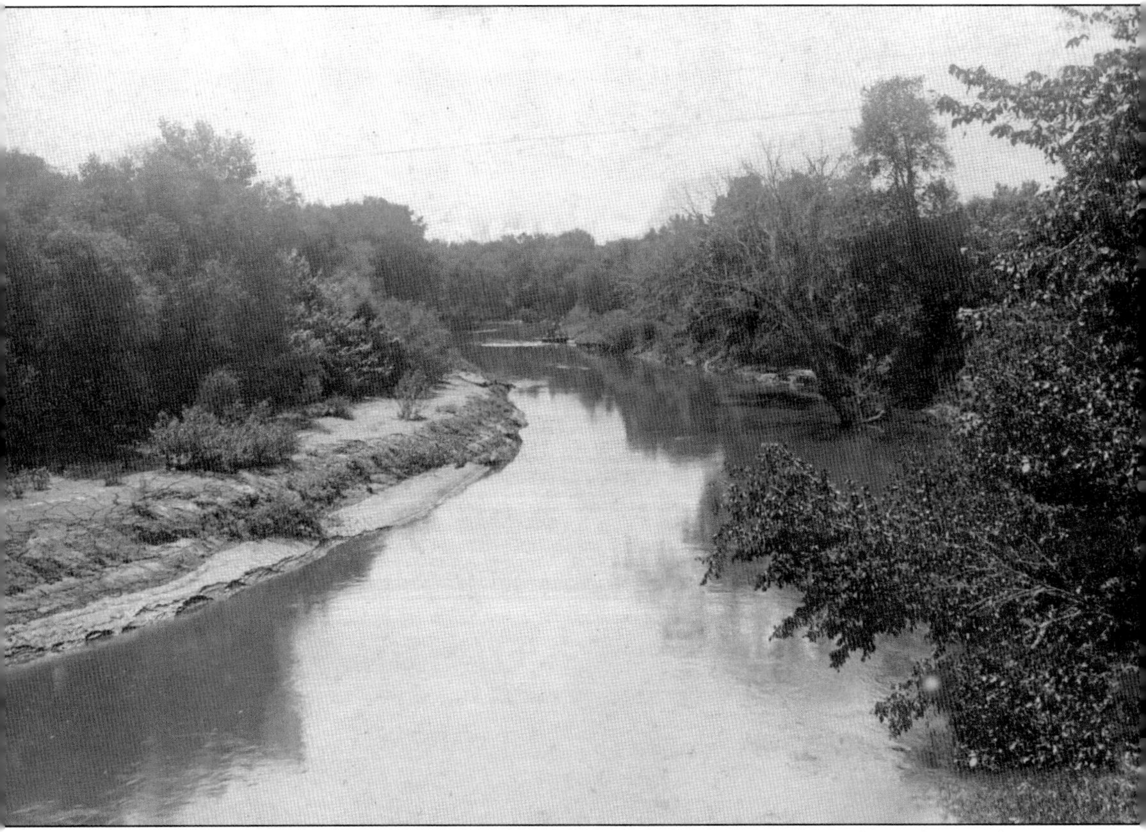

The Nishnabotna and the Nodaway are the two main rivers of Cass County. The Dakota Indians named them *nodaway*, meaning "crossed without canoe," and *nishnabotna*, meaning "crossed with a canoe." In the 1850s, this area had abundant antelope, deer, quail, prairie chickens, and a few elk and beaver. The rivers were well stocked with catfish and carp. Many types of trees, such as cottonwood, oak, elm, maple, hickory, and black walnut, grew along the riverbanks.

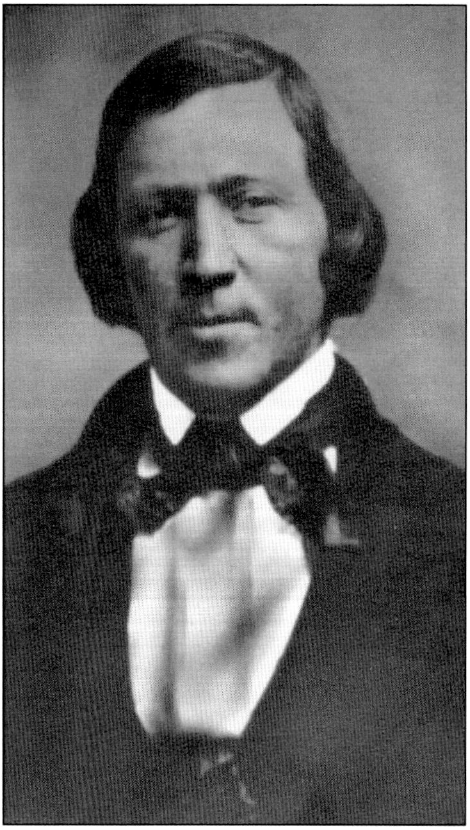

In 1844, Brigham Young took over the Mormon leadership following the death of Joseph Smith. Young wanted to lead his people westward to the desert wilderness of Utah where they could establish their homes and follow their way of life free from religious persecution. Many lives were lost on the journey westward, attested to by the number of graves that dotted the hillside just west of their temporary quarters near present-day Lewis.

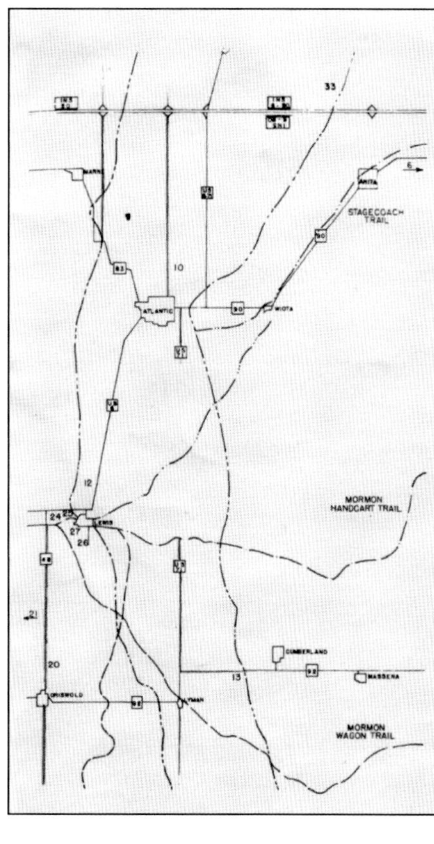

Cass County is crisscrossed with several famous trails. This drawing shows the path of three of those—the Mormon Wagon Trail, the Mormon Handcart Trail, and the Stagecoach Trail. Most of these paths crossed the Nishnabotna River at Cold Springs near present-day Lewis because the river was shallow there and the riverbed was largely rock. Most of the towns shown were not in existence at the time these trails were established but serve as points of reference.

Two

CASS TOWNSHIP

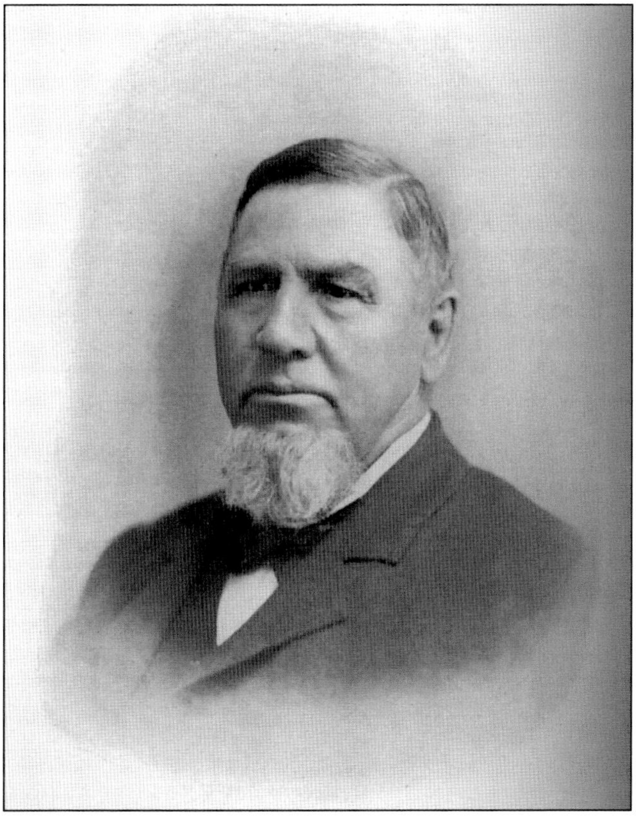

In 1857, Oliver Mills purchased land near Lewis. As a director and president of the Iowa Agricultural Society, he helped select the site for the Iowa State Agricultural College at Ames. In 1872, Mills was elected as representative to the 14th General Assembly for Cass, Montgomery, and Adair Counties. He was an ardent abolitionist and helped establish the Underground Railroad through Cass County. He was a personal friend of John Brown and frequently hid runaway slaves on their way to freedom in the North.

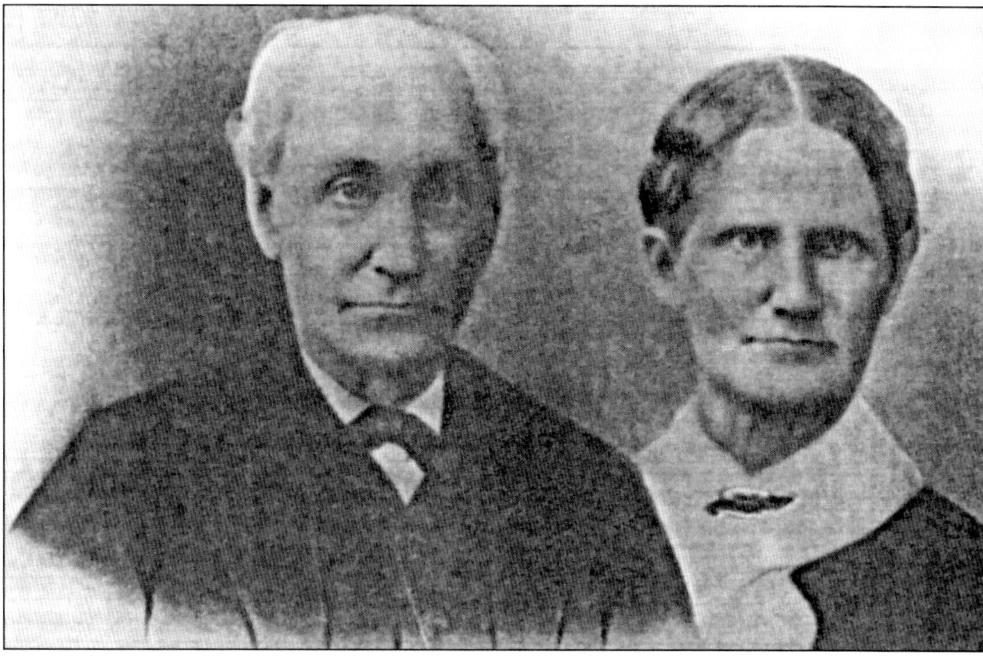

In 1850, Vincent M. Conrad arrived in Indiantown and built a log cabin. Conrad is credited with being the first white man to purchase land in Cass County for permanent settlement, as the Mormons were considered only temporary sojourners. In 1853, Conrad was elected as the first Cass County recorder and recorded the first deed filed in the county. He served as mayor of Lewis, and his residence housed the post office and a dancing school.

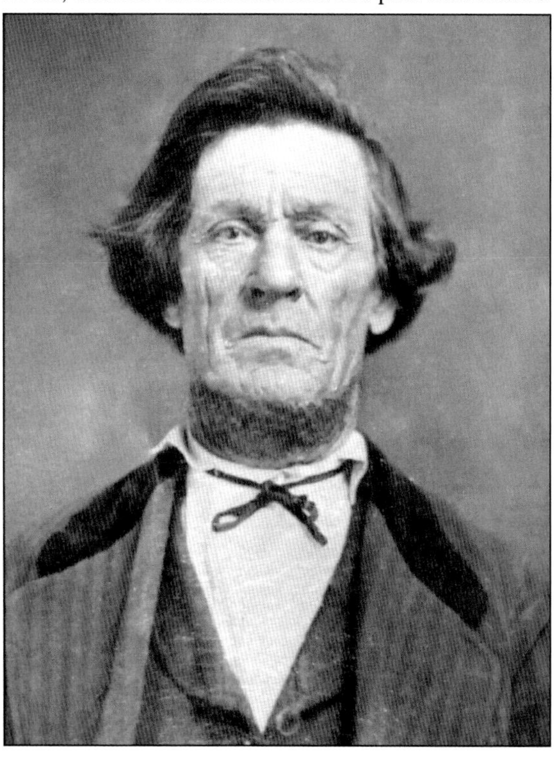

In 1851, Jeremiah Bradshaw, married to Eliza Doolittle, settled at Indiantown. He arrived with seven elk, four deer, two badgers, and a sandhill crane. He frequently harnessed two of the elk to a sleigh. In 1853, Bradshaw was elected as the first judge in Cass County. In 1861, he enlisted in the 4th Iowa Infantry and took part in the Battle of Pea Ridge. During the war, Eliza passed away, and in 1865, Bradshaw married Parmelia Ferrell.

In 1854, the Horatio Ferrell family settled east of Iranistan. In July 1856, Horatio's son Wilson died at the age of 17. Horatio's health soon failed, and he died in October 1857. The men were buried on their farm, and this photograph shows the original location of the graves. The graves remained there until Lawrence Pope reset them in the west side of Oakwood Cemetery at Lewis, where they can be found today.

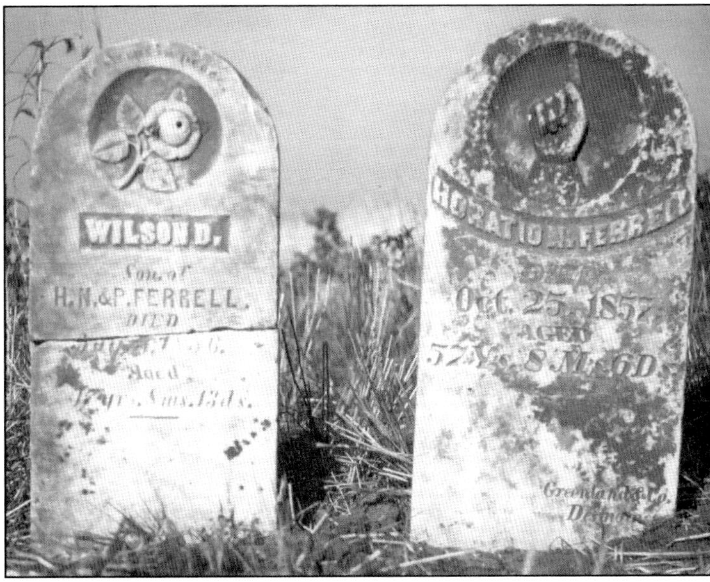

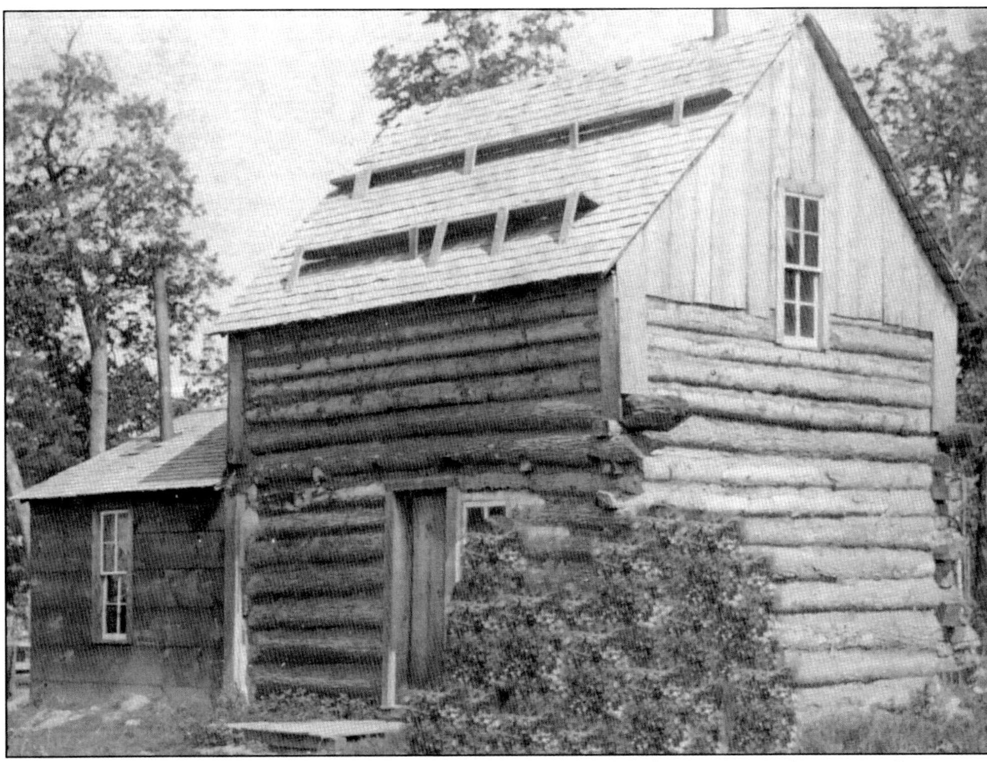

One real frontier character was A.J. Millslagel, or "Old Slagel." He arrived in Cass County in 1851 as the first professional prairie breaker in the area. As such, he was hired by settlers to clear land and open up the virgin prairies for cultivation. Millslagel was known for his prodigious appetite. Hunting parties refused to take him along because he would eat most of the kill. After he purchased a wife, Mrs. Frank Wilson of Douglas Township in Montgomery County, for one sow, two shoats, and a gun, indignant neighbors confronted him. Millslagel shot and killed John Snipes and wounded James Shores. He was sentenced to prison at Fort Madison for 14 years.

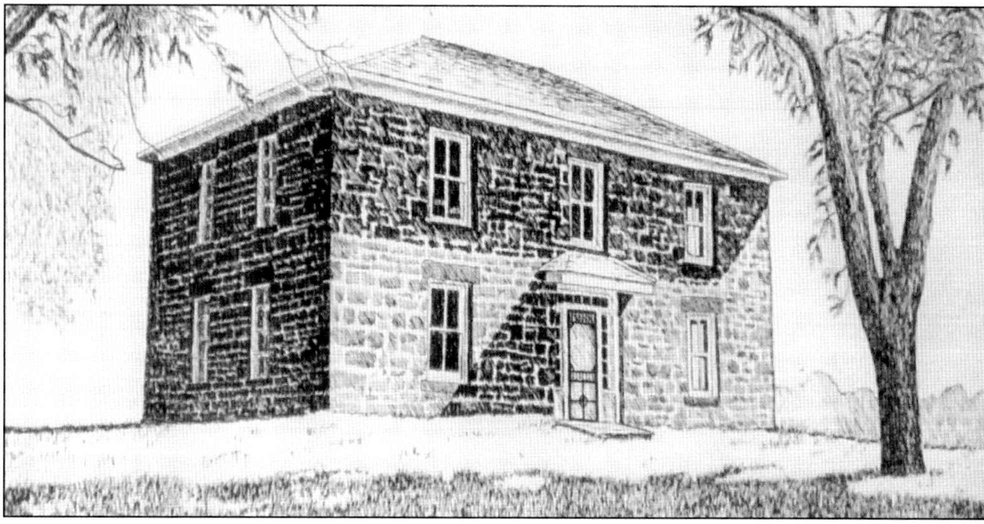

The Hitchcock House was called the "House of Mystery," "John Brown's Station," and the "Old Slave House." The Reverend George B. Hitchcock arrived in Lewis in 1853 and, in 1855, established the Congregational Church in Lewis. In 1856, he built a home on a scenic hill overlooking the Nishnabotna River. The home was built of native sandstone with walls that were 18 inches thick and contained a four-inch dead-air space between two layers of stone that provided excellent insulation. Hitchcock was very involved in the Underground Railroad and is credited with saving many lives. In his home, Reverend Hitchcock built a full basement containing a large fireplace that could be used for heating. Small rooms were constructed that could be shut off and cleverly concealed behind walls of shelving. These rooms provided safe hiding places for the runaway slaves passing through the area. (Drawing courtesy of Dana Kunze.)

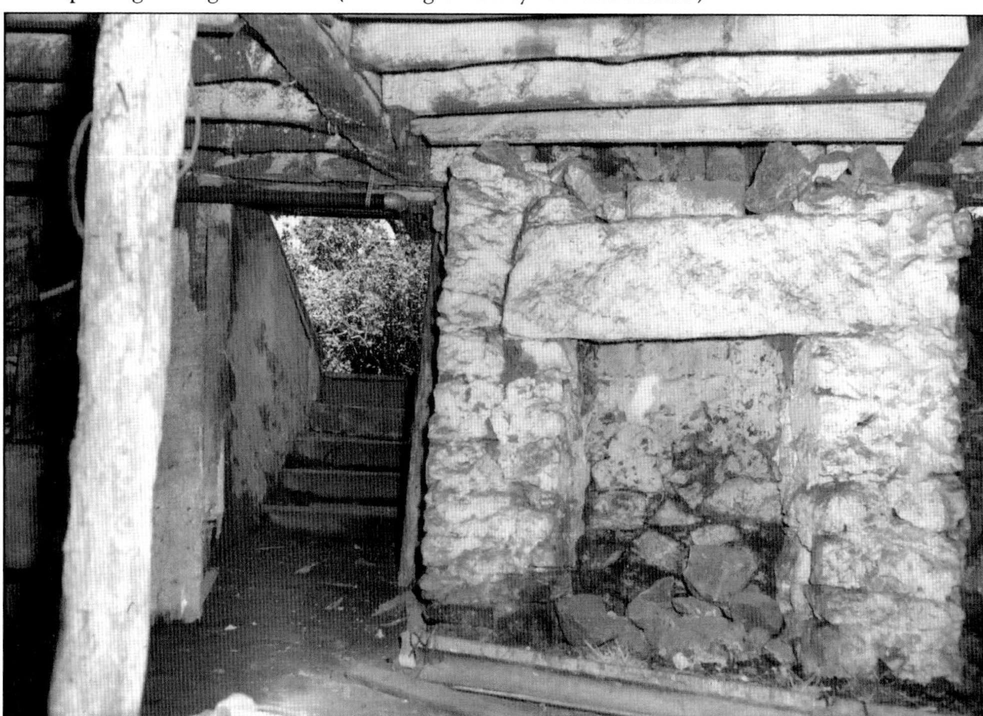

Rev. George B. Hitchcock left the area in 1865 and died in 1872. In 1977, his house was placed in the National Register of Historic Places. In 1984, the community took on the task of restoring the home. In 2006, it was designated a national historic landmark. It is open to the public, and the story of the Underground Railroad and the work of Reverend Hitchcock comes to life for visitors. He is pictured here with his wife, Caroline, and grandchildren.

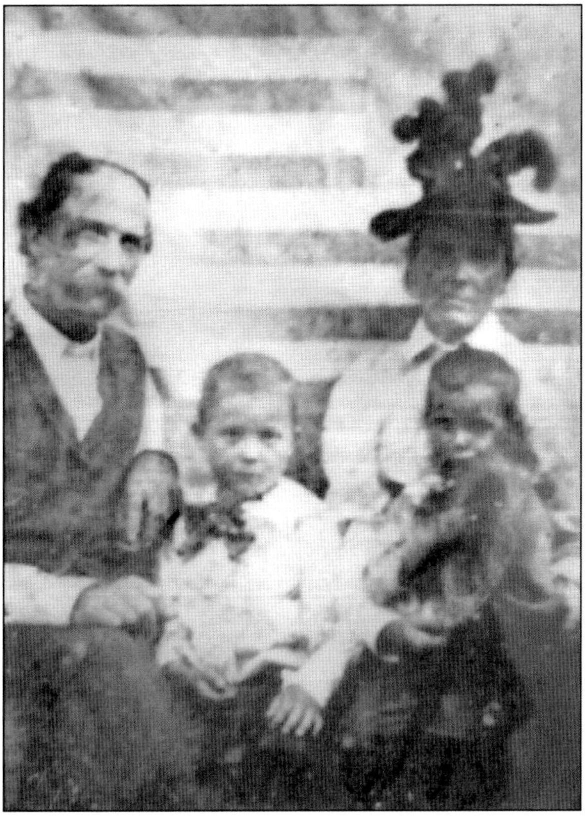

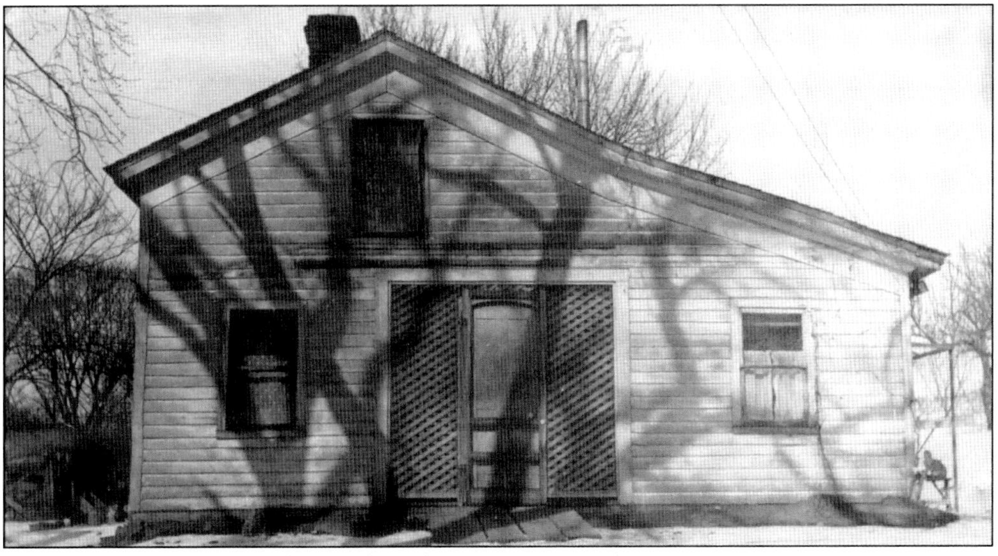

This ferry house is historically significant because it was on the main transportation route crossing the Nishnabotna River. In 1859, two male slaves were tracked to the Lewis area, where Sheriff John Keyes and S.H. Tefft, the ferryman, were alerted. On his way to church, abolitionist James Baxter drove his wagon to the ferry escorting two "veiled females." Baxter and his passengers were ferried across the river. The escapees continued on to Adair County and safety on the Underground Railroad.

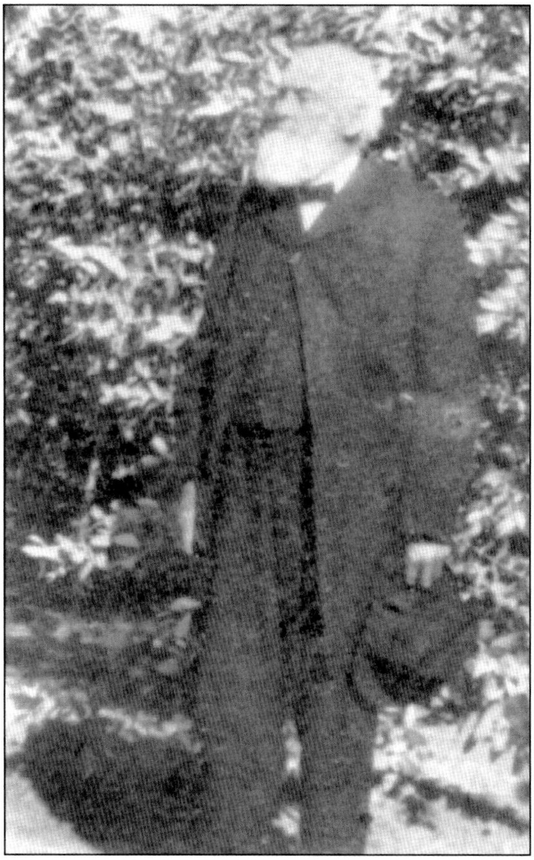

This photograph is of James M. Baxter, and below is an etching of his stock farm and residence from A.T. *Andreas' Illustrated Historical Atlas of the State of Iowa.* Baxter, a pioneer of Cass County, was born in Vermont in 1831. He received the education commonly given to sons of Vermont farmers following agricultural pursuits. He arrived in Cass County in 1856 and worked as a farm laborer. Baxter started buying land southwest of Lewis. He purchased and improved 2,000 acres of prairie soil over the years, built many homes, and completed at least 25 miles of fence. In 1858, he married Euphemia Richardson. The civic-minded Baxter served as supervisor of District No. 4 in 1880 and, in 1883, was elected chairman of the board of supervisors. He also served as a school director for Lewis District No. 1.

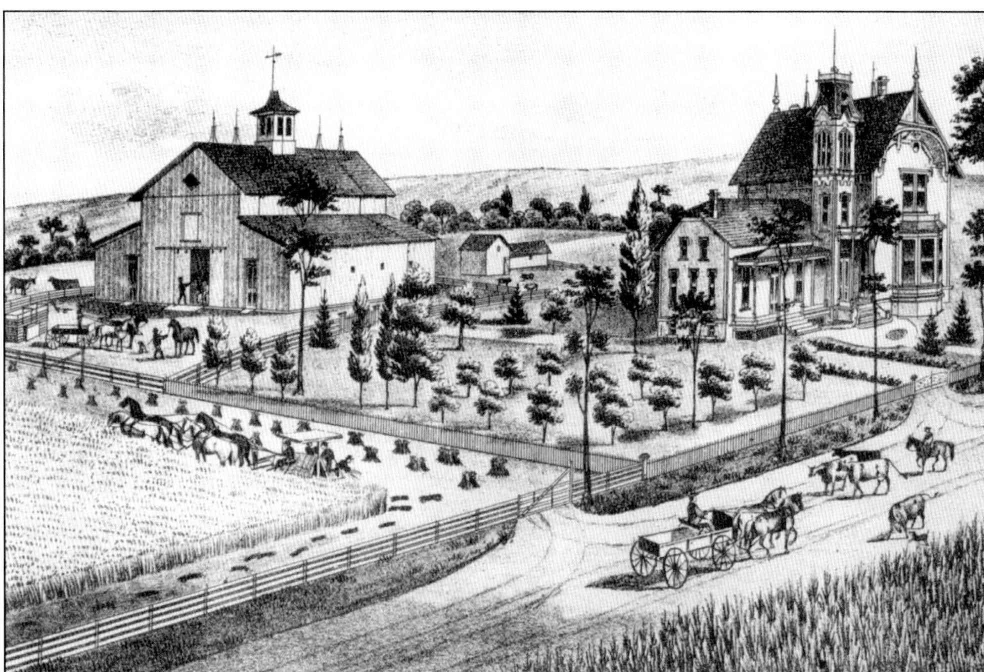

John Keyes, a local merchant, saw the need for a gristmill in Lewis, with the Nishnabotna River available as a source of power. Keyes, with his partner Edward Peck, organized the building of a dam and the gristmill, pictured right. The workers, shown below, completed the project in 1856. Later, the wooden dam was rebuilt using rocks and concrete. Settlers traveled long distances to have wheat and corn ground into flour, as corn bread and cornmeal mush were staples in the mid-1800s. Upon completion of the dam, farmers who came from the west would cross the Nishnabotna on the ferryboat built by Keyes and Peck. The mill was sold to Thomas Jones, a Lewis storekeeper, who operated it until his death in 1863. After 73 years as a Lewis landmark, the mill was torn down in 1929.

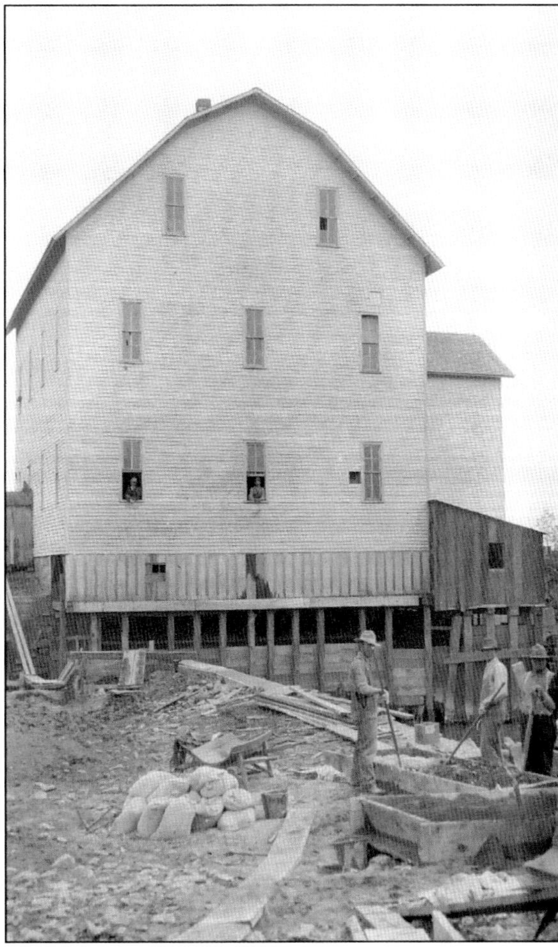

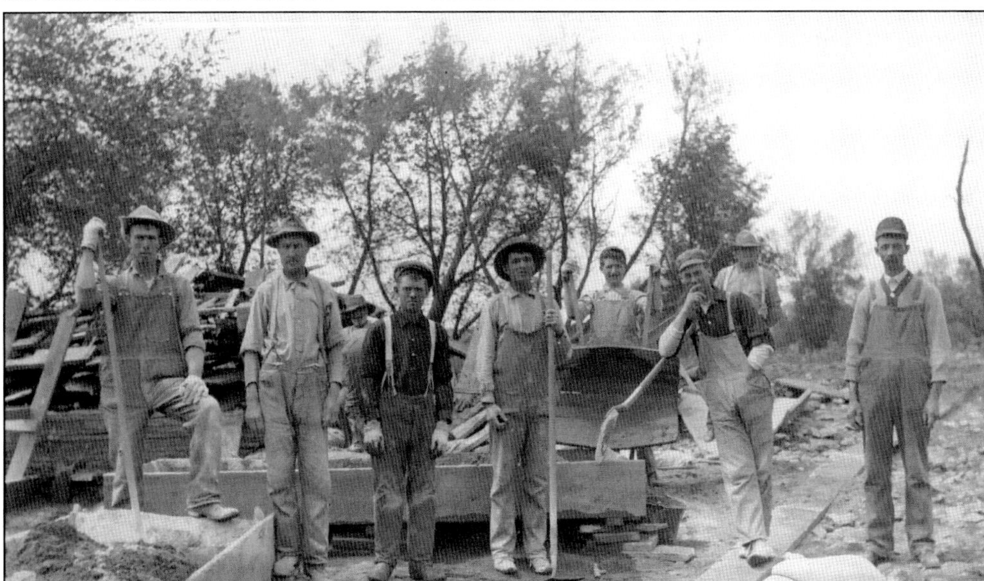

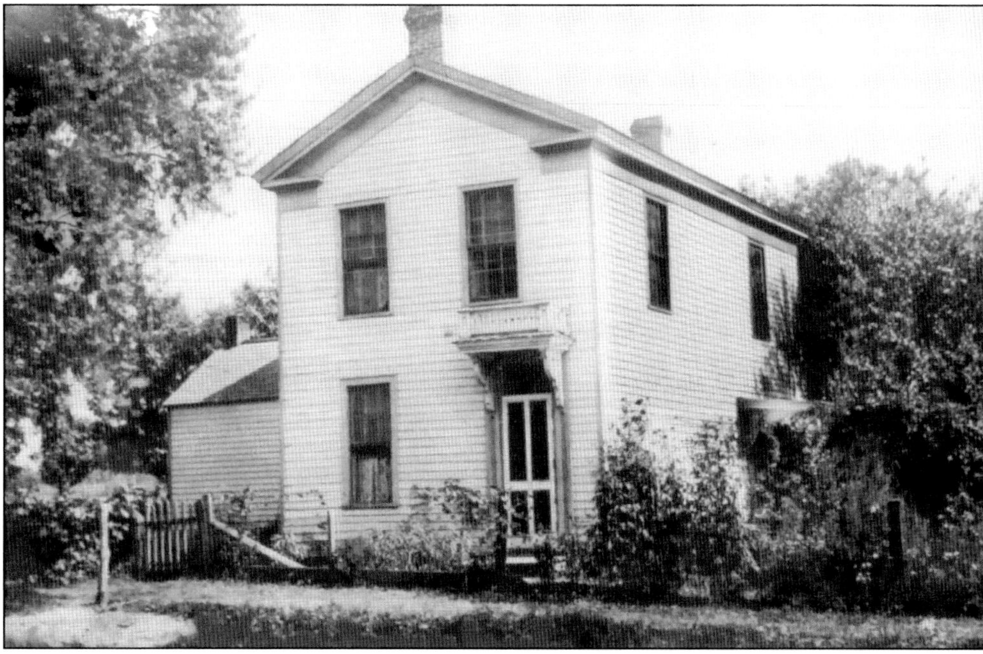

Cass County's first courthouse was a simple frame building erected in Lewis in 1856. When two of the three appointed commissioners voted to establish the county seat at a site one mile away from the village of Indiantown, lots were sold, businesses were moved into the new town, and it prospered. Eight years later, a stone structure was built to house the Cass County Treasurer's Office. In 1869, the county seat was moved to Atlantic.

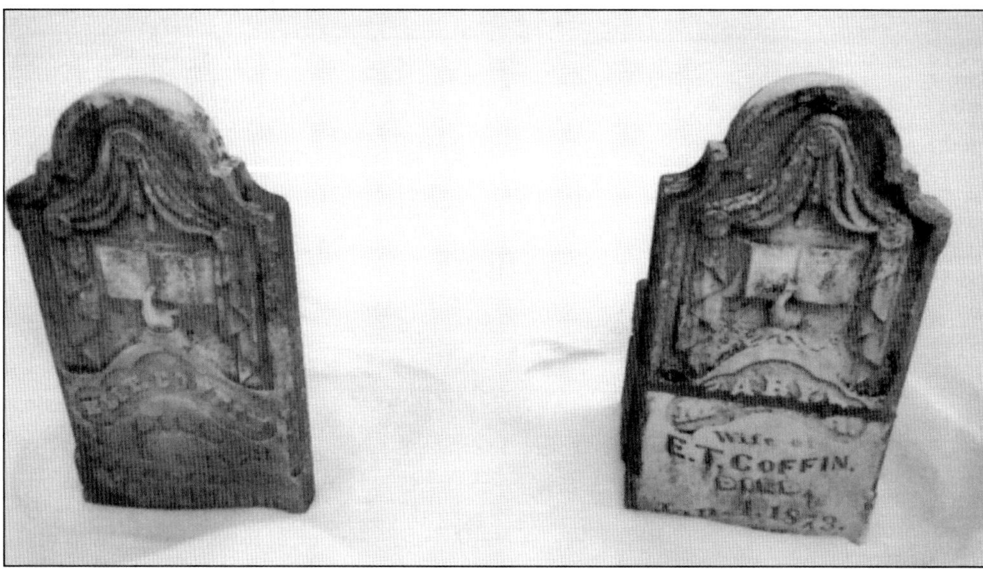

Mary Coffin, the wife of Ely Coffin, died January 1, 1873. Neighbors demanded an inquest, and findings showed that Mary had died of exposure, starvation, and neglect. Her husband was charged with murder. His trial was postponed several times, and neighbors, fearing Coffin might get away with murder, took matters into their own hands. John Tuttle, crossing over Turkey Creek, found the body of Ely Coffin, hands and feet bound together, hanging from a bridge support. The perpetrators were never identified. The Coffins are buried together in the Oakwood Cemetery at Lewis.

Belle Macomber, a schoolteacher in Cass County, married William S. Reynolds in 1860. Reynolds served in the Civil War, and she accompanied him. At the Battle of Pittsburg Landing, she ministered to the sick and wounded, earning their esteem and gratitude. Governor Yates of Illinois, upon hearing of her bravery, awarded her with a commission as a major in the US Army. It is thought that no other lady in America had ever received such a distinguished honor.

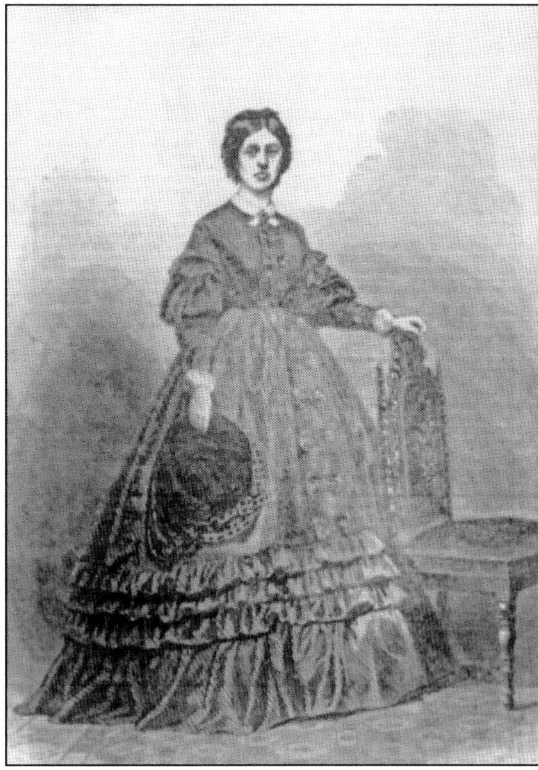

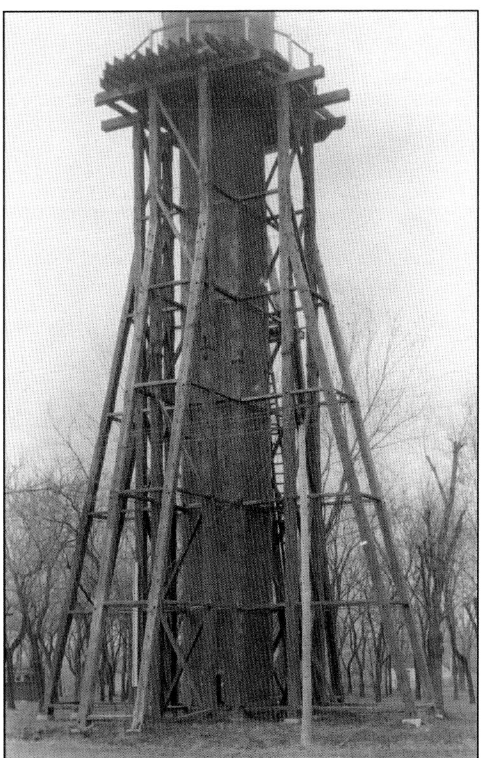

The wooden water tower served the town of Lewis for many years. In 1902, water rates included a $5 annual charge, an extra $3 for a water closet, and yet another $3 for a bathtub. If residents wasted water, the supply would be cut off. The tower crashed to the ground in 1906 when the hoops around the tank broke apart; it created quite a flood in downtown Lewis. This photograph was taken in 1900 and developed from a badly scratched glass photographic plate.

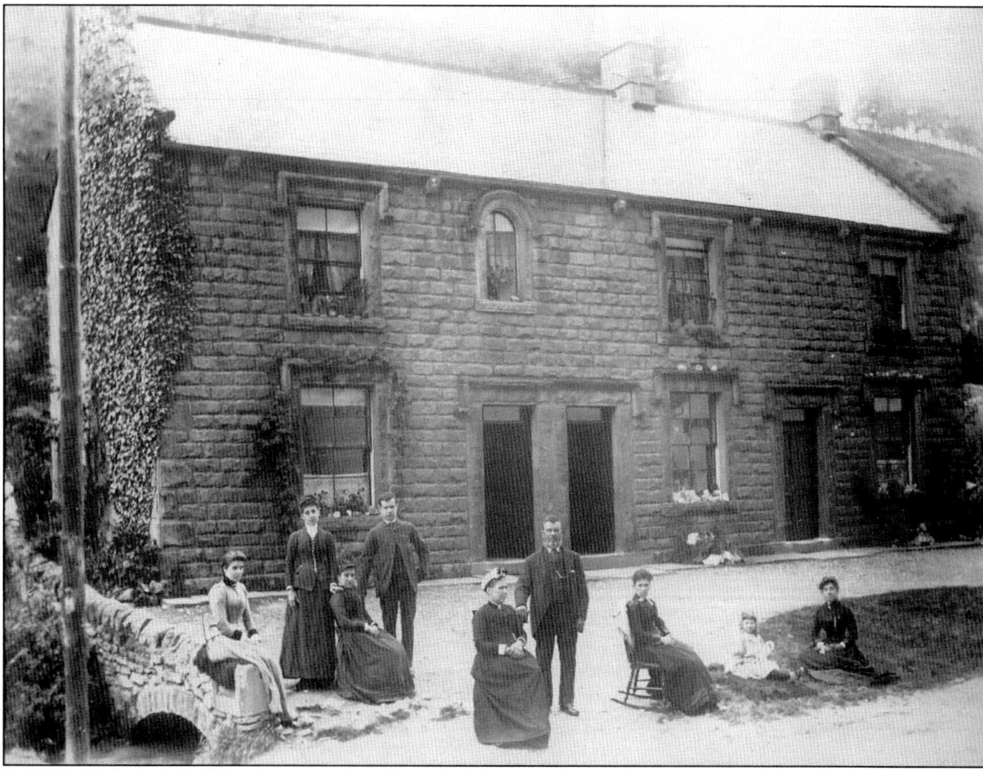

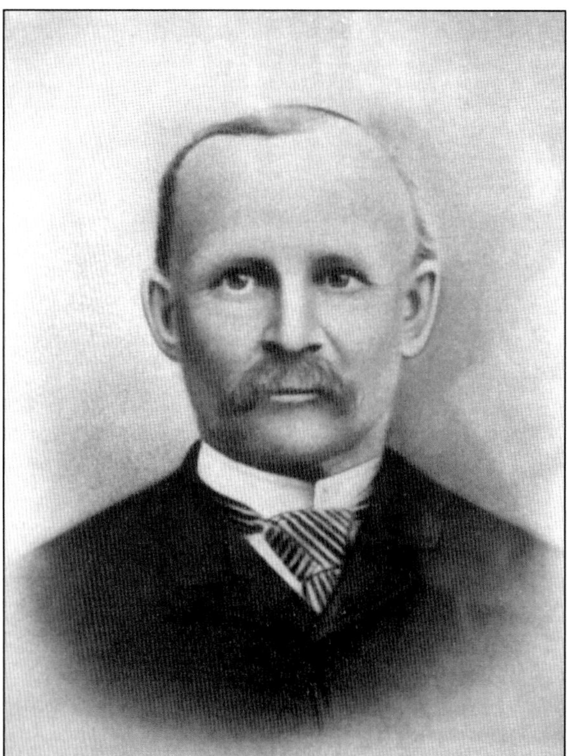

The above photograph is of the Morton home in Derbyshire, England, with several members of the Morton family posed in a manner typical of the time. Henry Morton, pictured left, was born in Derbyshire in 1832. As a young lad of 12, he was indentured to George Hibbert, a tailor by trade, for a period of nine years. The indenture agreement states that "Henry diligently attend to the concerns of his master." He received no pay but was provided housing, food, and clothing. The indenture system was a commonly used method of learning a trade and provided many individuals a chance to eventually earn a better living.

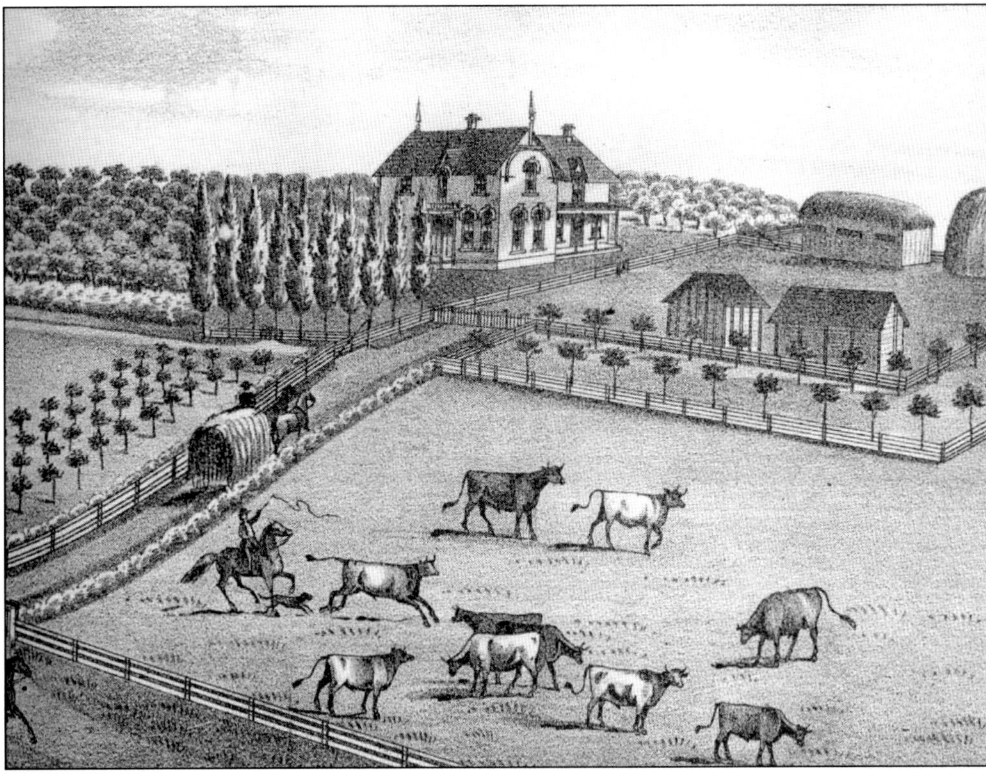

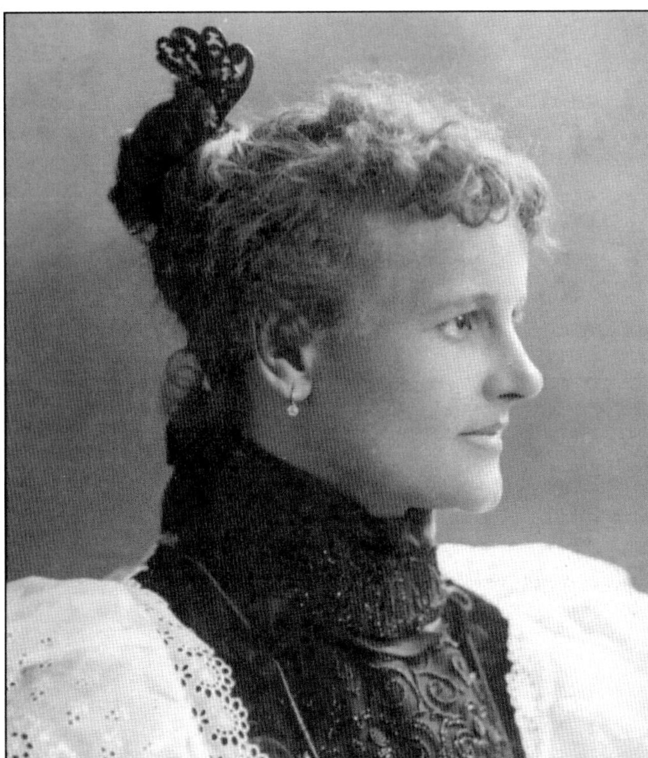

In 1865, with his wife, Jane, and several of his children, Henry Morton moved to the United States to improve himself financially and to give his children the advantage of the new continent. He settled first in Kewanee, Illinois, but soon decided to move farther west. In 1867, the family traveled by covered wagon to Cass Township in Iowa, where Morton was able to purchase a 320-acre farm. Morton made a success of his enterprise as the above engraving of his Cass County home from A.T. *Andreas' Illustrated Historical Atlas of the State of Iowa* clearly shows. Morton operated his stock farm until his death in 1887 of malaria fever. Pictured at right is Morton's sister Clara.

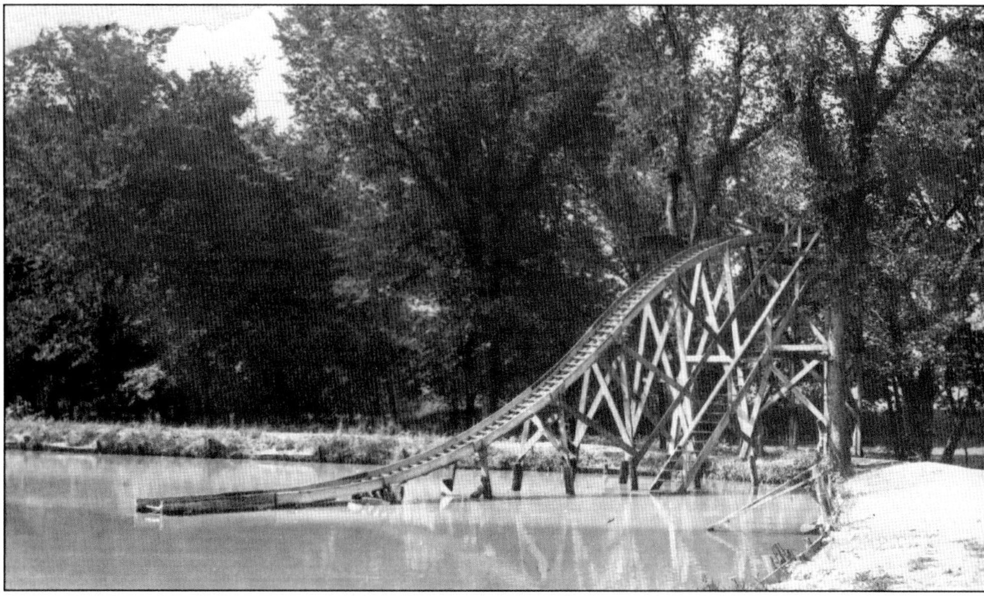

A dream of Chet Woodward was the creation of a recreation area he named Crystal Lake. Work began in 1896, and the lake was soon deep enough for a steamboat to operate. A boat ramp, boat rental, roller-skating rink, pavilion, and concession stand were built. Visitors from nearby towns packed into trains to travel to the lake in order to enjoy its many activities. In 1931, Crystal Lake was selected as an Iowa State Fish Hatchery. After the Depression and the onset of World War II, the park fell into disrepair. In 1948, Iowa state representative Gus Kuester and state senator Jay Coburn were key figures in restoring Crystal Lake. It is now named Cold Springs State Park. The 1899 photograph shown below was taken at the area of Crystal Lake known as "the Ripples," a favorite "wooing spot." Shown are, from left to right, Charlie Taylor, Perry Robinson, Birde Taylor, Mabel Taylor, Leonard Gardner, and Nellie Taylor.

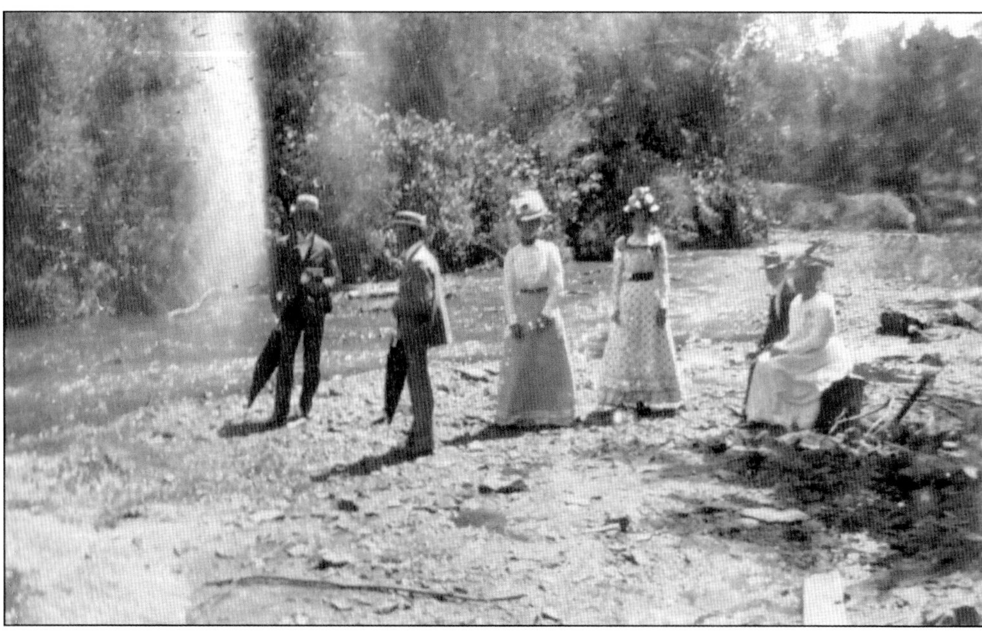

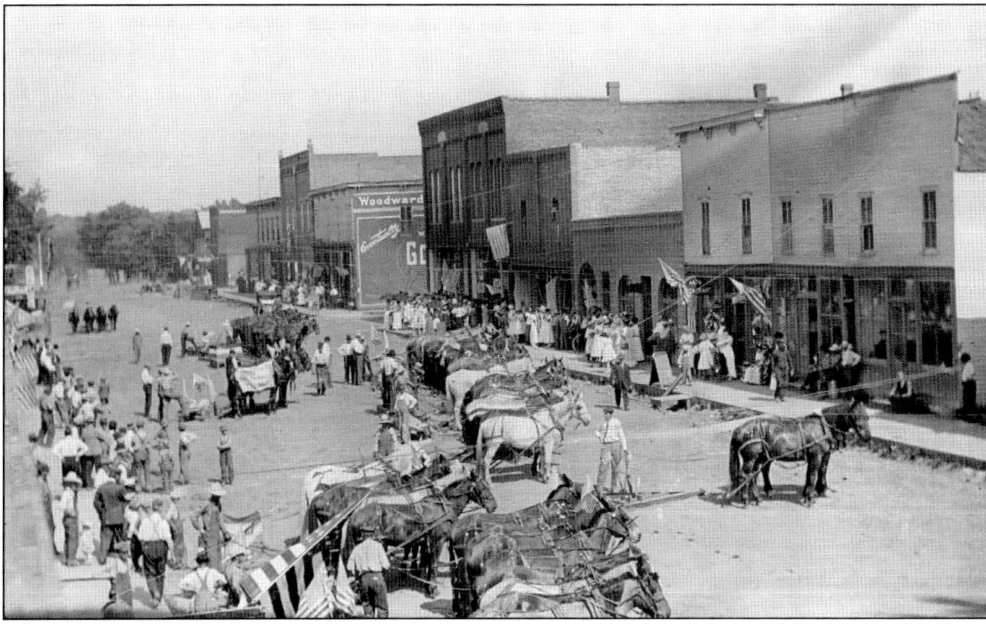

Dirt streets and roads demanded maintenance, and in Lewis this was done once a year on "Drag Day." This was not a celebration but a real workday. Residents brought their horse teams downtown, hooked on wooden drags, and smoothed out the ruts in the streets. Naturally, the activity brought out a lot of "sidewalk superintendents" to oversee the work. This photograph was taken on the main street of Lewis in 1911.

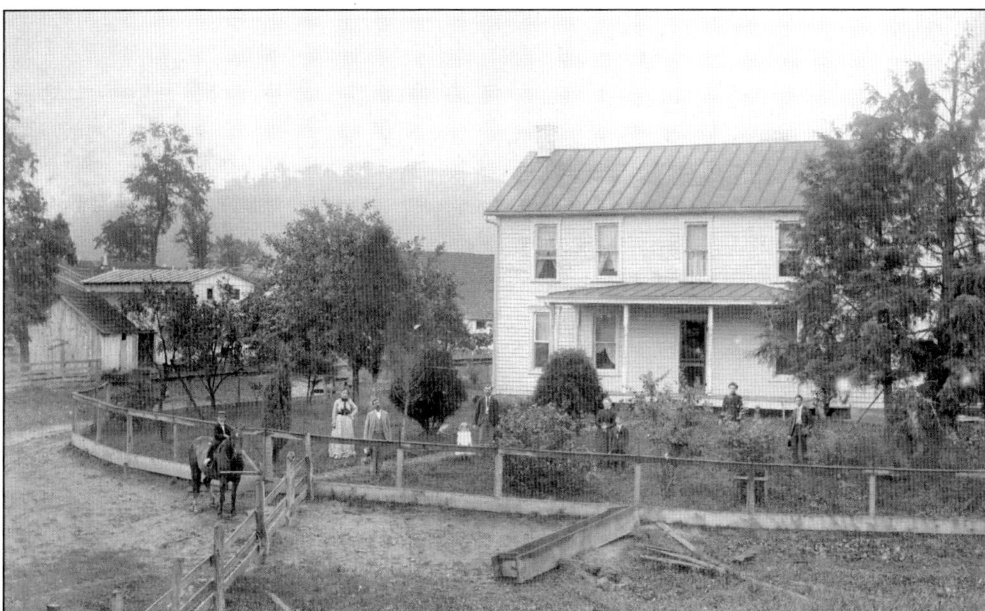

The Cass County landscape is dotted with prosperous farms. Note the pine-board fencing; pine was used as it was plentiful and inexpensive. Barbed wire was introduced in Iowa as early as 1858 but was not commercially produced until sometime later. Low-cost barbed wire helped advance the diversification of farming, and Iowa farmers bought into the raising of cattle. The lack of indigenous forage plants brought about the introduction of clovers to the state.

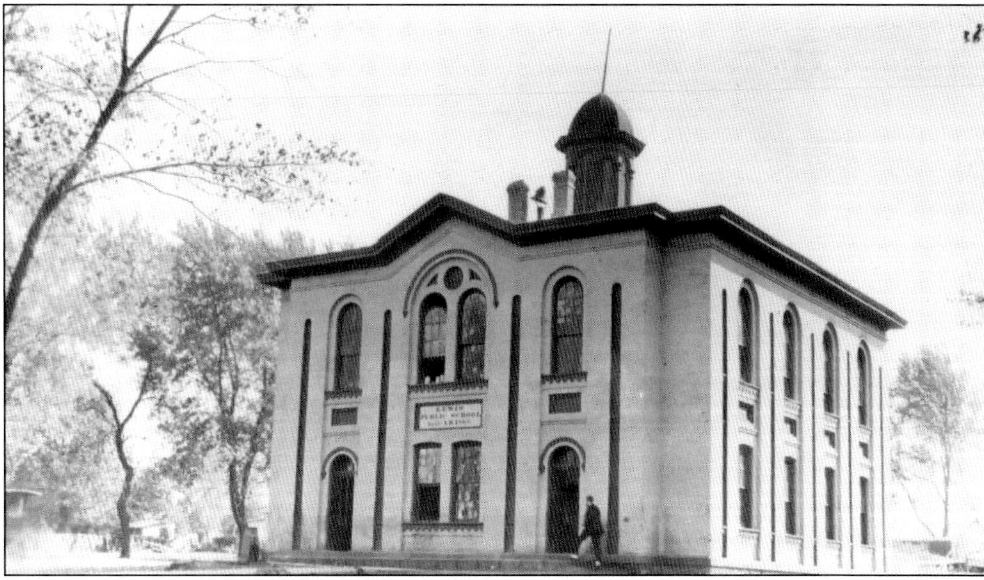

In 1868, at a cost of $9,200, this school was constructed in Lewis. The first principal was S.R. Manning, who established high standards. Lewis was not always that fortunate in its choice of principals. An 1884 history of Lewis, referring to the sixth principal, states, "J.W. James left no trace of any good school work." A new school was constructed in 1916. This new building was destroyed by fire in 1960, and Lewis became part of the Griswold Community School District.

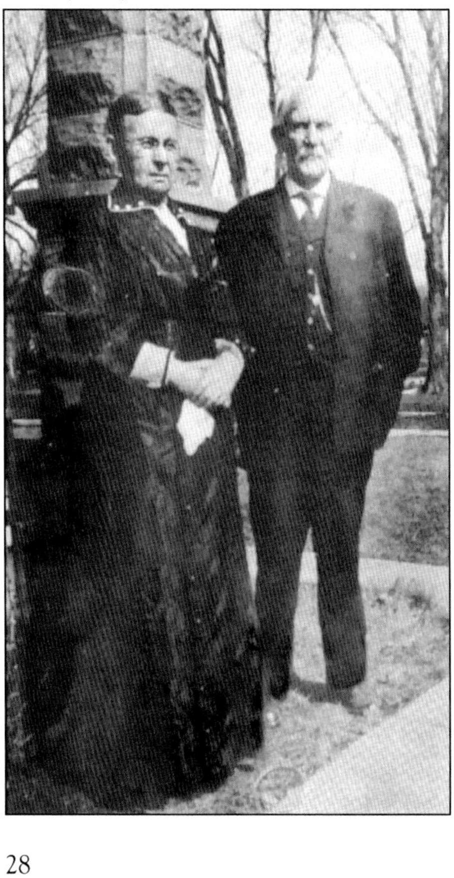

Fremont C. Jones, better known as "Grandpa Jones," moved to Lewis in 1872 and married Georgia Anna Tefft in 1877. The photograph was taken on their 50th wedding anniversary. Georgia was the first female born in Lewis. They had four children, one of whom was Carlyle R. Jones, a prominent doctor who practiced in Lewis and Atlantic. Grandpa Jones built houses, grandfather clocks, and intricate miniature furniture. Many of his pieces are now in collections and are treasured mementos.

Three

Grove Township

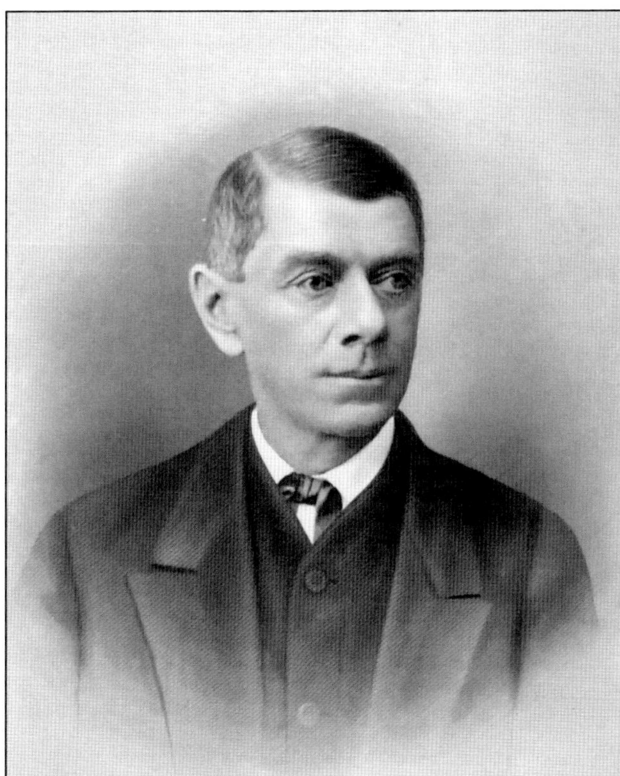

Franklin H. Whitney founded the city of Atlantic. He established the Atlantic Town Company in 1868 and was instrumental in laying out the town. Trained as a surveyor, Whitney assisted in the plotting of the Chicago, Rock Island & Pacific Railroad route. He was instrumental in the location of the depot, a designation that insured that Atlantic would become a thriving community as well as the seat of Cass County.

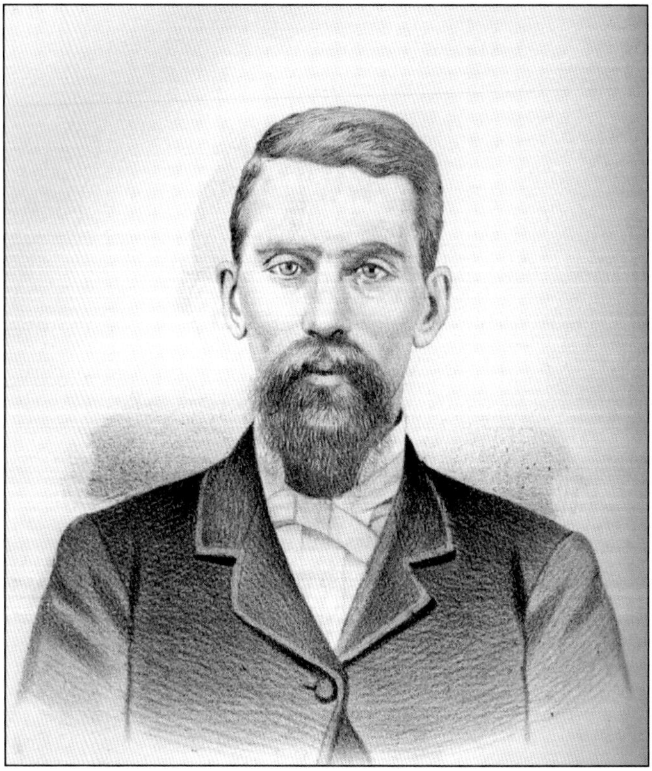

Albert Wakefield was a teacher in Maine when he decided to move in 1853 to Cass County, Iowa, where he purchased 600 acres of land. He built a sawmill on Turkey Creek in which he kept an interest for 10 years. Wakefield later bought the land where Grove City once stood. On this site, he planted a large orchard and vineyard. Wakefield was a respected civic leader and served as treasurer for Grove Township for 14 consecutive terms.

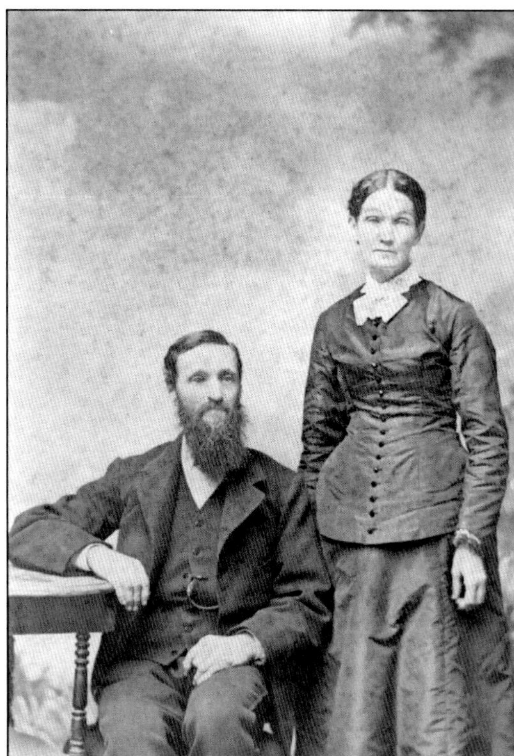

George Reeves and his wife came to Cass County in 1851. Reeves was known to be a rather cantankerous man. He served on the first jury in Cass County that tried the case of *David Weliman v. William Wood*. In 1852, Reeves was asked by Mrs. Jesse Marshall to go to Indiantown to purchase a coffin for her dead husband. It took Reeves five days to return with the coffin due to a five-day drinking spree.

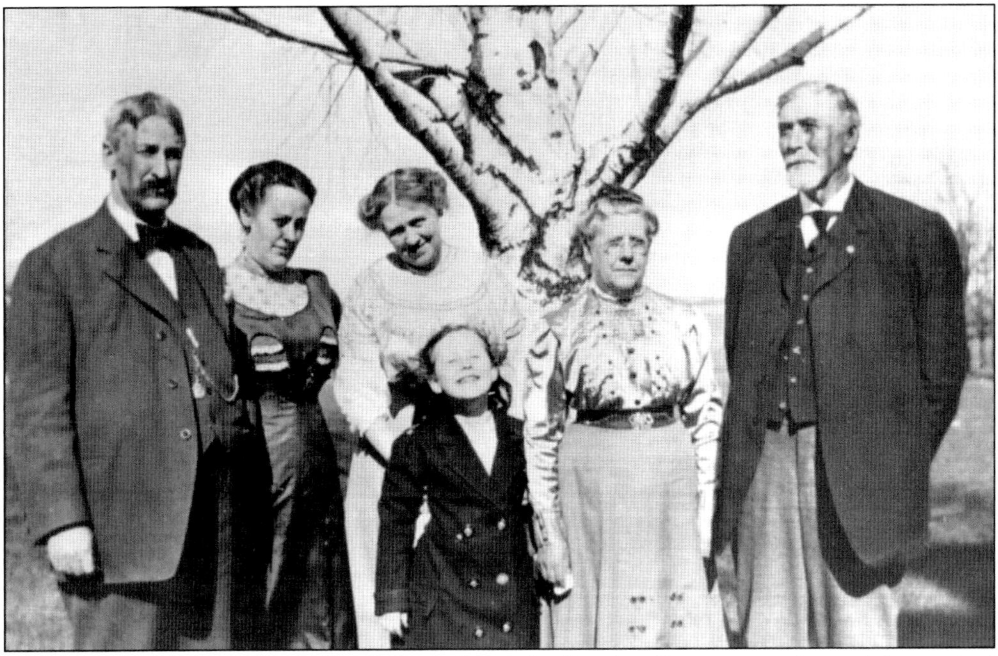

Edward Shaw was a partner in the Shaw and Crombie Lumber Company and one of the original investors in the Light Company of Atlantic. The Shaws built the home on Chestnut Street that was later called the Cuykendall House. Shown in the 1911 photograph above are, from left to right, Edward A. Shaw, Leila E. Mullins, Emma H. Shaw with Louise Mullins as a small child standing in front, Elizabeth J. Mullins, and Capt. Lafayette F. Mullins. Captain Mullins served during the Civil War under Gen. Ulysses S. Grant and fought at the siege of Vicksburg, which was where he was badly wounded. Mullins later served as Cass County sheriff, postmaster of Atlantic, and county treasurer. He and his wife, Elizabeth, had one son, Dr. U.S. Mullins, who practiced medicine in Atlantic until 1936. The 1901 photograph below shows Sarah Cuykendall and her daughter Virginia in their carriage at the Shaw/Cuykendall House.

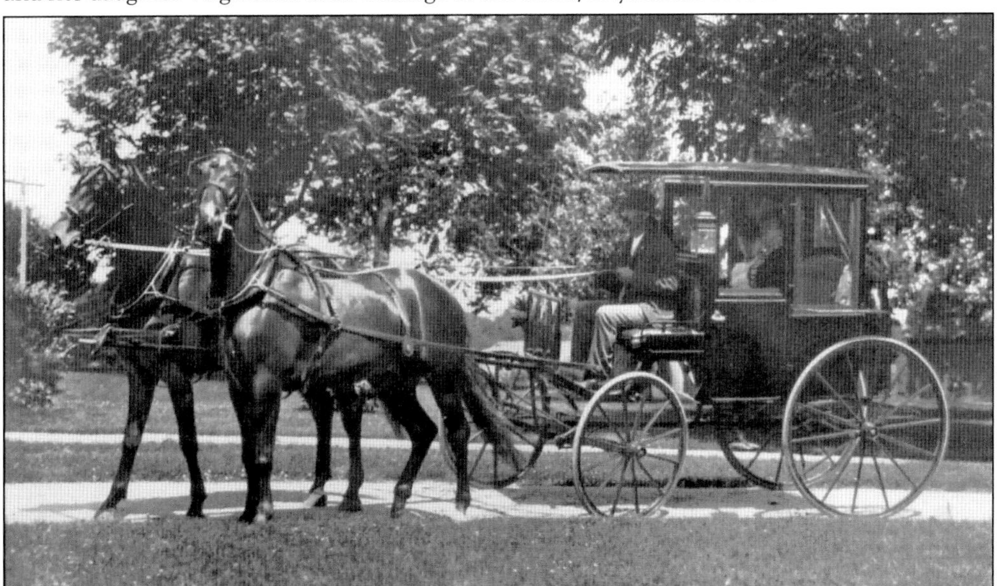

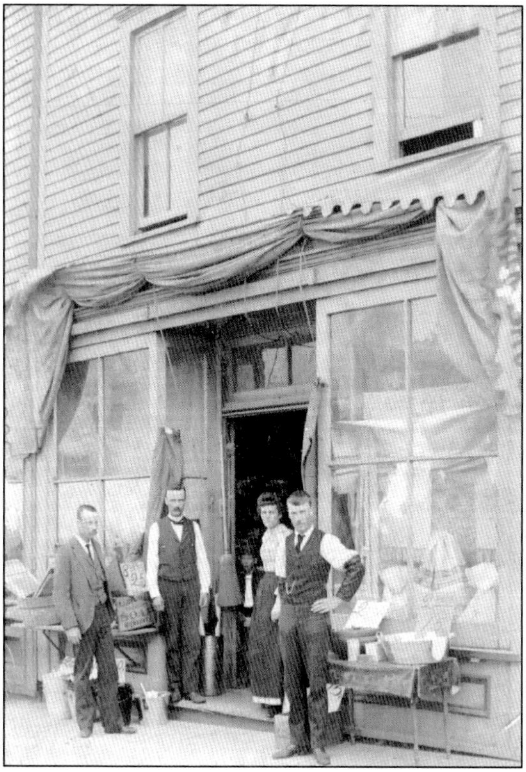

Albert Beech came to Atlantic at the age of 38 with $190 worth of general merchandise in his possession. He proved to be a good businessman and established a successful store at 312 Chestnut Street. Beech was not a joiner, but from the time he settled in, until the time he closed his doors, he could always be relied upon to support endeavors that led to the improvement of his adopted city. The people shown in the left photograph, taken outside the store around 1917, are, from left to right, unidentified, Albert Beech, Margaret Beech, and clerk Earl Beech.

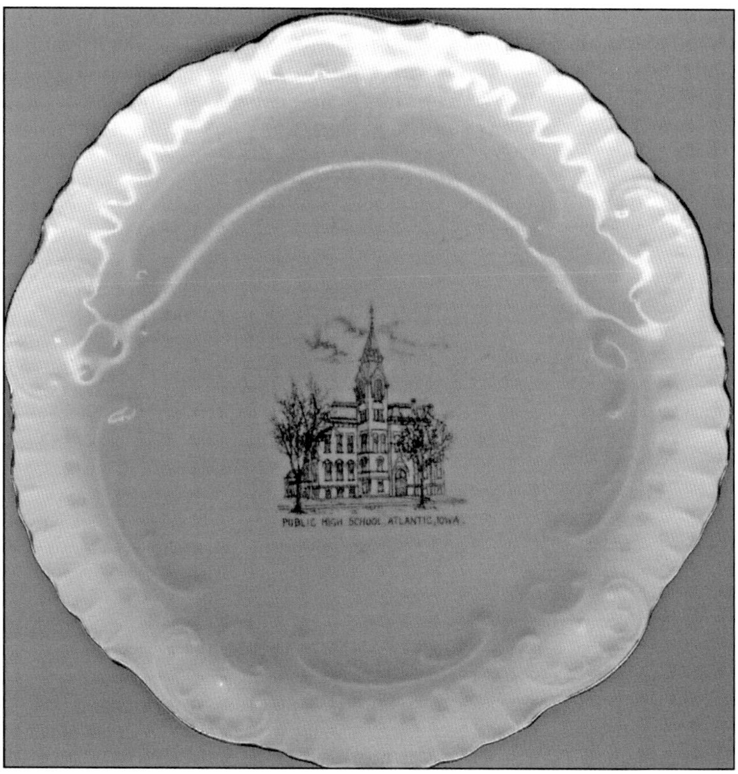

This photograph shows a china plate made specifically for the Beech Store as a customer appreciation gift, a fairly common practice at the time. On the back, the mark states, "Wheelock China made in Austria for A.G. Beech, Atlantic, Iowa," and the front features a rendering of the first Atlantic High School.

Franklin H. Whitney was an extremely good businessman, and as he was always looking to bring more people into the area, it should come as no surprise that he ran a successful real estate operation. The advertisement at right shows land selling from a low of $10 per acre up to $25 per acre in March 1887.

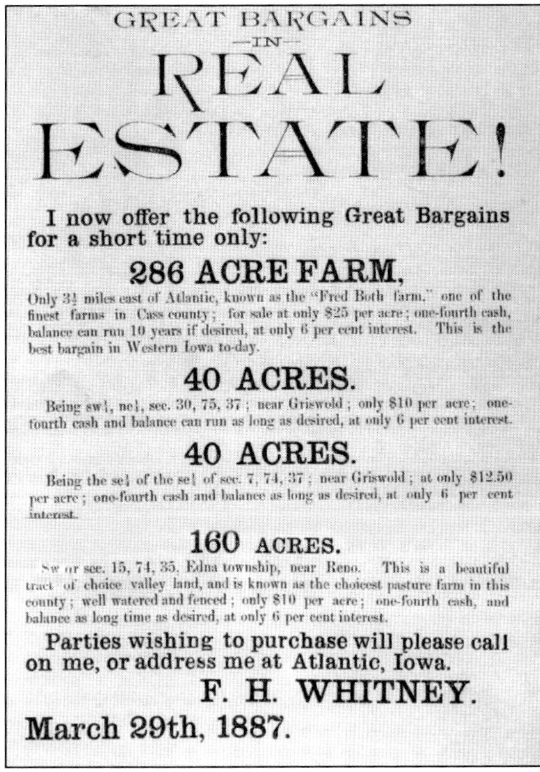

GREAT BARGAINS
—IN—
REAL
ESTATE!

I now offer the following Great Bargains for a short time only:

286 ACRE FARM,

Only 3½ miles east of Atlantic, known as the "Fred Both farm," one of the finest farms in Cass county; for sale at only $25 per acre; one-fourth cash, balance can run 10 years if desired, at only 6 per cent interest. This is the best bargain in Western Iowa to-day.

40 ACRES.

Being sw¼, ne¼, sec. 30, 75, 37; near Griswold; only $10 per acre; one-fourth cash and balance can run as long as desired, at only 6 per cent interest.

40 ACRES.

Being the se¼ of the se¼ of sec. 7, 74, 37; near Griswold; at only $12.50 per acre; one-fourth cash and balance as long as desired, at only 6 per cent interest.

160 ACRES.

Sw¼ of sec. 15, 74, 35, Edna township, near Reno. This is a beautiful tract of choice valley land, and is known as the choicest pasture farm in this county; well watered and fenced; only $10 per acre; one-fourth cash, and balance as long time as desired, at only 6 per cent interest.

Parties wishing to purchase will please call on me, or address me at Atlantic, Iowa.

F. H. WHITNEY.

March 29th, 1887.

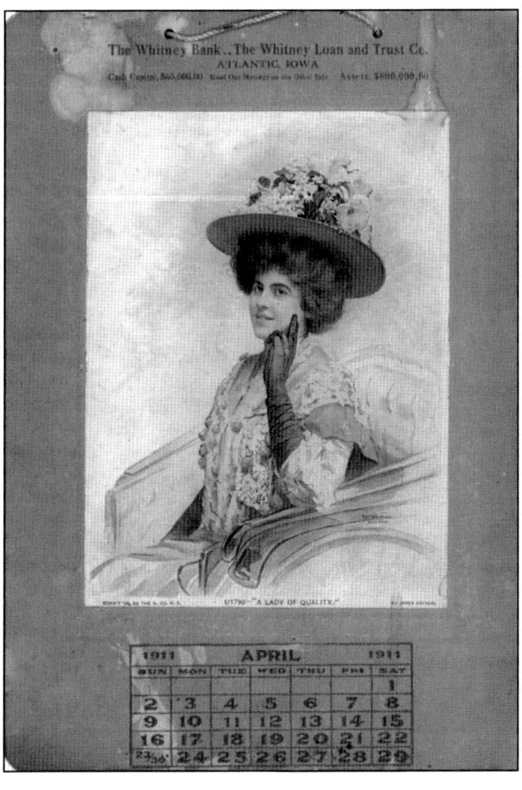

Calendar art came into vogue in the early 1900s, and much of it was quite elaborate. The 1910 calendar, shown left, was a customer appreciation gift of the Whitney Bank and Whitney Loan and Trust of Atlantic. One of the most famous and successful calendar art businesses in the world, the Thomas D. Murphy Company, was located close to Atlantic in Red Oak, Iowa. Calendars such as this are now collectibles.

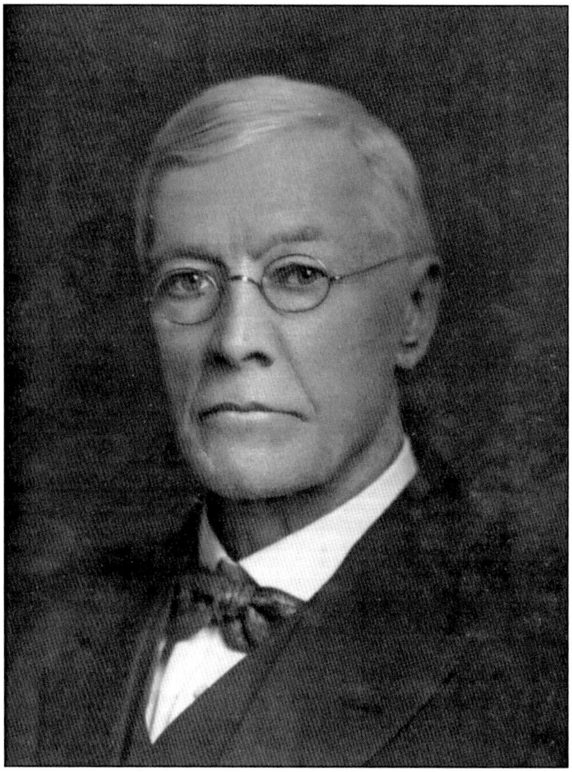

S.F. Martin, pictured left, operated a hardware store in Lewis but moved into Atlantic in 1869. In 1882, he was instrumental in establishing the Atlantic Canning Company with partners J.A. McWaid and Dr. R.D. Wilkin. This was an extremely successful enterprise, but Martin sold out his interest to McWaid in 1890. The business, which became the largest canning company in the world, was eventually sold to J.A. McWaid's son William and J.W. Cuykendall.

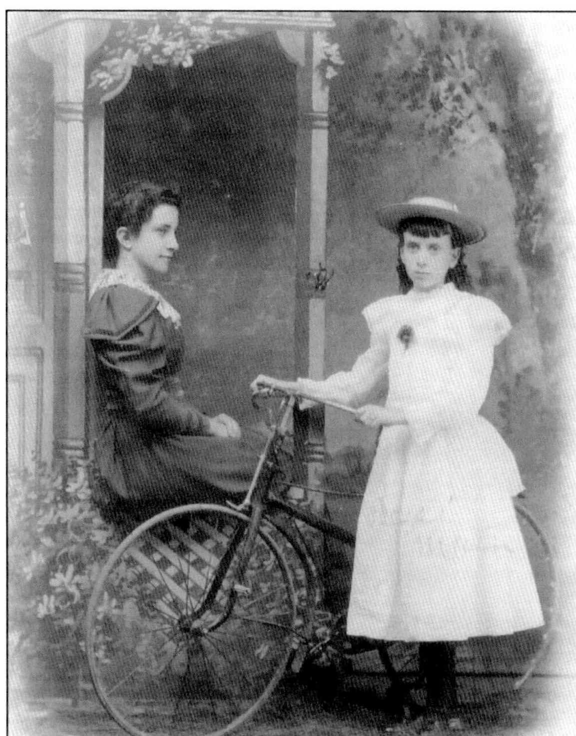

In 1872, Martin built an impressive Second Empire–style home on Fifth and Poplar Streets that is still known as the S.F. Martin House and is currently being restored. Martin left Atlantic in 1893 to operate another canning factory in Carroll, Iowa, but eventually moved to Blair, Nebraska, where he had other business interests. Pictured at right are two of Martin's nieces, Elizabeth Reeves (seated) and Arselia Martin.

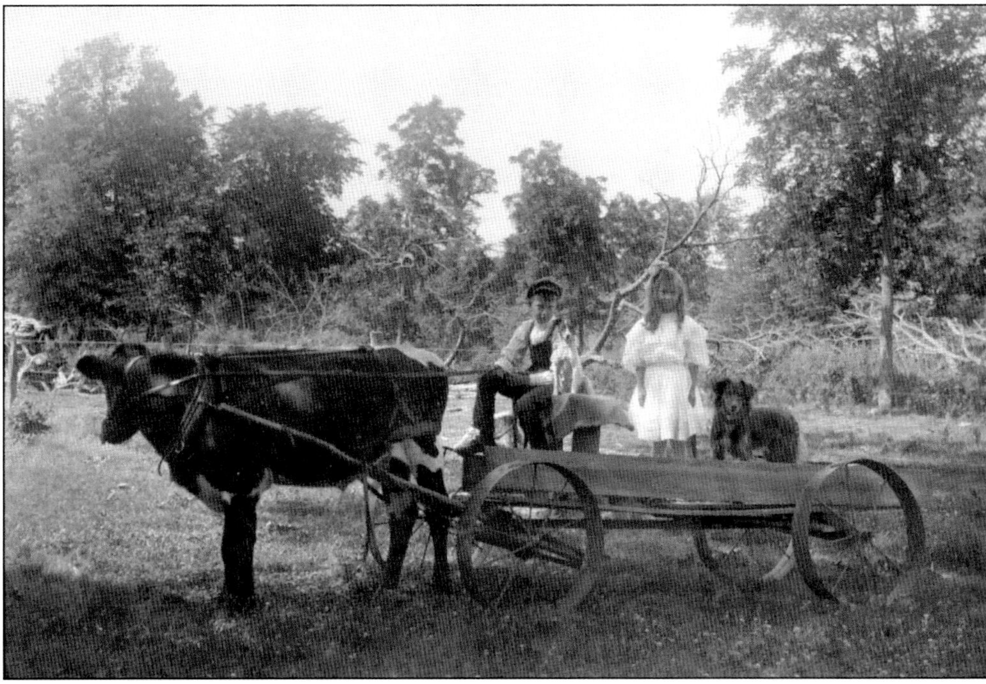

Virt Anderson was born in a log cabin in the northeast section of Atlantic in 1898. His parents farmed, but, after a few years, they sold everything by auction and looked for greener pastures in Washington State, where Virt's sister Sadie was born. The Andersons did not care for the climate in Washington and returned to Iowa. The family moved many times over the years and finally purchased a rooming house at 301 Maple Street in Atlantic in 1920. The above photograph, taken in 1908, is of Virt and Sadie. The photograph below shows Virt and Sadie's father in the buggy that is harnessed to Jim, the steer. Note the advertisements on the side of the barn; most contain a reference to steers, such as, "He will steer you to C.P. Meredith for buggies and coal."

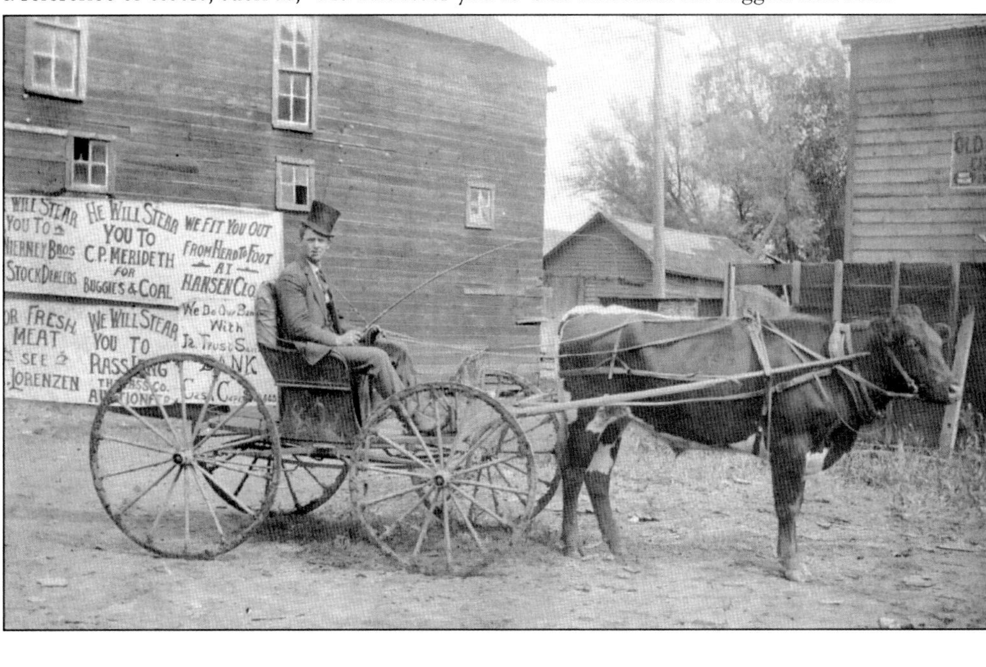

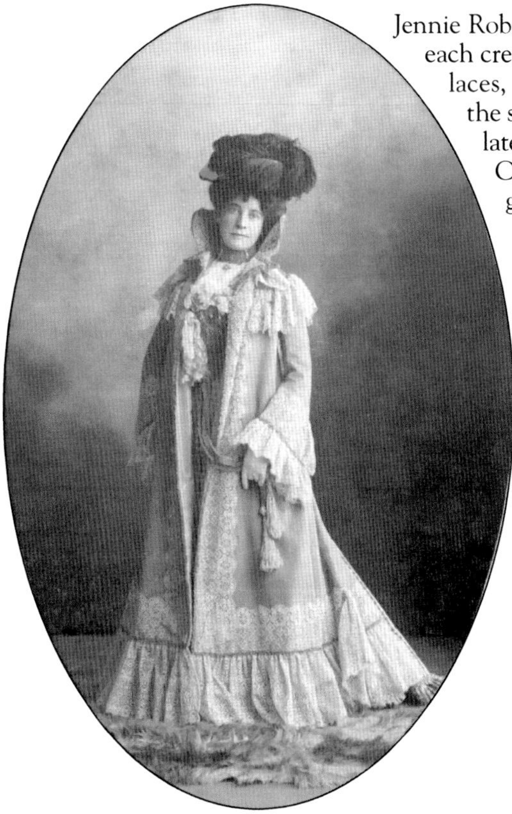

Jennie Roberts was a designer of couture at a time when each creation was made-to-order. The use of brocades, laces, tassels, ruffles, pleats, and elegant fabrics set the style of the day, and a hat was de rigueur in the late 1890s. She lived at 613 Poplar Street. Zeta and Corrie Osborne were both married in Roberts's gowns; Zeta's can be seen in the Cass County Museum in Griswold.

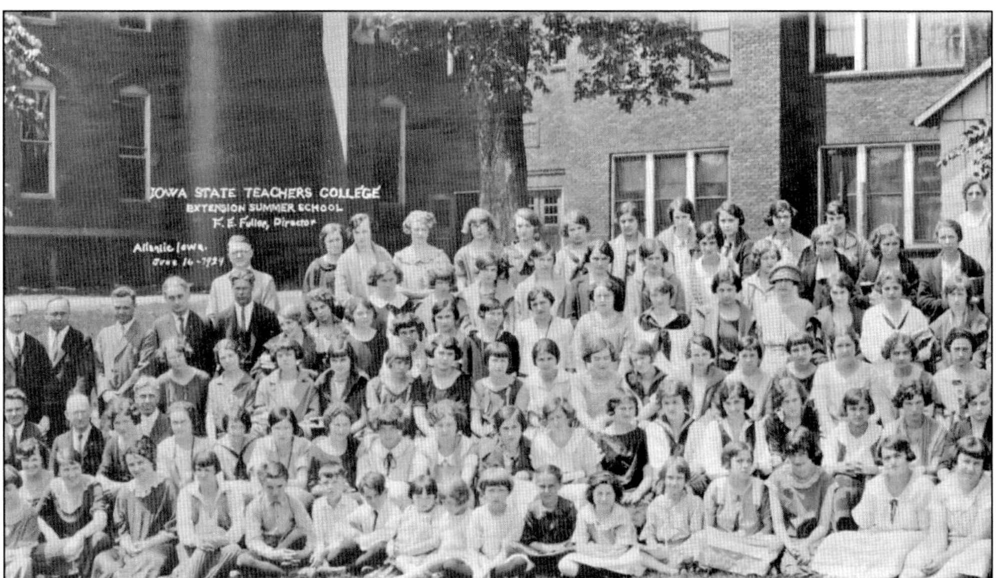

Iowa State Teachers College conducted extension summer schools around the state. The college sent out professors to teach certain subjects for students and other subjects for teachers. Atlantic hosted such a school in June 1924 with F.E. Fuller as director. Over 300 people attended, and this photograph shows a portion of the group.

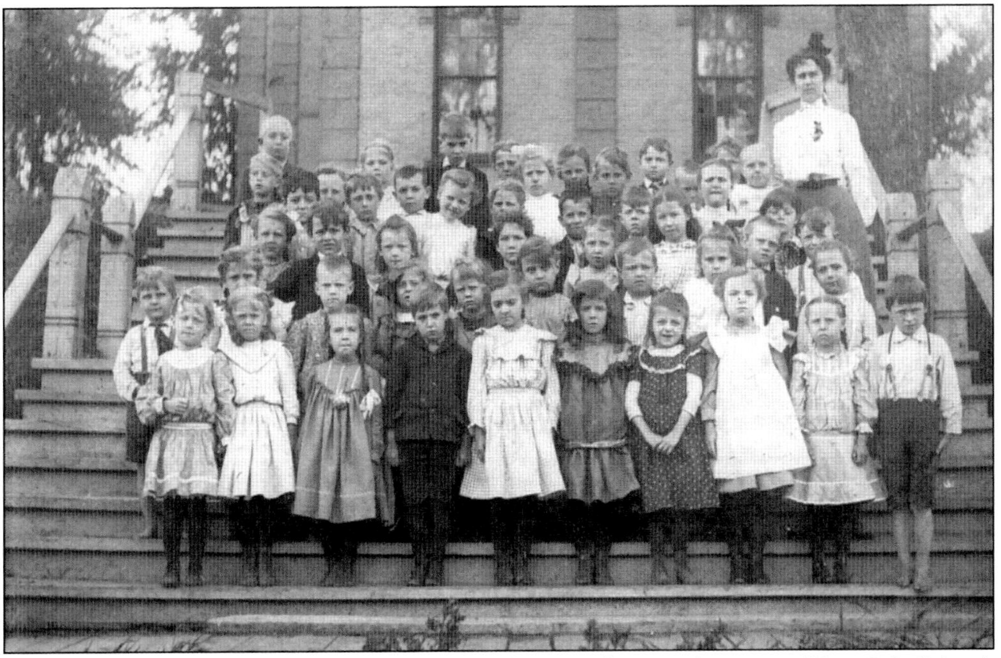

This 1903 photograph shows a group of first graders standing on the steps of East Side School. This building was erected in the 1870s. The continual growth of Atlantic, particularly during the next decade, required an ongoing expansion of school facilities. Note that the boys on both the left and right sides of the photograph are not wearing shoes.

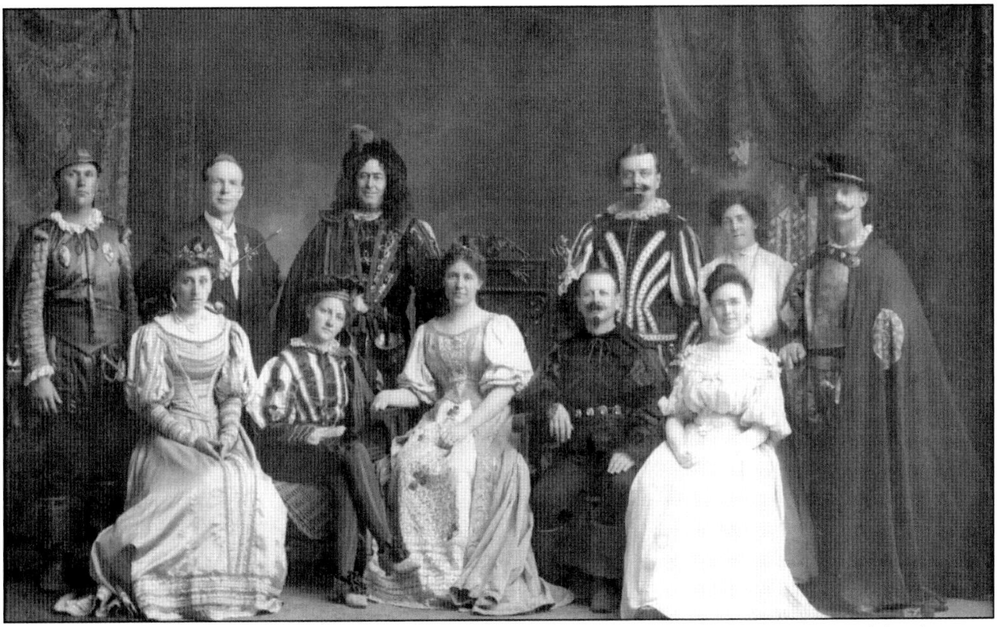

This 1906 photograph shows members of the Atlantic Choral Union. The group posed for this cast picture when they were performing the operetta *Maritana*. From left to right are (first row) Lizzie Hoenke, Rose Danvenport, Mrs. Wilson, Mr. Welch, and Mable Taylor Whitney; (second row) Ira Painter, Dave Shuter, Billy McConville, Thomas Whitney, Elizabeth Daly, and unidentified. Tom Whitney was the younger son of Atlantic founder Franklin H. Whitney.

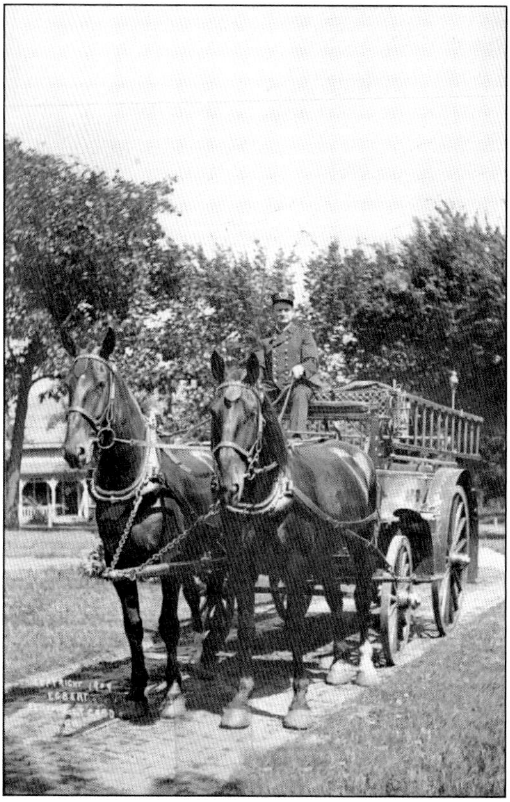

At the 1909 Atlantic Firemen's Fair, Atlantic's Fire Team No.1 poses for this photograph taken by the prestigious Egbert Studio. Patch and Dan are the horses, and they featured prominently in the numerous state awards won by the Atlantic Fire Department. The driver is identified as Hillman Wright. Different towns held firemen's fairs in which the firemen and their teams competed for honors in such events as ladder climbing.

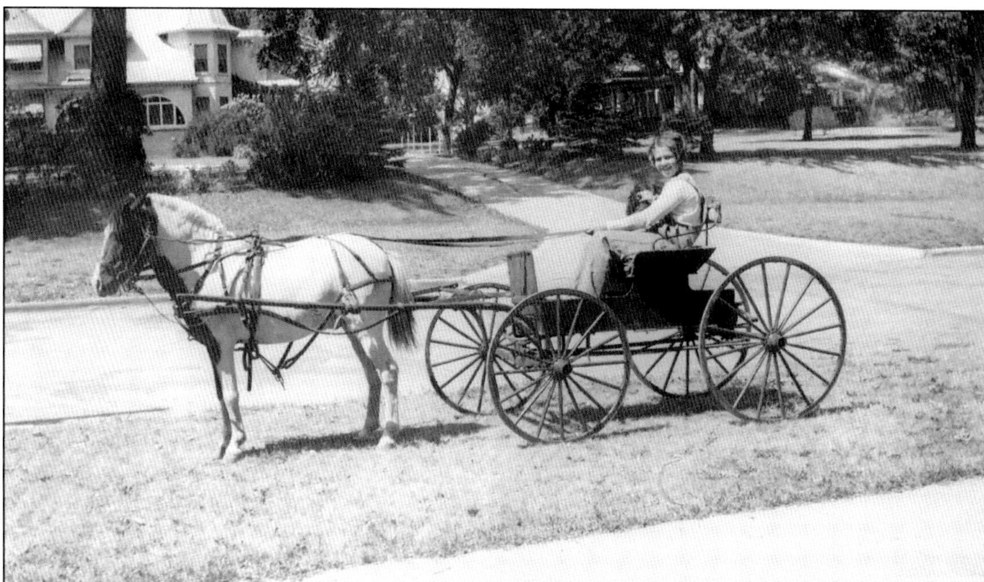

Phyllis Otto is shown here in front of the Dick Bell home in Atlantic. On August 27, 1945, she won the Western Amateur Golf Tournament in Chicago over golf celebrity Babe Didrikson Zaharias. Otto was responsible for starting junior golf at the Atlantic Country Club. Her parents were Oscar and Eloise Otto; Oscar Otto served as president and later as chairman of the board of the Whitney Bank.

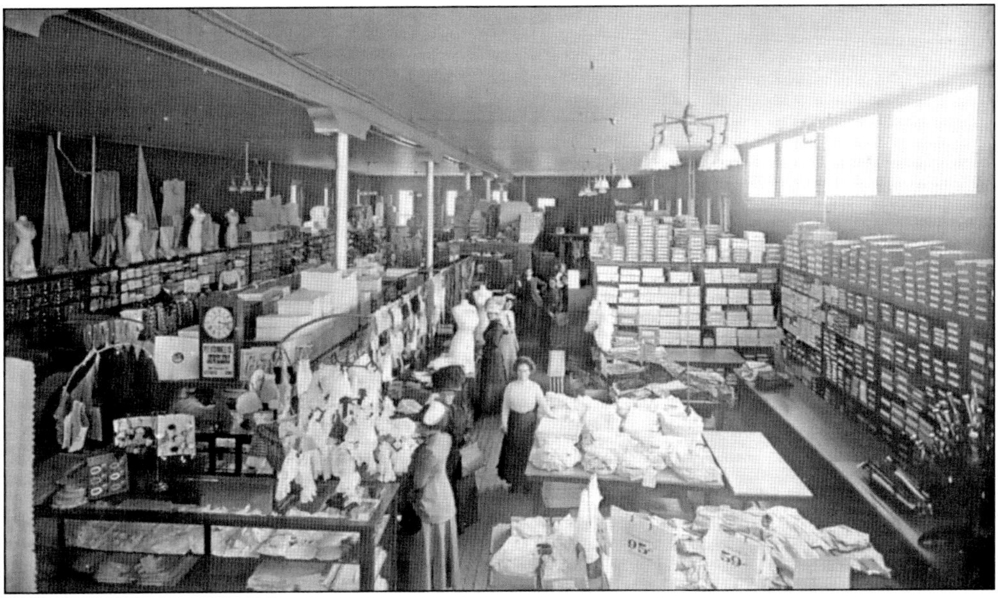

L. Oransky and Sons, commonly called Oransky's, was a very popular department store in Atlantic in the early 1900s. It was located at 501–503 Chestnut Street. One of its advertisements in the *Atlantic News Telegraph* reads, "The bargains offered to you in our Ladies' Ready-to-Wear section during this bargain fest will reach far beyond your anticipation." The store offered "Highest grade Wooltex Coats, lustrous Astrakhans, beautiful Caucasians . . . All priced at your choice. $11.95." The photographs show the interior and exterior. Oransky's served as the Santa Claus headquarters in Atlantic, and large crowds gathered each December to visit Santa. In March 1925, Oransky's was sold to A.D. Bullock and his son Wayne, of Anita.

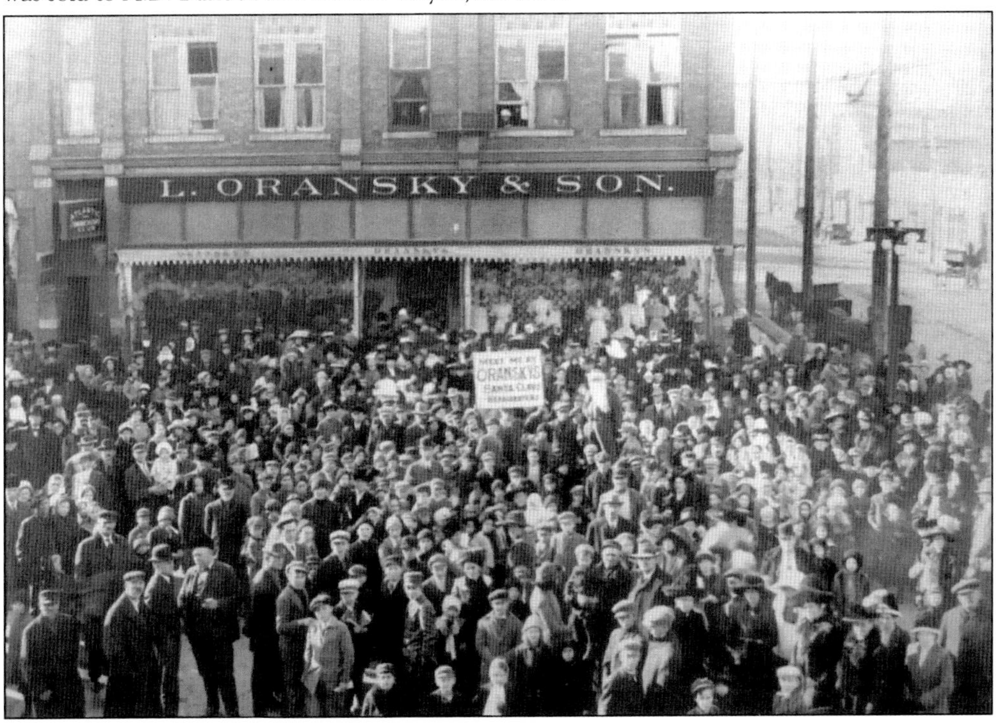

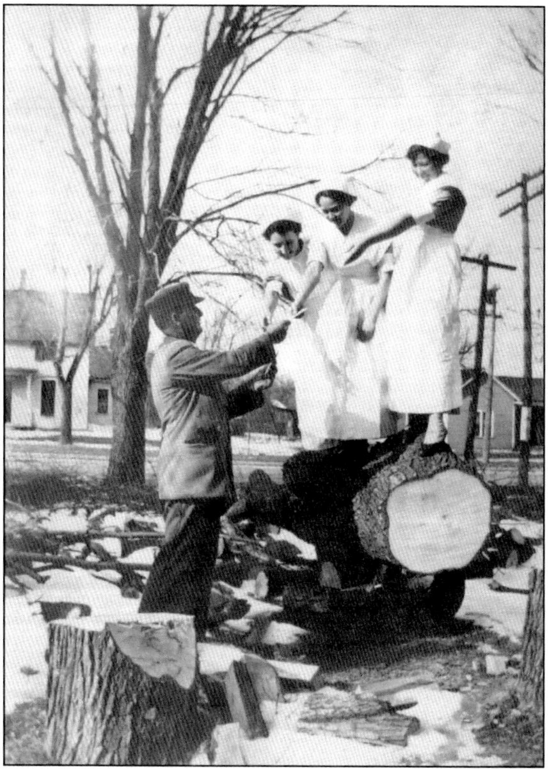

The nurses at the Carlyle Jones Hospital in Atlantic loved it when the postman arrived. The student nurses underwent their training at the hospital, which was also where they took room and board. Letters from loved ones were treasured. Pictured in 1919, they were not above giving the postman a hard time and themselves a little break from the serious responsibilities of their chosen profession.

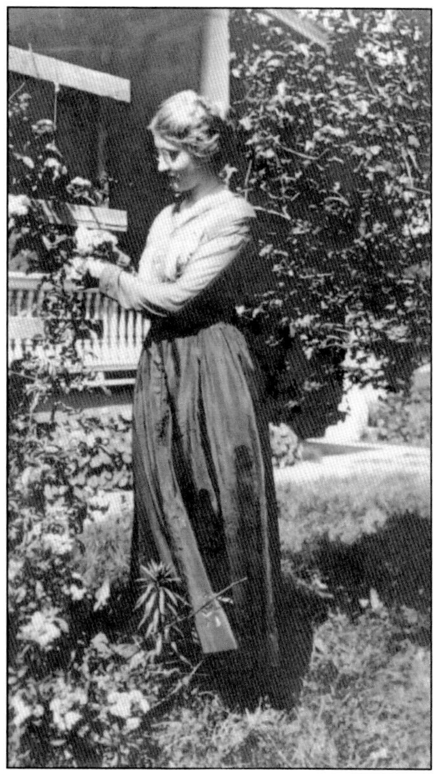

In 1910, Dr. Carlyle Jones opened a medical practice in Lewis. He moved his practice to Atlantic in 1916 and established the Jones Hospital on Walnut Street. Jones was married to Jessie Caulder of Omaha, and they established a home in Atlantic. The photograph at right shows Caulder-Jones in her rose garden.

Dr. W.S. Greenleaf delivered many children, such as the three pictured right, during his tenure in Atlantic. He served at the Atlantic hospital that was located at Fifth and Oak Streets. This facility was affiliated with the University Hospitals of Iowa City and had a medical, surgical, and teaching staff of 11, including Dr. Greenleaf and Dr. U.S. Mullins. Greenleaf served as secretary of the Atlantic Hospital Corporation.

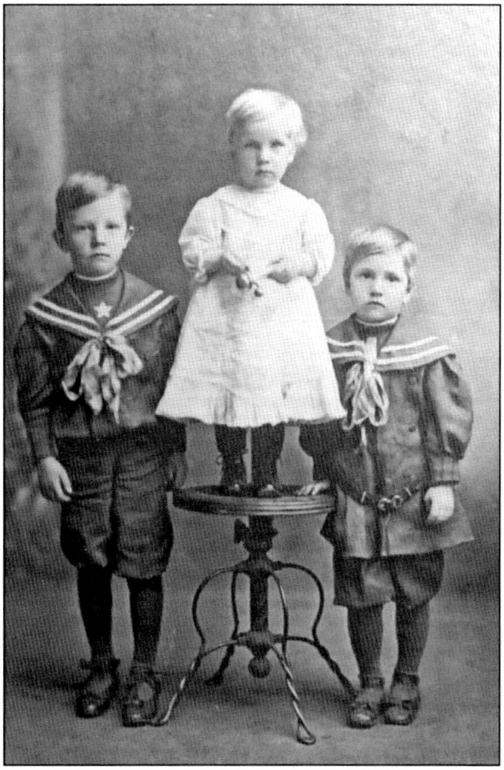

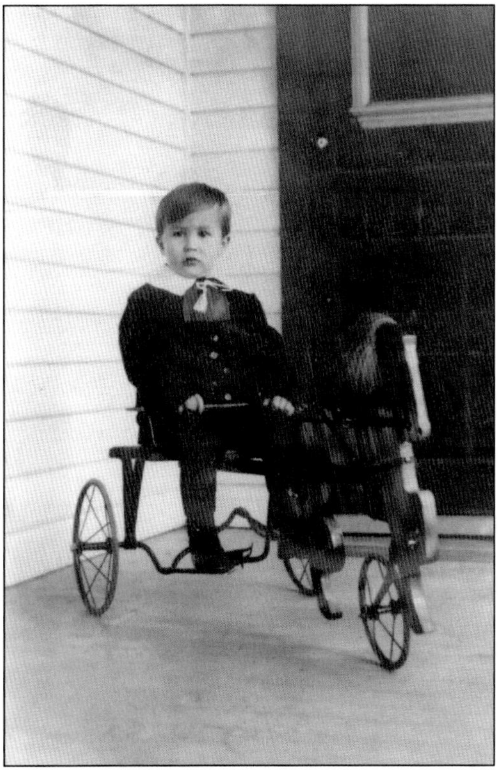

This appealing young lad is George Onken, son of Walter Onken, a great-uncle of Richard MacCauley of Atlantic. The photograph shows a serious-minded young George dressed in his Sunday best, posed on his tricycle. In the early 1900s, many toys were still handcrafted, but elaborate tricycles were manufactured in the United States as early as the 1880s.

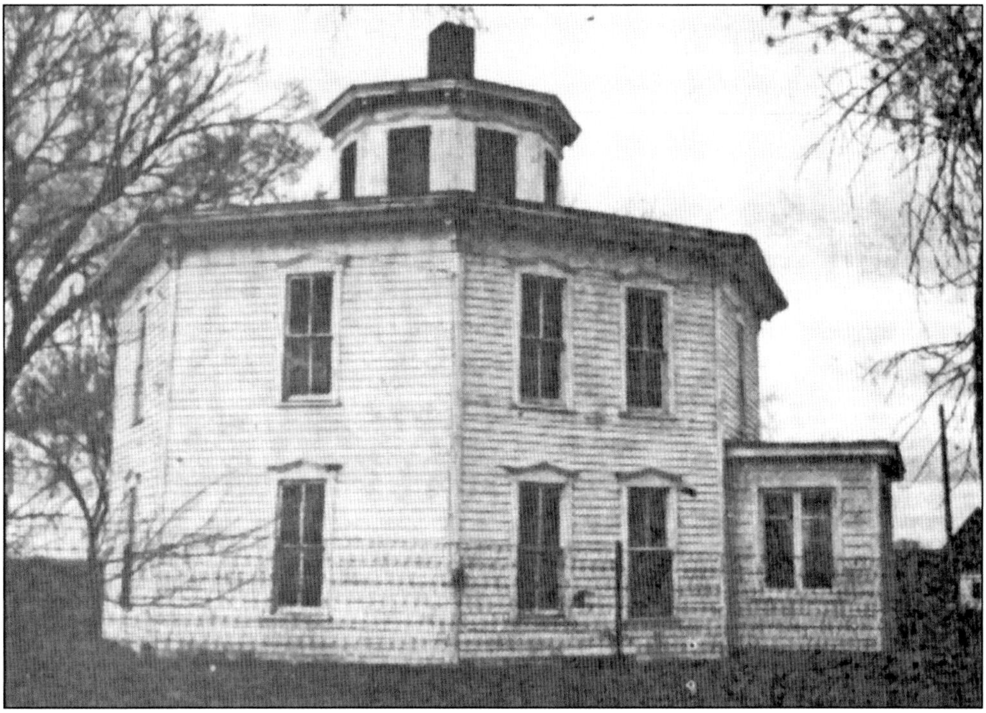

William Duncan built this eight-sided house in Atlantic after the Civil War. While legend says he built it to please his eight daughters who all wanted a "room with a view," it is known that he had only one daughter, Addie. In 1878, she was the first girl to graduate from Atlantic High School. The interior featured a beautiful spiral staircase built by William McElwain, an Atlantic cabinetmaker. A model of the staircase can be seen at the Cass County Museum.

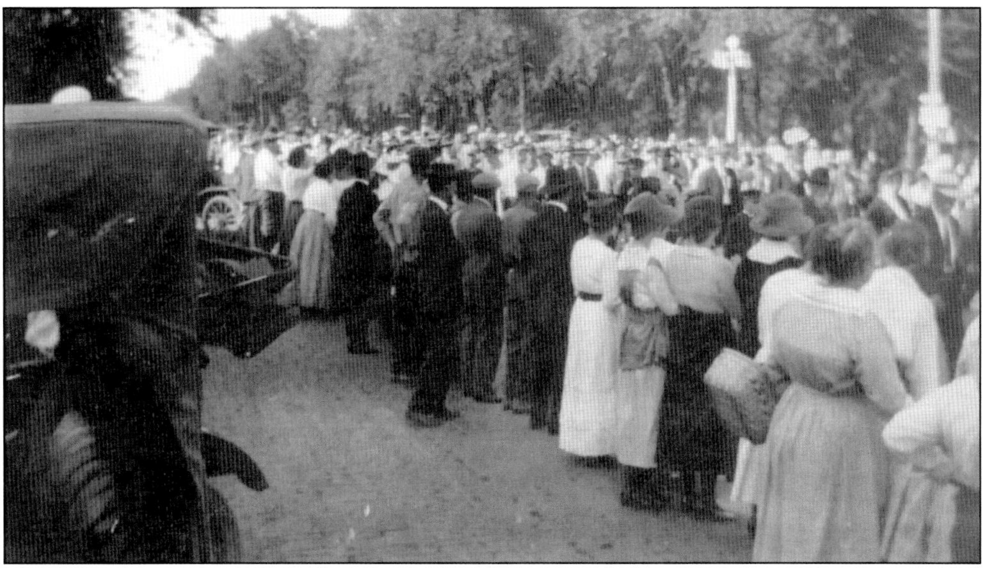

According to an early edition of the *Atlantic News Telegraph*, the end of World War I in 1918 was the highlight of the decade: "It touched off the greatest and wildest celebration Atlantic had ever seen. When word reached Atlantic at 3:00 a.m., the fire bells rang, whistles blew, and people rushed into the streets to hear the news . . . The celebration continued throughout the day."

In 1869, Belle Tiffany, who was originally from Waukegan, Illinois, established the first private school in Atlantic. She had no trouble getting students, but obtaining books was another story. The students brought whatever books they could spare from home, and one can imagine the confusion that ensued. Tiffany did not deal with the problem for too long, because she caught the fancy of a prosperous local civic leader and businessman, Cyrus B. Osborne. The couple married in Chicago in 1872. They had two daughters, Zeta and Corrie. Zeta married Hugh Reinig in 1898; Corrie married Delmar Herbert in 1908.

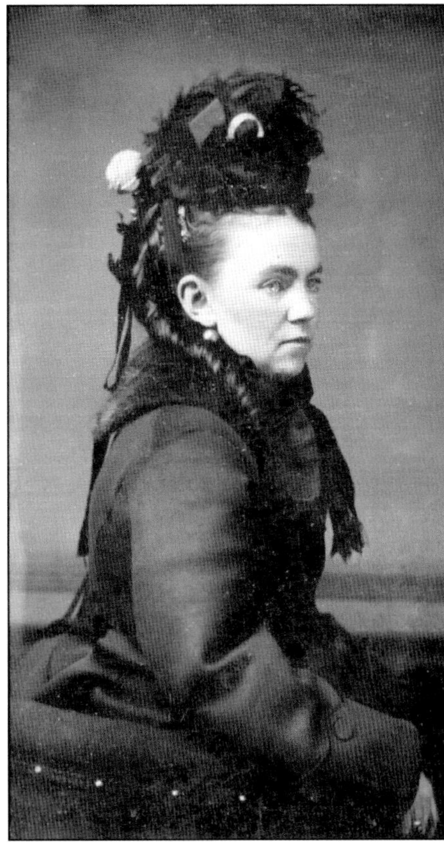

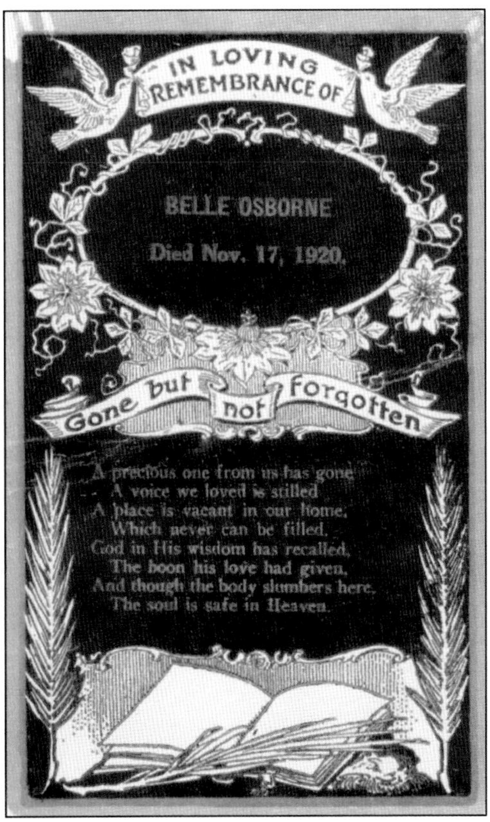

Hugh Reinig was the son of L.O. Reinig, who came to Cass County in 1867 and was a respected businessman in Lewis. Delmar Herbert was the son of Franklin Herbert, an early Cass County recorder. A remembrance card for Tiffany-Osborne is shown at left.

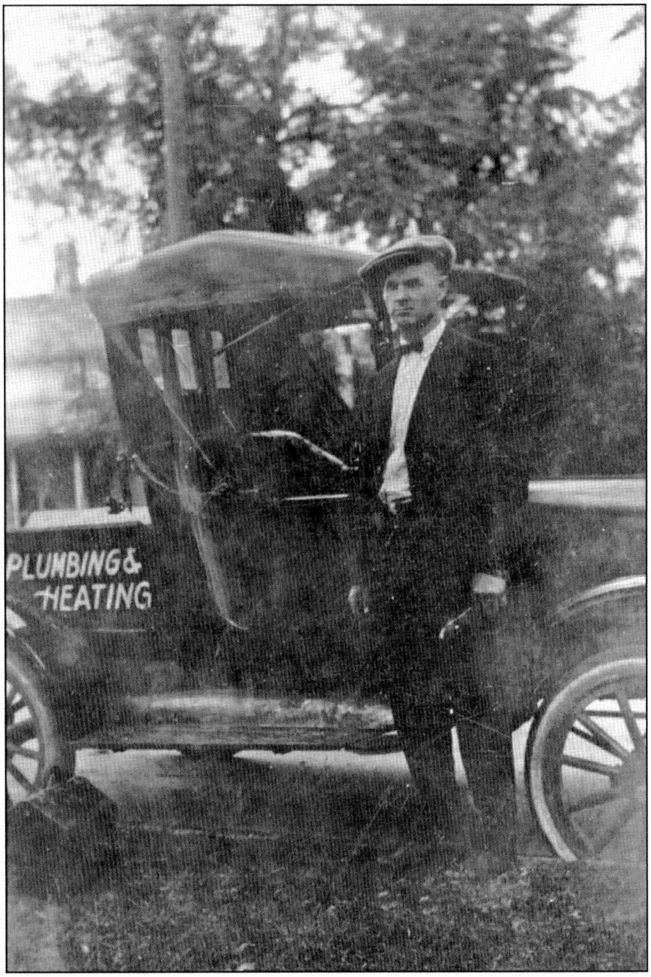

Lou Camblin started his plumbing and heating business in Atlantic in 1919. This photograph shows Camblin standing beside his Ford Model T truck. The office and warehouse began in his home at 604 Fifth Street. As business grew and prospered, he moved downtown to the basement of the Wood and Savery Abstract Office at Sixth and Chestnut Streets, shown below. In the ensuing years, Camblin installed both plumbing and heating in practically all the newly constructed homes in and around Atlantic. At this time, coal was a popular source of heat, and many people were delighted when a mechanical coal stoker was developed. This apparatus had a fire pot, an auger, a blower, and a hopper. With the hopper filled with Iowa coal, "the heat was on," and the only thing left to do was watch out for clinkers.

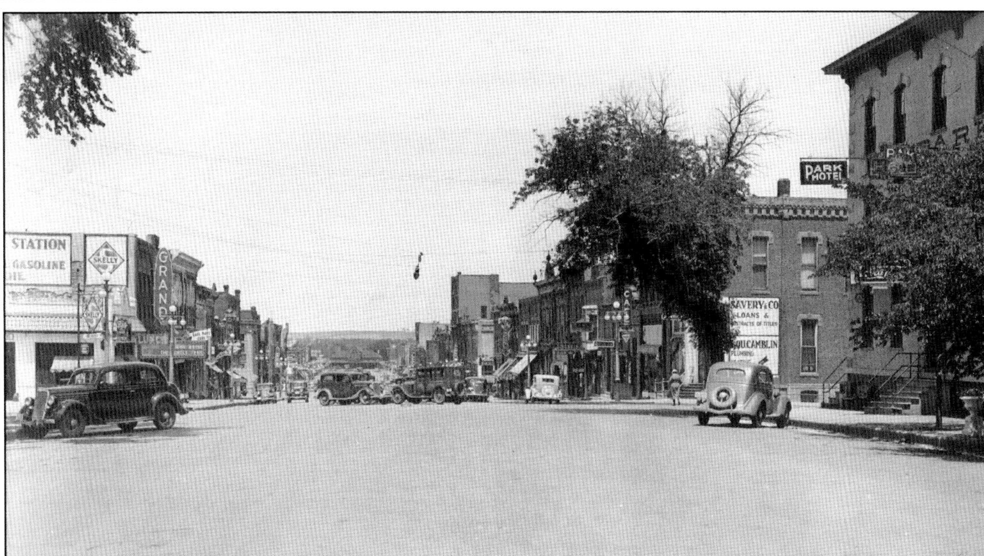

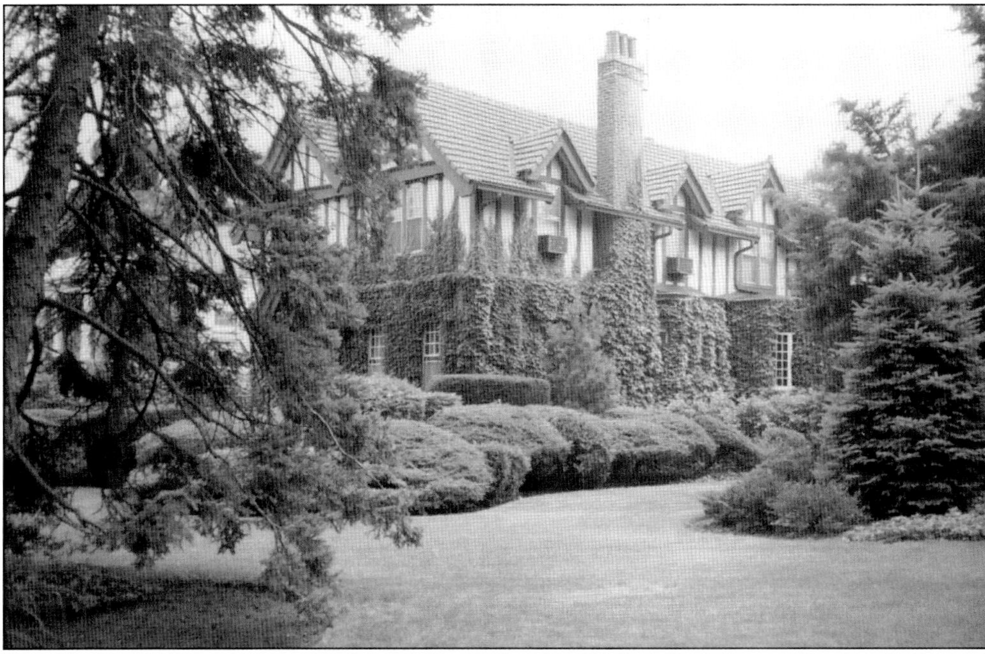

The land at 1200 Chestnut Street has a story to tell. Loring L. DeLano, a prominent Atlantic attorney, built the first of three homes on the property. It was sold to local banker and financier Edgar S. Harlan, who proceeded to tear it down in 1910 and build the second residence. Business prompted the Harlans to move to Chicago, Illinois. When Harlan informed his wife, Ethel, of the move, she stated that she would only go if the house went with her. The home was taken apart and transported by rail to Chicago in 1918. The above photograph of that reconstructed residence was taken in Chicago in 2008. The third home, shown below, was built by Frank M. Nebe in 1922. Nebe was a well-known Atlantic businessman who operated a very successful shoe company. The house he built is now beautifully restored and owned by Roland and Sandi Landsness.

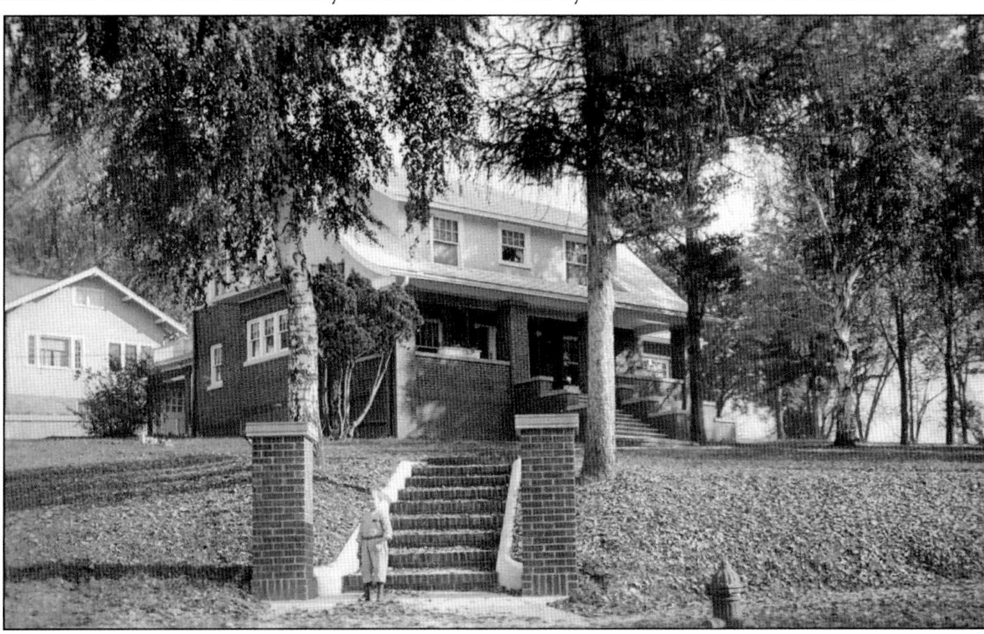

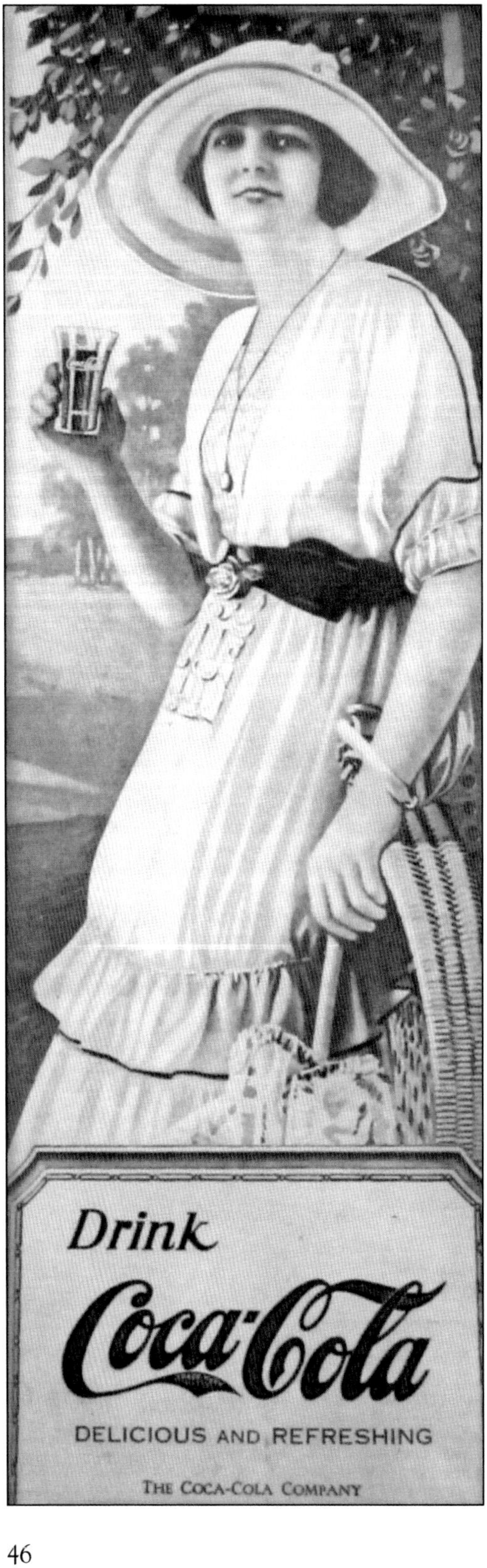

Atlantic is the Coca-Cola capital of Iowa. Three generations of the Tyler family have been instrumental in building this successful Atlantic business and in advancing the interests of the city. The family secured the franchise contract when it was found in the safe of a creamery they had purchased in Clarinda. Coca-Cola was not known in Iowa at the time, but the Tyler family introduced it, and the rest is history. The company built a new plant in 1940, located on Second Street in Atlantic. Besides Coca-Cola, the facility has bottled 7 Up, Like, Tab, Dr. Pepper, Frostie, Fresca, Squirt, and Tyler flavors such as orange. The Coca-Cola Company has always been in the forefront of quality advertising. This early advertisement is typical of the refinement adhered to by the company over the years. Coca-Cola items are collectibles, and a great variety can be seen in the Atlantic Coca-Cola Center and Museum.

Four

Brighton, Pymosa, and Washington Townships

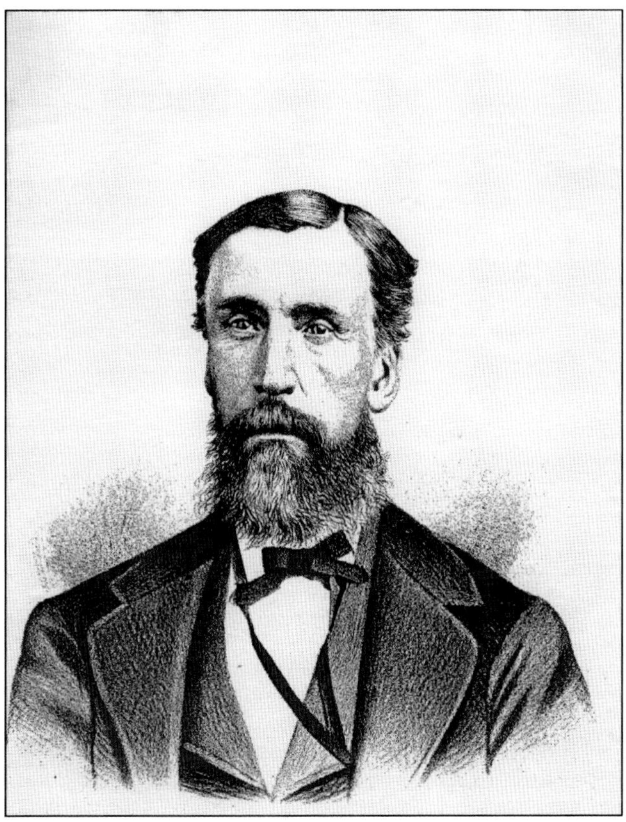

Thomas O. Meredith epitomized the pioneer breed of men who settled in Cass County. He helped his father break the virgin prairie and clear the forests. Meredith made his home in Marne, where he farmed and operated a general store. In 1861, he served on the first board of supervisors of Cass County. Meredith was involved in naming the township and suggested it be called Brittain (Britain). Judge Lorah vetoed the name, and a compromise was made; the township was called Brighton.

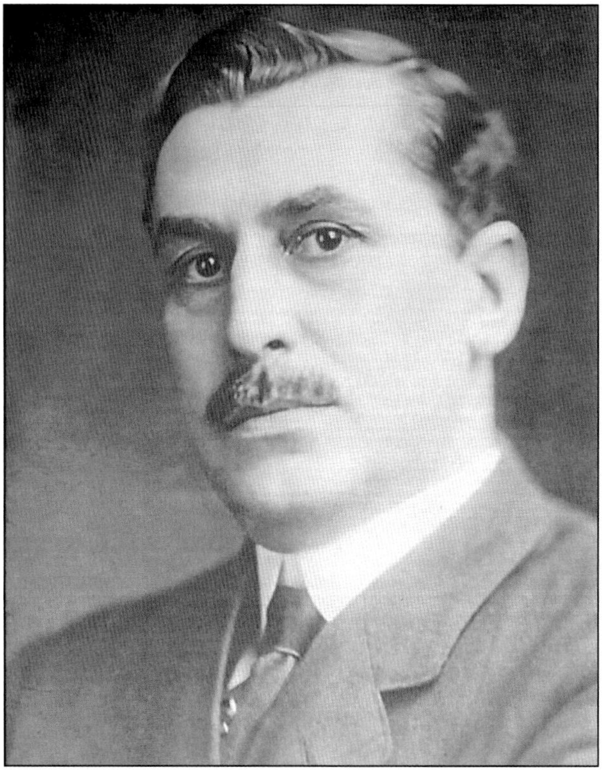

Edwin T. Meredith, son of Thomas O. Meredith and Minerva March Meredith, was a Marne High School graduate. He served as both Iowa secretary of agriculture and later the United States secretary of agriculture in the administration of Pres. Woodrow Wilson. Edwin Meredith founded the Meredith Publishing Company of Des Moines, now known as the Meredith Corporation.

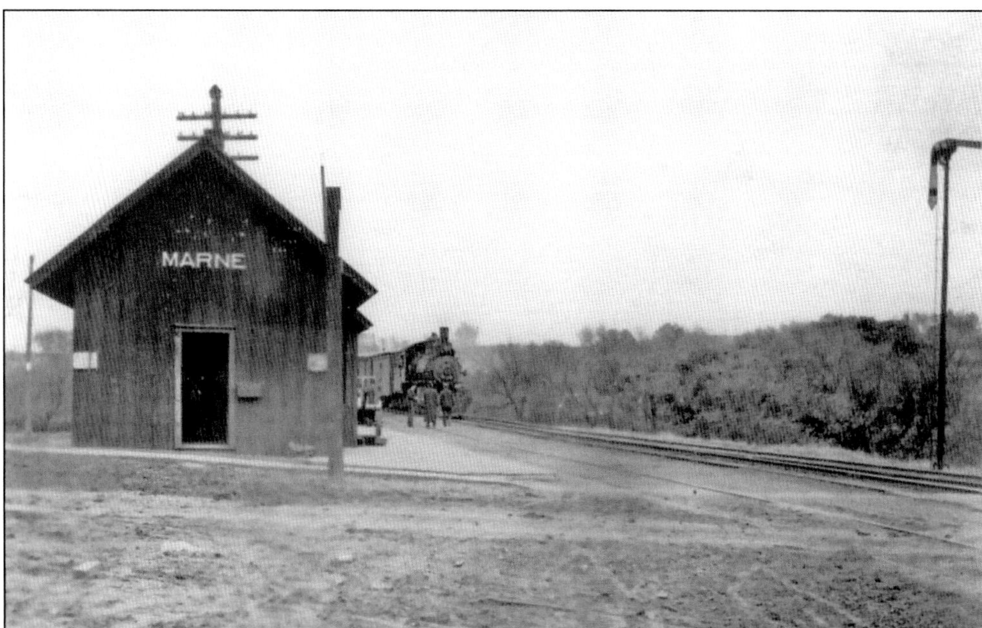

The Rock Island Railroad pushed its line through Brighton Township in 1868 prior to the incorporation of the town of Marne. Once established, the town grew rapidly, becoming a shipping center for grain and livestock. This 1909 photograph of the Marne Depot shows the stationmaster and two local men as a train enters the station.

Samuel J. Kirkwood, pictured at right, served three terms as governor of Iowa. In 1875, James B. Weaver, pictured below, thought he had the nomination for governor secured when Dr. Samuel Ballard of Brighton Township nominated Kirkwood. In an unprecedented vote, Kirkwood, not even a candidate, was elected to a third term.

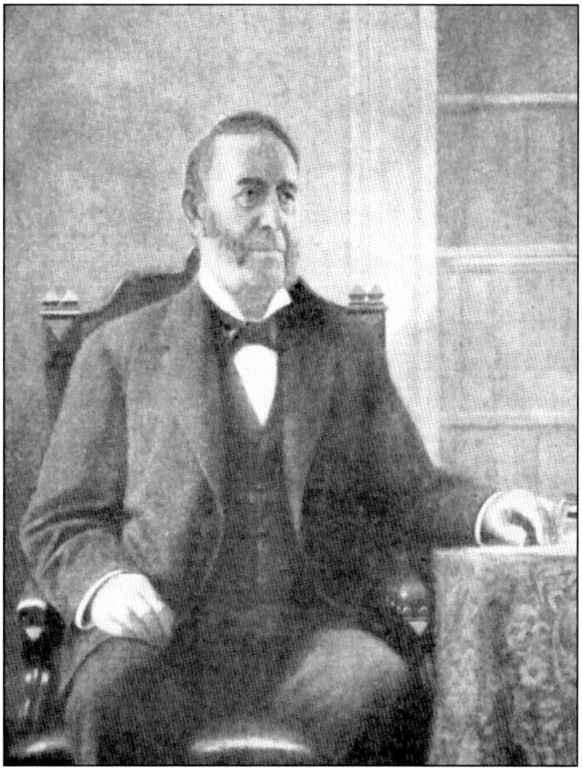

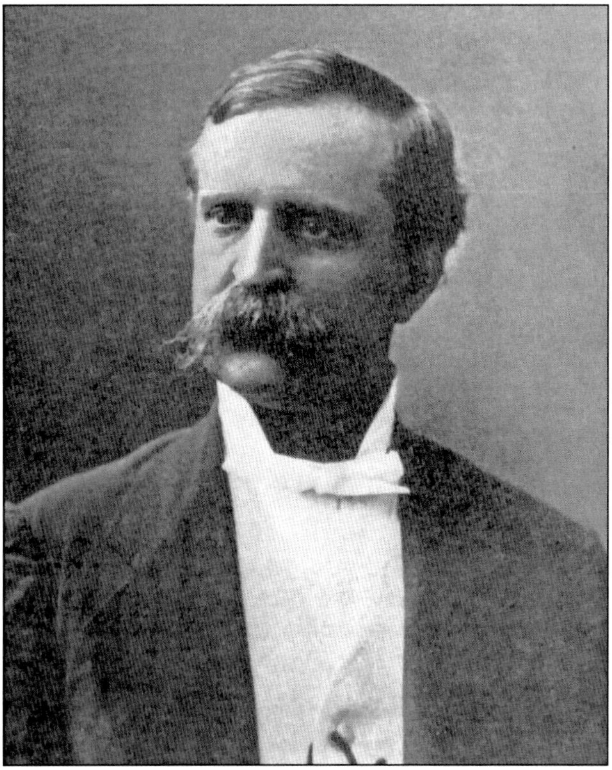

Ballard helped found the Republican Party of Iowa. He had come to the area in 1881 and practiced medicine in Cass and Audubon Counties. Often working 20 out of 24 hours and frequently sleeping in the saddle as he made his rounds, he amassed great wealth that he put into land and property in Brighton and Pymosa Townships. He spent only enough to provide the bare essentials. At one time, Ballard kept large herds of cattle. He was frequently robbed, and it is thought that the culprits were members of the notorious Crooked Creek Gang led by "Old Knowlton."

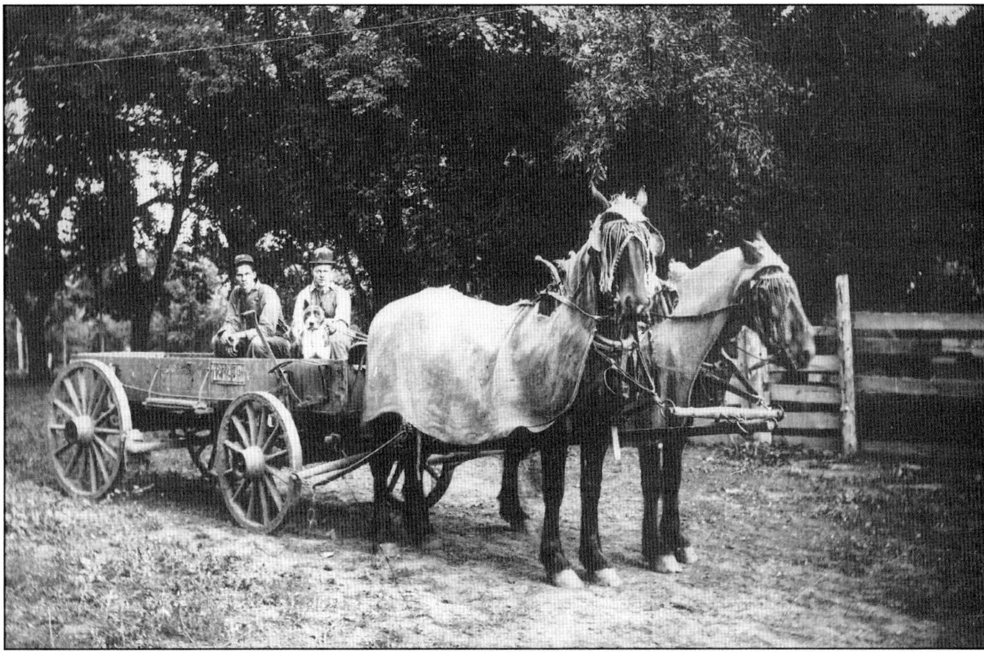

At a time when horses were used as a means of transportation and as beasts of burden, they also provided the power needed to farm the land, which made them very valuable commodities. Flies were known carriers of disease and were a terrible irritation to the horses. Some horse owners solved the problem by draping their stock in fly nets that provided protection from the pests.

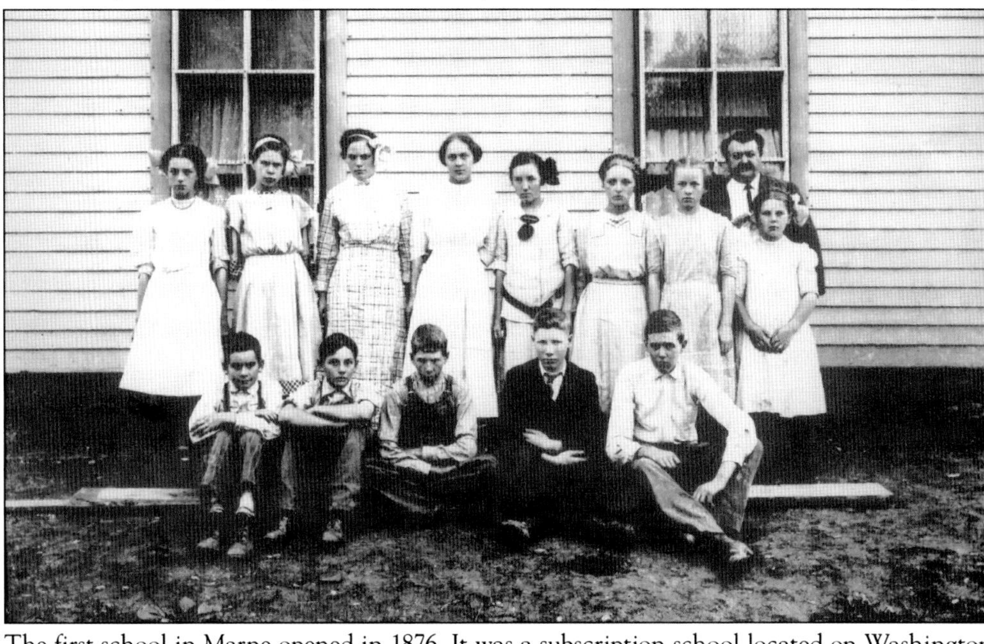

The first school in Marne opened in 1876. It was a subscription school located on Washington Street until the structure shown here was erected in 1877. The only two individuals identified are (standing) Edna Kellogg Brindley, fourth from left, and Mildred Swinburn Rogers, fifth from left. This school was used until 1951, when a brick school was erected. Marne joined the Atlantic School District in the 1960s.

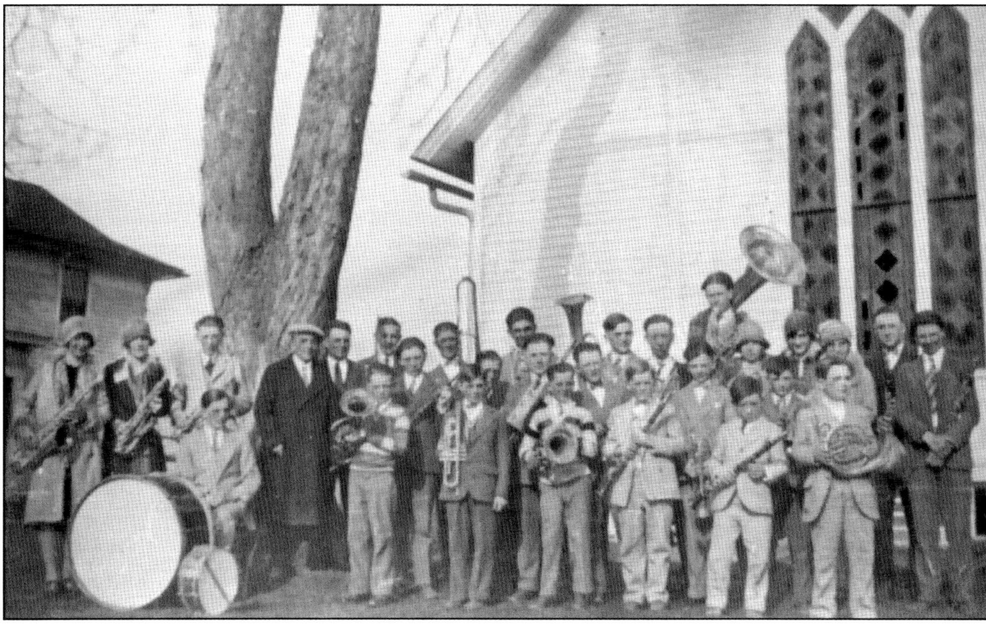

Under the leadership of Jim Smith, the Marne Community Band played weekly concerts at the town bandstand in the late 1920s. In 1927, the band performed on the Anita radio station sponsored by Walnut Grove Products of Atlantic, originally an Anita company. The band was very popular at county fairs and around southwest Iowa. Band member Vernon Wheatley formed his own group, the Marionettes, which featured locally popular singer Dorothy Kilgallen.

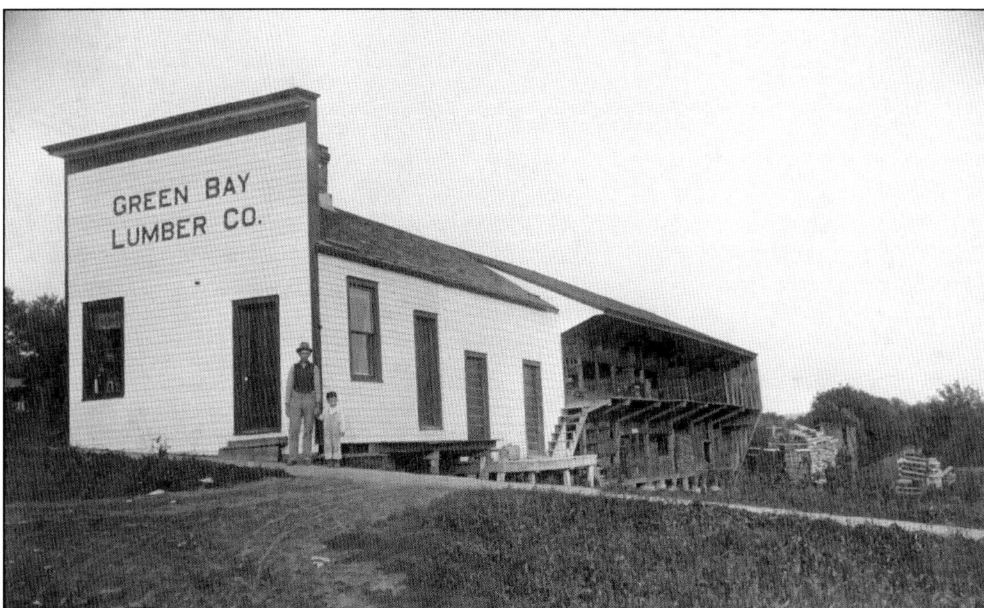

The Green Bay Lumber Company was located on the southeast corner of Main and Washington Streets in Marne. The lumber business opened in 1887 and continued to operate for over 50 years. The election to incorporate the town was held in this store in 1892. In 1973, the ballots from this election were found at the Cass County Courthouse. Several had been disqualified due to colorful remarks that had been written on them by voters.

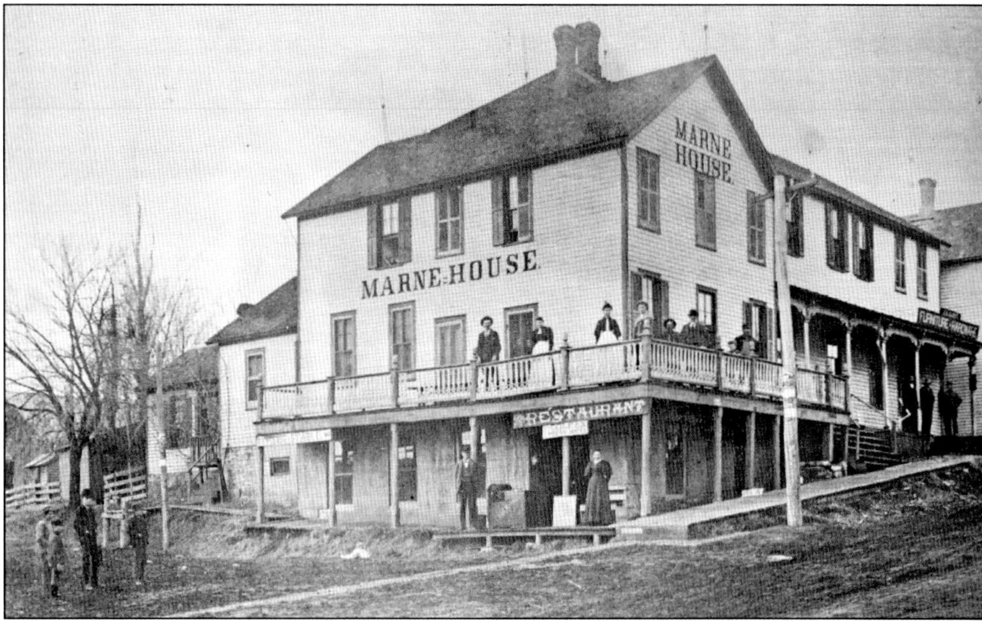

This 1908 photograph shows the Marne House Hotel, located on the corner of Main and Washington Streets. It accommodated passengers using the Rock Island Railroad. Hans Simonsen, a local businessman, built the hotel in 1878. An early newspaper, the *Marne Message*, describes the Marne House as being well furnished and having good accommodations for travelers. Entertainment was close at hand as a dance hall was located in the basement.

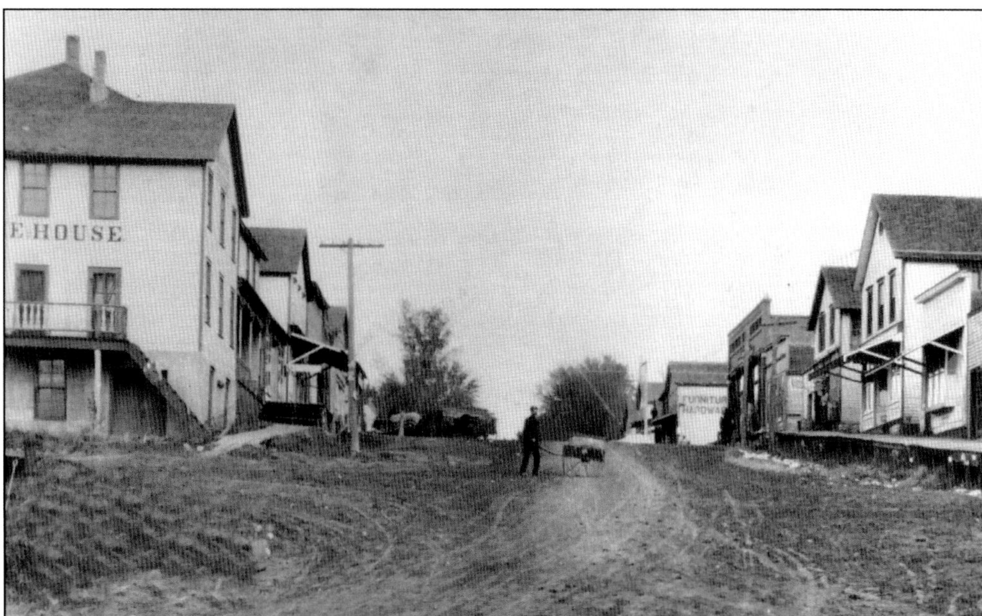

The Marne Post Office was established in 1876. The first postmaster was Julius Langfelt. The office changed locations several times through the years. In this 1909 photograph, Joe Lasker is crossing Main Street with his mail cart. The office was designated as a money order office in July 1878 and issued about $15,000 in orders per year.

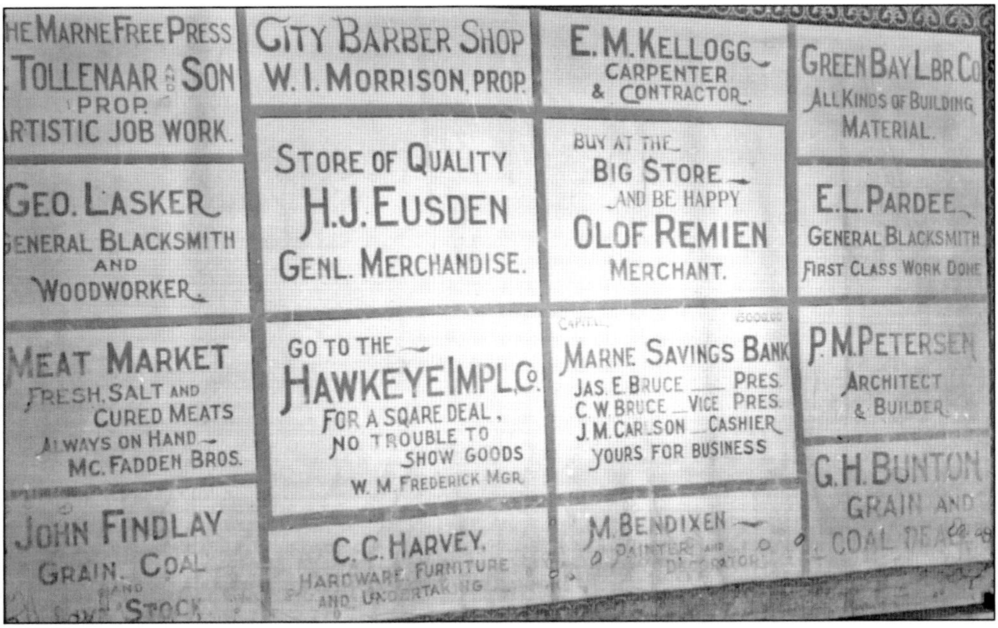

Thomas Meredith owned the Brighton House Hotel in Marne that became the home of Grove Lodge No. 492 of the Masonic Order in 1892. This canvas stage curtain was used at the lodge for many years. It advertised the many businesses operating in the 1890s when Marne was a thriving community. The play *The Little Clodhoppers* was performed on this stage in 1909. This historic building was razed in 2009. Grove Lodge No. 492 continues as the oldest fraternal organization in Marne.

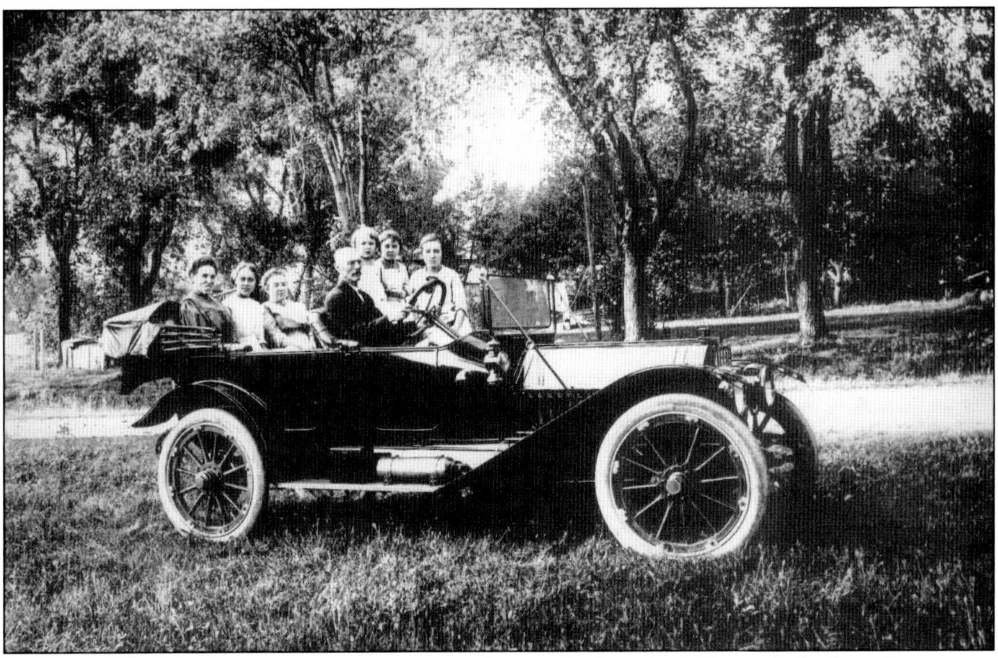

The horseless carriage was frequently met with outright hostility. Horses bolted, and runaways were common when cars approached with their raucous bulb horns and constant noise. In this image are, from left to right, (front seat) Edward Kellogg, Neoma Brindley Ridlen, Leah Brindley, and unidentified; (backseat) Maude Brindley, Edna Brindley, and Grandma Brindley.

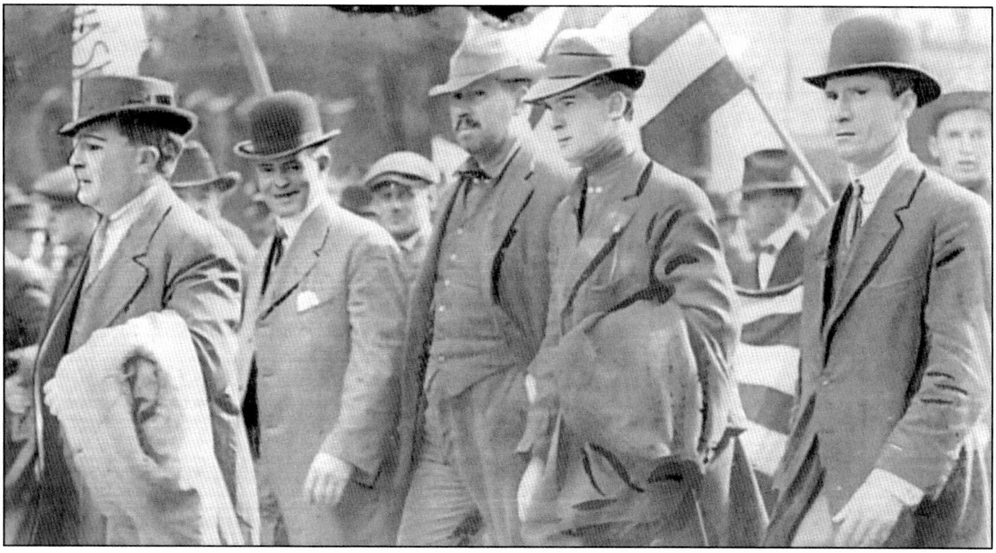

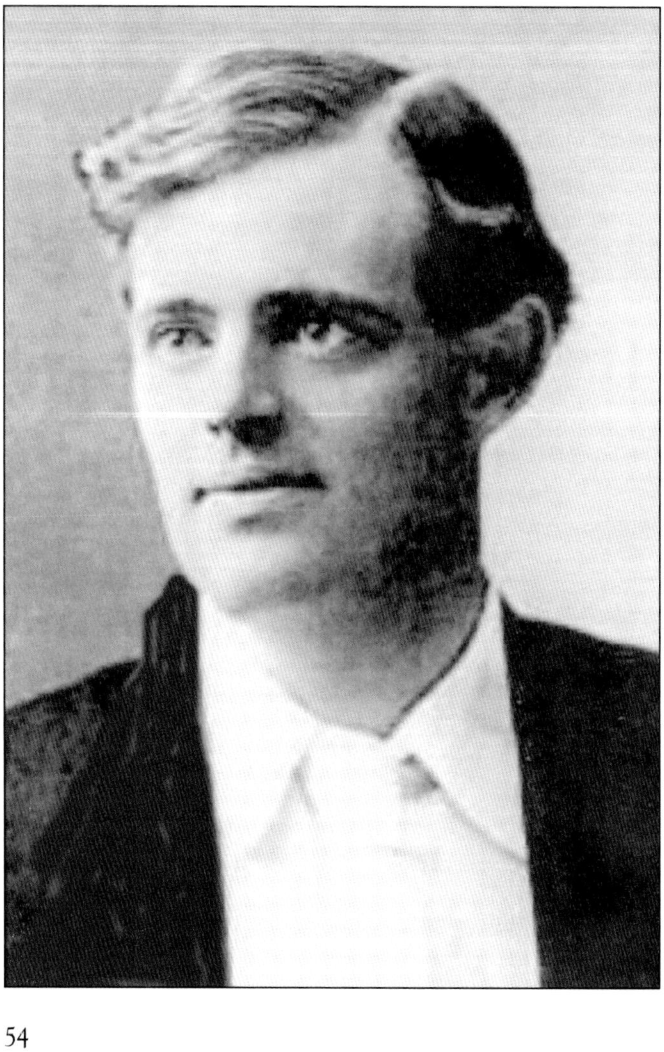

In 1894, Iowa experienced one of the worst droughts in its history; there were no crops, farmers shot livestock they could not feed, and hogs were rushed to a glutted market. Iowa was in the depths of a financial depression. Gov. Frank Jackson received word that an army of 2,000 unemployed men under the command of "General" Charles T. Kelley had arrived in Council Bluffs en route to Des Moines. They planned to go on to Ohio to meet up with Jacob Coxey and his Populist Party army and together march to Washington, DC. Kelly's army marched through Marne and made a stop in Atlantic. One of the army members was a young adventurer who was destined to become one of America's outstanding novelists, Jack London. London, shown left, saw greener pastures, deserted the group, and headed to Chicago to the world's fair that had opened the previous year.

Five

Franklin and Benton Townships

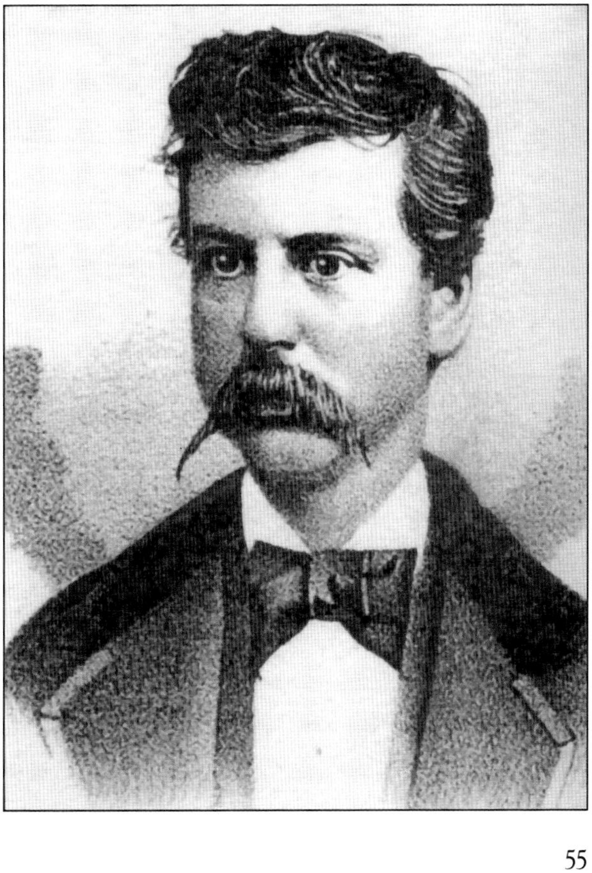

Oliver Coomes was a successful writer of dime novels in the late 1800s. He came to Cass County in his early 20s. Hawkeye Harry and Old Optic were two characters he created. Coomes was usually paid about $100 per book, but for *Omaha, Prince of the Prairie*, he received $1,000. Coomes preferred life on his Cass County farm to the many editorial offers he received. He wrote over 100 Western adventure novels. (Photograph courtesy of A.T. *Andreas' Illustrated Historical Atlas of the State of Iowa.)*

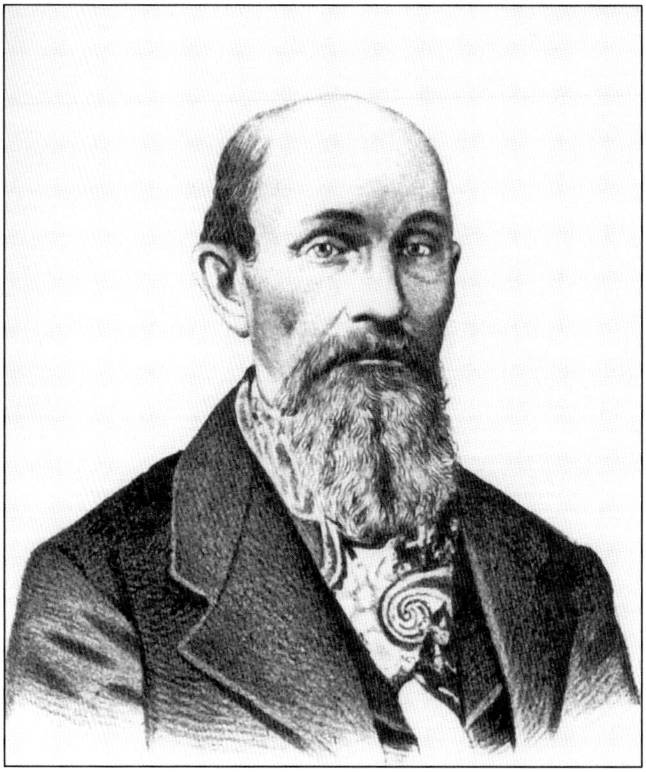

W.W. Jameson, shown at left, and his brother R.L. Jameson settled in Franklin Township in 1855. R.L.'s daughter Evaline died in 1855 and was buried on the land the Jameson brothers had purchased. Her death was the first recorded in Franklin Township. Two of Jameson's brothers served in the Civil War, and one, Reed, died in the Belle Isle Confederate prison camp in Virginia. W.W. Jameson later established the Jameson Cemetery on land where his niece was buried.

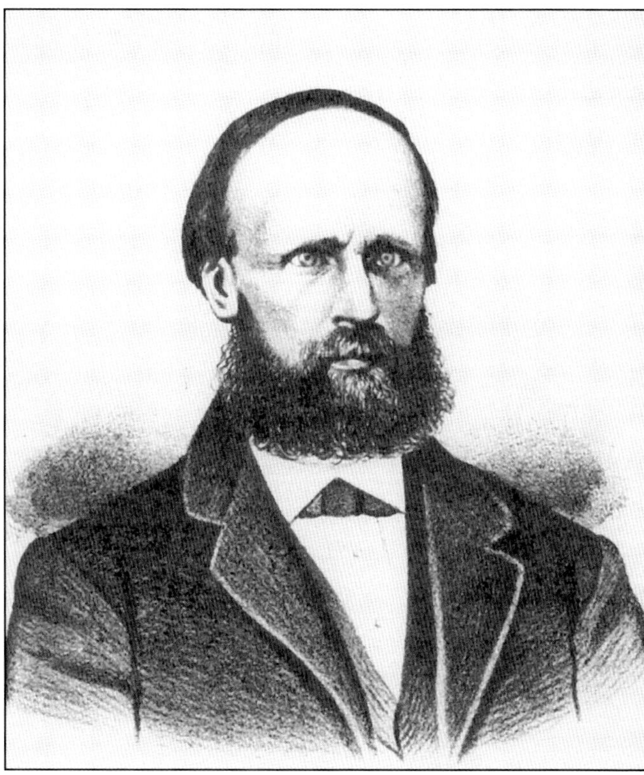

Joseph Turner, an Englishman, was a farmer who arrived in the Wiota area in the 1860s. In 1878, he moved into Wiota after the death of his parents and, having learned this trade from his father, opened a blacksmith shop. Wiota was incorporated in 1884, and Turner was elected mayor at that time. He lived in one of the finest homes in the town and was well respected.

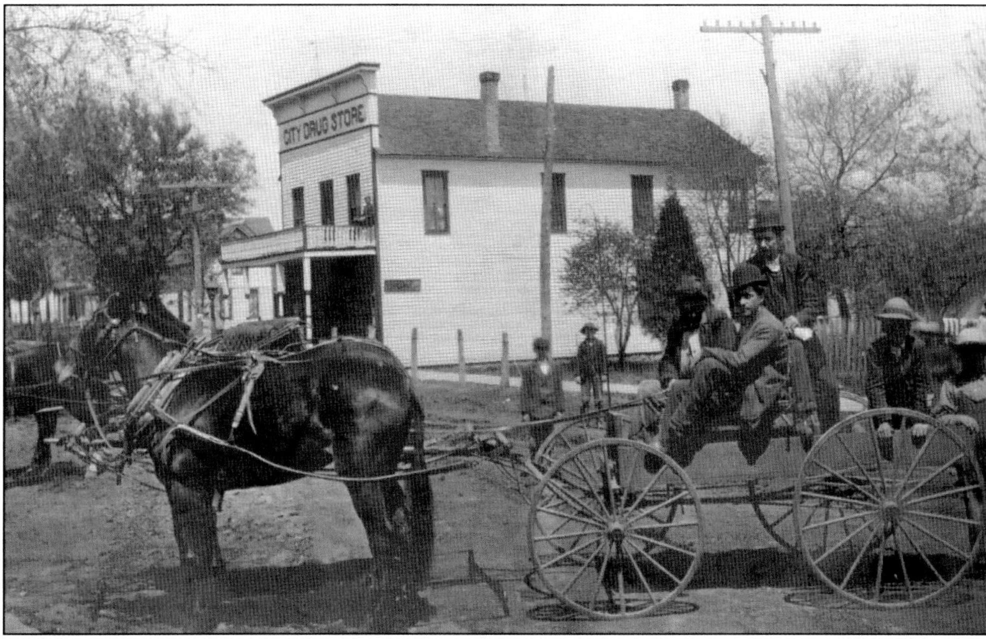

By 1900, Wiota had progressed from a typical one-horse town to a thriving county trading center. This photograph shows Warren Jordan and his mule team, May and Molly, as they pause on Wiota's Main Street in 1900. The City Drug Store is in the background at the present-day site of the Wiota Steak House.

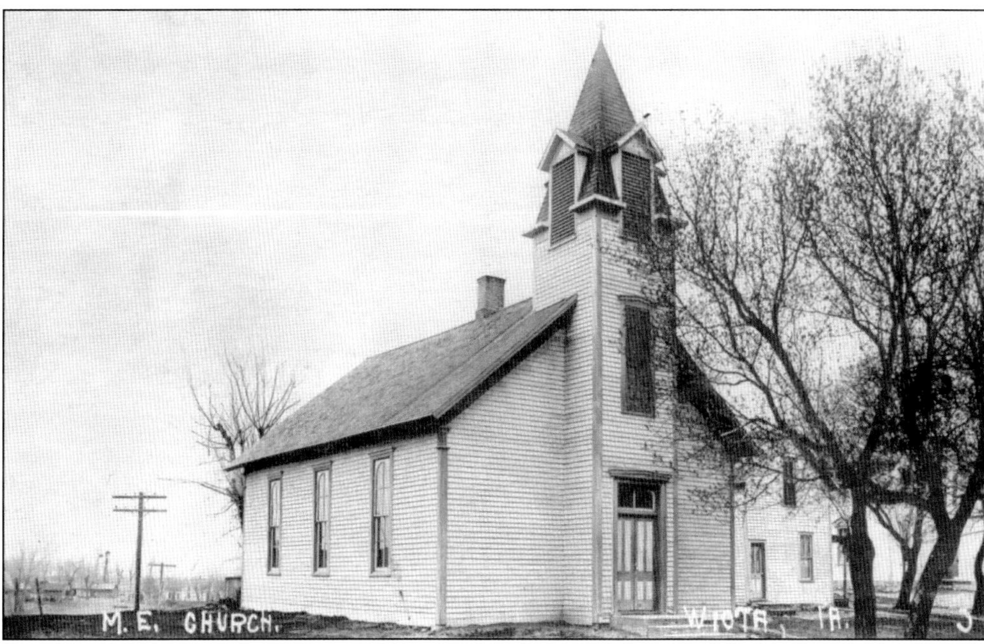

Wiota did not exist until 1872, but as early as 1866, Methodist families were meeting in a log cabin in the area. The Methodist church pictured here in 1912 was built in 1879. Franklin H. Whitney donated the land for this church. The cost of the structure was $1,200. Ambrose Ostrander served as the first Sunday school superintendent, and the first trustees were William Taylor, Charles Whitmore, Oliver Coomes, A.J. Roe, and G. Hornby.

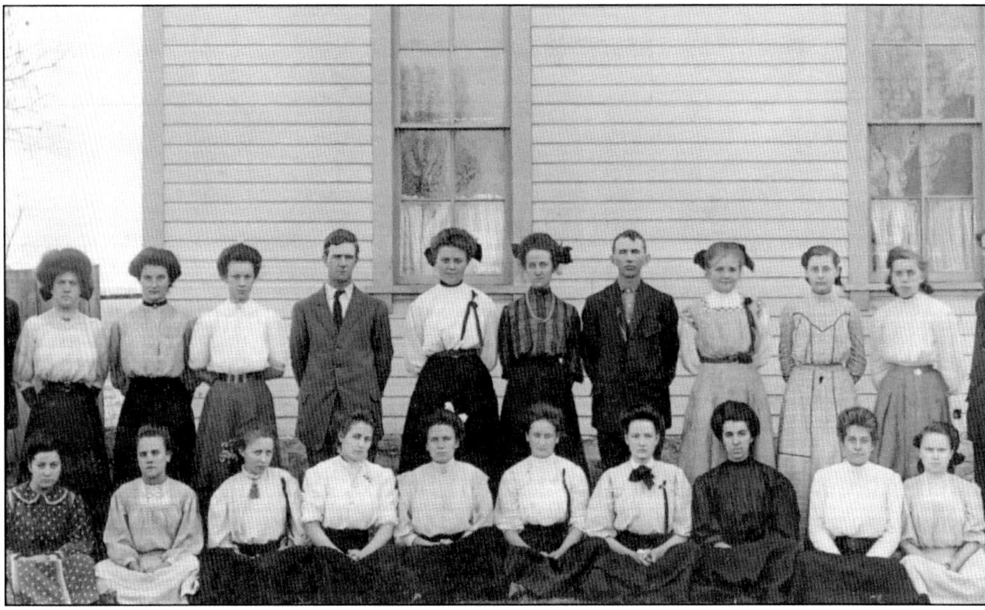

The Wiota School was erected in 1880, and an addition was built in 1895. It was a common practice to take a yearly photograph of the pupils, teachers, and the school. The photograph above is of a group of Wiota students before the turn of the century. The students obviously have dressed for the occasion, as the clothes they are wearing do not reflect the common dress of a normal school day at that time. In the photograph below, note the student hanging out of the second-story window. In 1920, a bond issue was passed that provided funds for a brick schoolhouse to replace the old wooden structure.

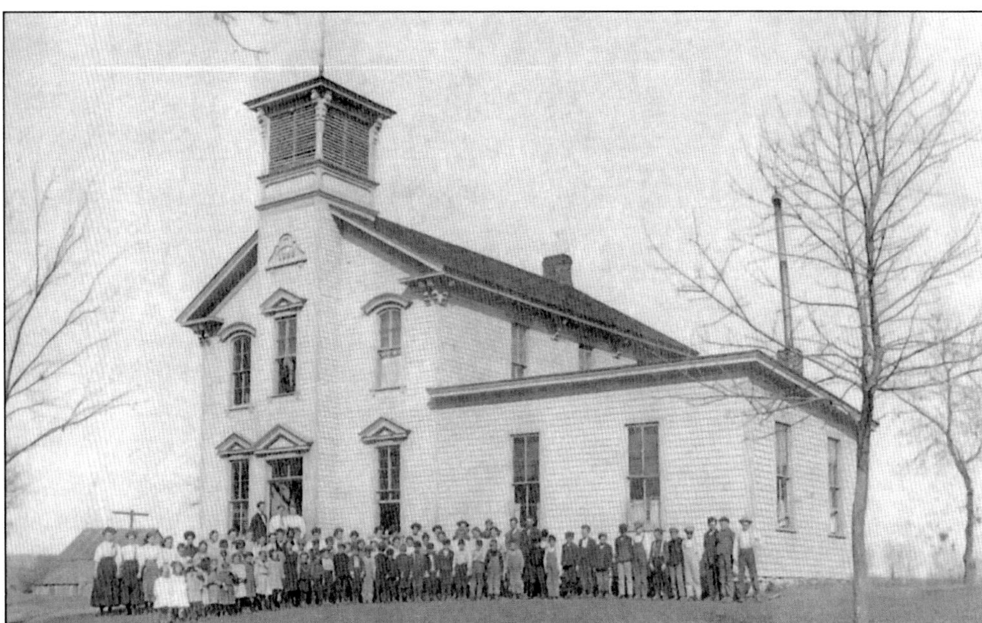

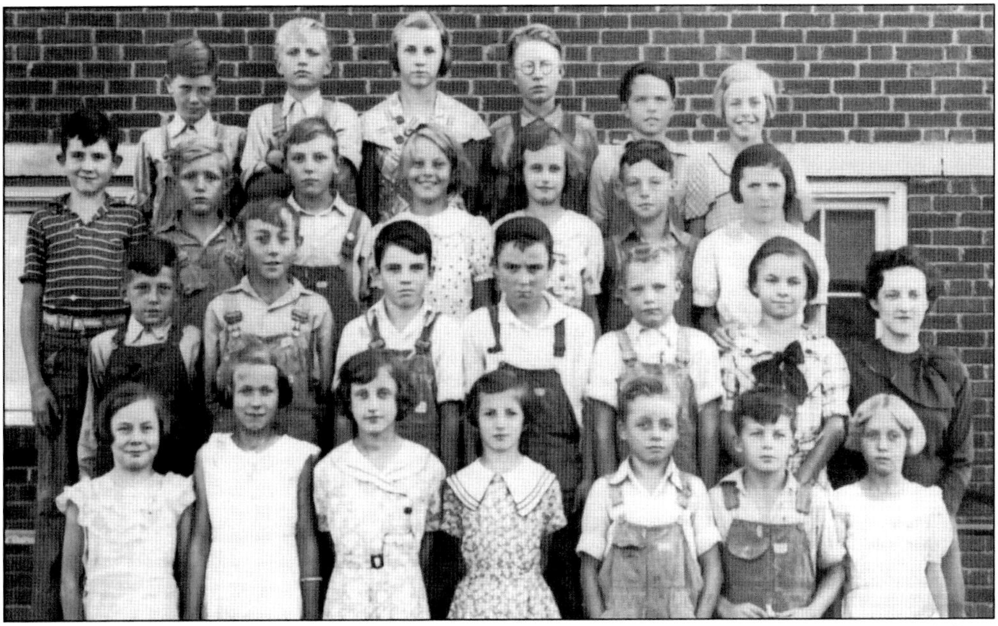

This 1936 photograph is of the Wiota fifth and sixth grade students and teacher. From left to right are (first row) Frances Earl, Delores Herkleman, Genevieve Foster, Marion Hunter, Richard Reed, Lloyd Reed, and Iona Campbell; (second row) Randall Baier, Robert Steutelberg, Dale Odem, Gail Wilson, Merle Welton, Mildred Jorgenson, and teacher Eileen Shay; (third row) John Collins, Joe Neins, Henry Miller, Marilyn Coomes, Gertrude Foster, Howard Malone, and Maxine Armstrong; (fourth row) Paul Steffens, Richard Pedersen, Lela Mae Anderson, Carrol Snyder, Bobby Brown, and Leone Campen.

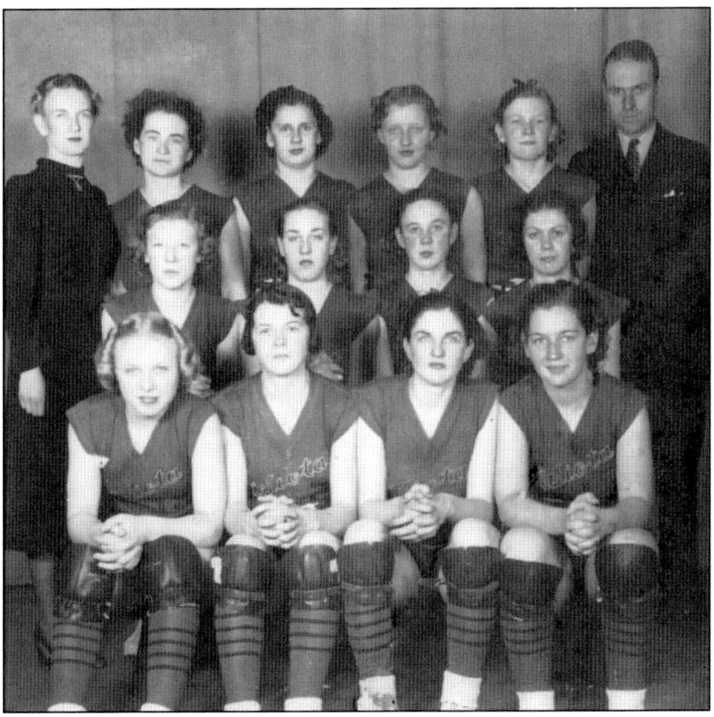

These Wiota basketball players won the Cass County championship three times during their high school years. They won two Nishna Valley conference titles and two second-place finishes in the sectional meets. From left to right are (first row) Leah Beebe, Marge Armstrong, Luella Brown, and Lucille Morgan; (second row) Nadine Wood, Elsie Reed, Mary Malone, and Belle Armstrong; (third row) Miss Logan, Mary Gibson, Mardelle Barnholdt, Viola Miller, Helen Neiens, and coach Joe O'Conner.

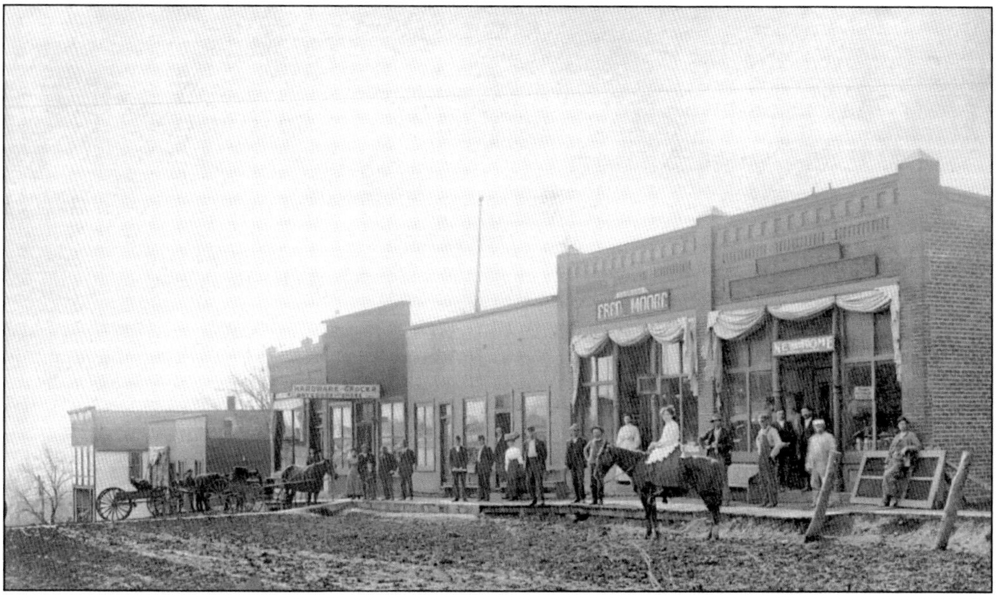

This 1908 Wiota photograph shows many elements typical of Midwestern towns at the turn of the century. While Main Street was not yet paved, more substantial brick buildings had replaced the wooden structures. Boardwalks served as sidewalk store entrances. The livery stable and the blacksmith shop were popular places for the men to gather for conversation and camaraderie.

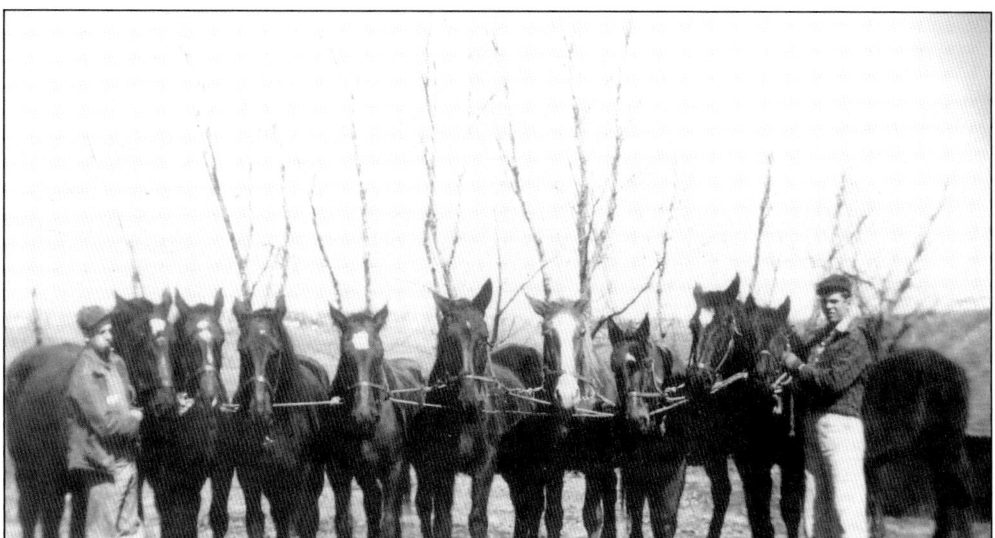

Arnold Baier (left) and Mahlandt Baier are pictured with a string of workhorses. This photograph was taken on a farm southwest of Wiota. Breaking horses was a constant job in the life of a farmer prior to the mechanization of agriculture. Two of the common working breeds used in this area were Belgians and Percherons.

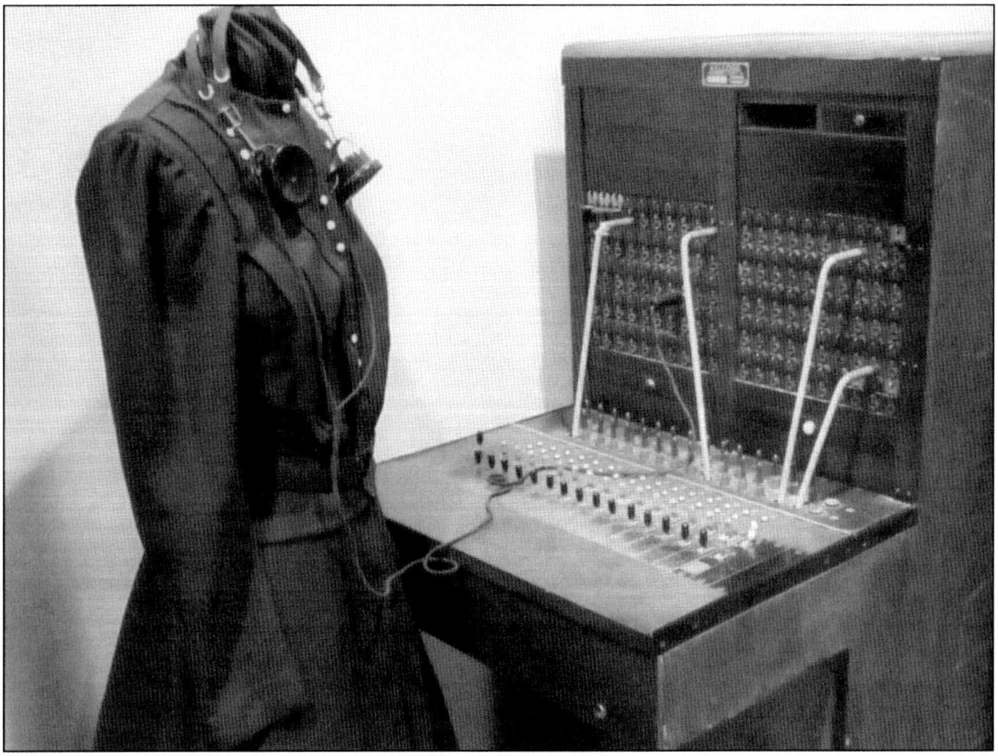

The Wiota Telephone Company was started in 1900. The switchboard, pictured, was purchased for the sum of $2,155.14 and can be seen at the Cass County Museum. The first line the company ran was to Cumberland, followed by two short lines, the Sunnyside and the Franklin. Pearl Wood was an operator for the company in the 1920s.

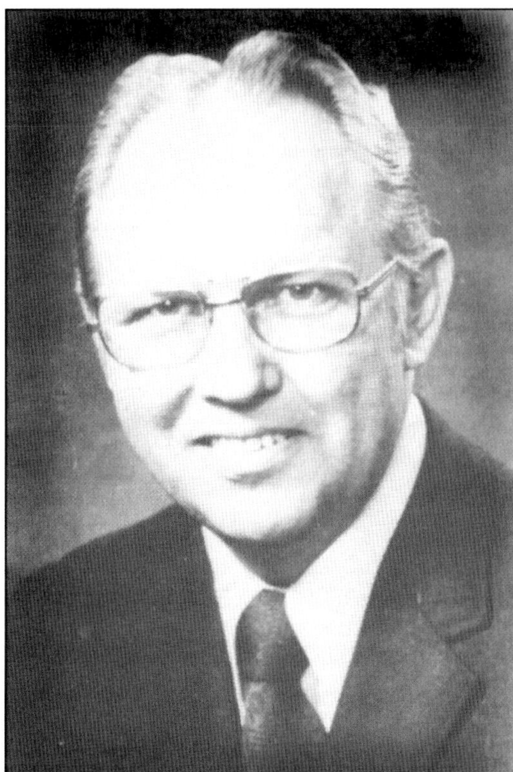

Dr. Merrill Ostrus Staton was born in 1918 in Franklin Township. After graduating from Wiota High School in 1936, he received a doctorate from Columbia University. During his career, he sang with the Fred Waring, Paul Whitman, Arthur Godfrey, and Robert Shaw orchestras. He also formed the Merrill Staton Voices. Staton performed on radio and on television, including the *Steve Allen*, *Dinah Shore*, *Voice of Firestone*, *Ed Sullivan*, and *Julie Andrews* shows. He received 10 gold records, each signifying over a million copies sold.

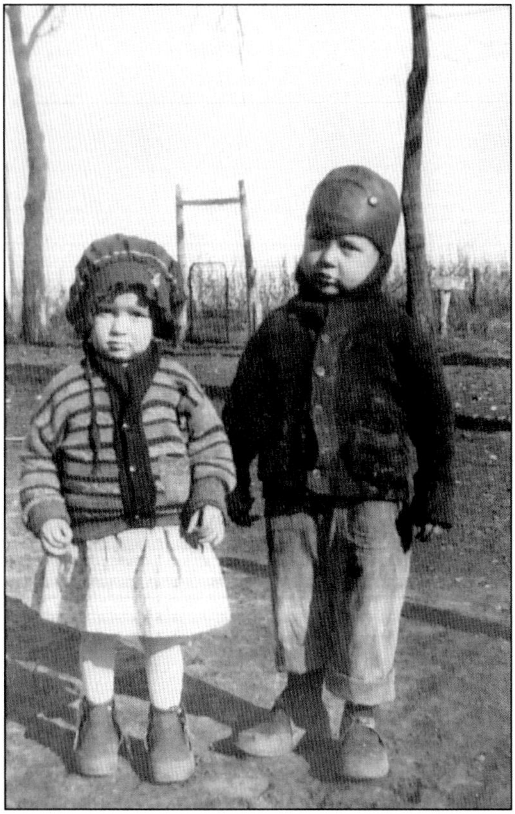

This young brother and sister are the children of Fred H. and Goldie D. Baier. The photograph was taken in 1929 on their farm southwest of Wiota. The children, Dorothy and Randall, are dressed in clothing typical of the time period. Even though it is obviously quite cool, note that Dorothy is wearing long stockings but no long pants; in 1929, little girls wore skirts.

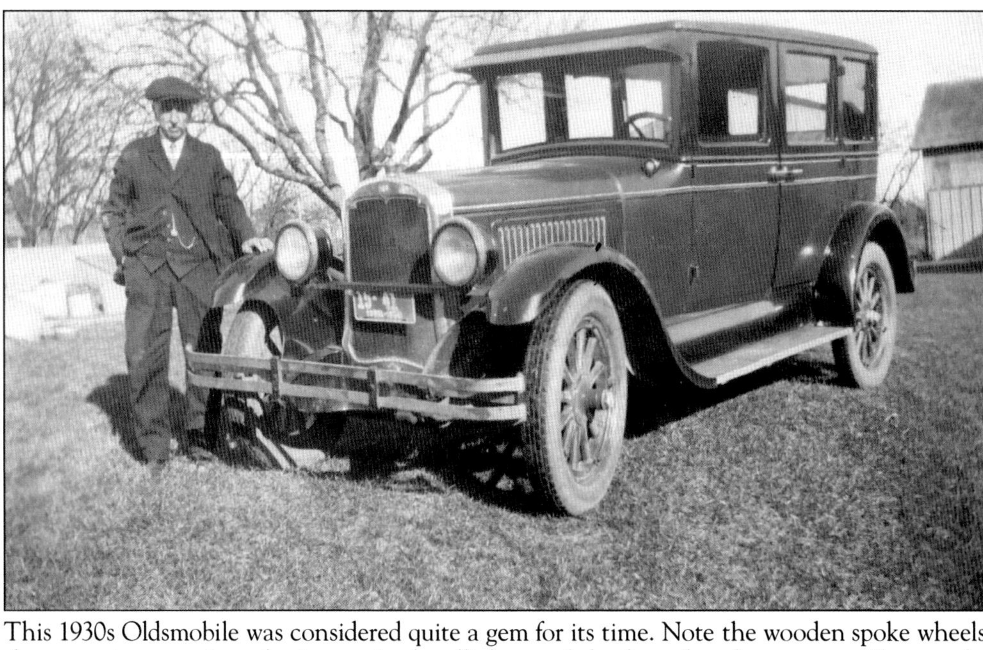

This 1930s Oldsmobile was considered quite a gem for its time. Note the wooden spoke wheels, the extension sun visor, the impressive headlights, and the fancy hood ornament. The car also sported a rear trunk and a luggage carrier that are not visible in the photograph. Standing beside the car is its proud owner, George Daughenbaugh.

Six

Grant and Lincoln Townships

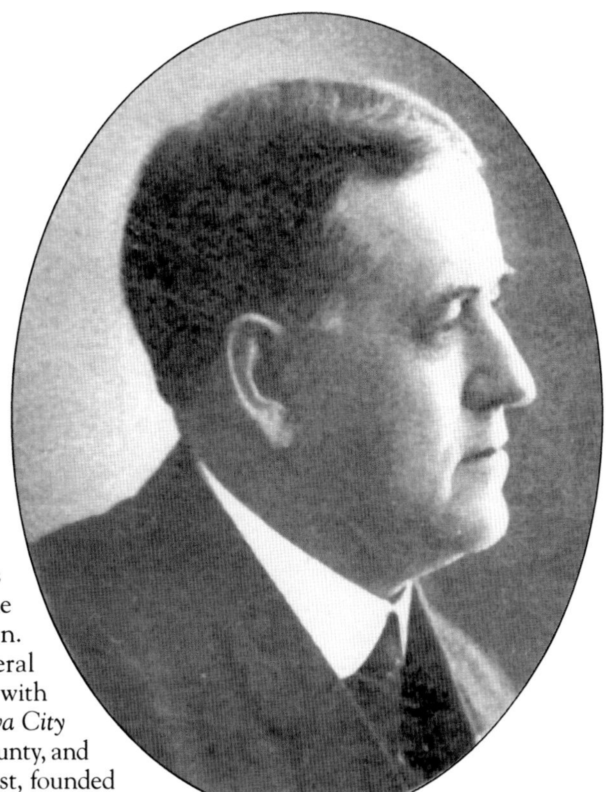

Charles F. Chase was born to be a newspaperman. At the age of 10, Chase began work as an apprentice, more commonly known in the business as a printer's devil, in the office of the *Prairie du Chien Union* in Wisconsin. After working at the paper for several years, he moved to Iowa and worked with the *Davenport Democrat* and the *Iowa City Press*. In 1877, Chase moved to Cass County, and with his business partner Claude Faust, founded the *Anita Times*.

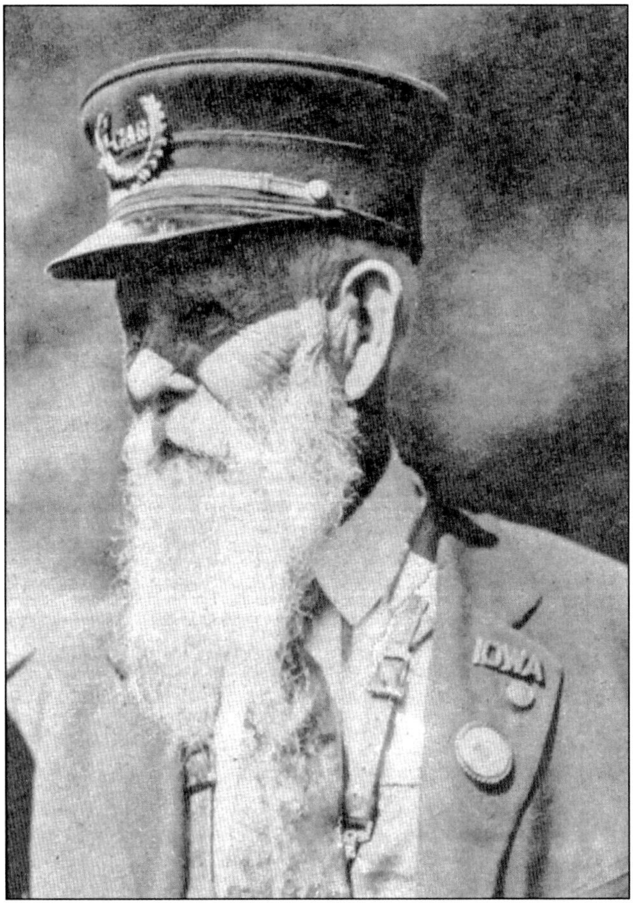

The left photograph is of R.D. McGeehon, an early Grant Township pioneer. McGeehon, Peter Kanawyer, J.R. Kirk, and Dr. Gershom Morrison staked out a road from Guthrie County to the Nishnabotna River near Indiantown. In May 1855, Morrison's home became a station on the Western Stage Company's regular route. Morrison abandoned his medical practice in favor of improving the land. He and his men were not paid, as there was not enough tax money to cover the improvement projects. He built bridges and roads and kept his family alive by use of his hunting skills. In the winter of 1856, he reportedly killed 150 deer. Below is an early Anita street scene. Anita was surveyed and platted in 1869 by Lewis Beason. The land was sold to Franklin Whitney, B.F. Allen, and John Cook who filed the plat in November 1870. Anita was incorporated in June 1875.

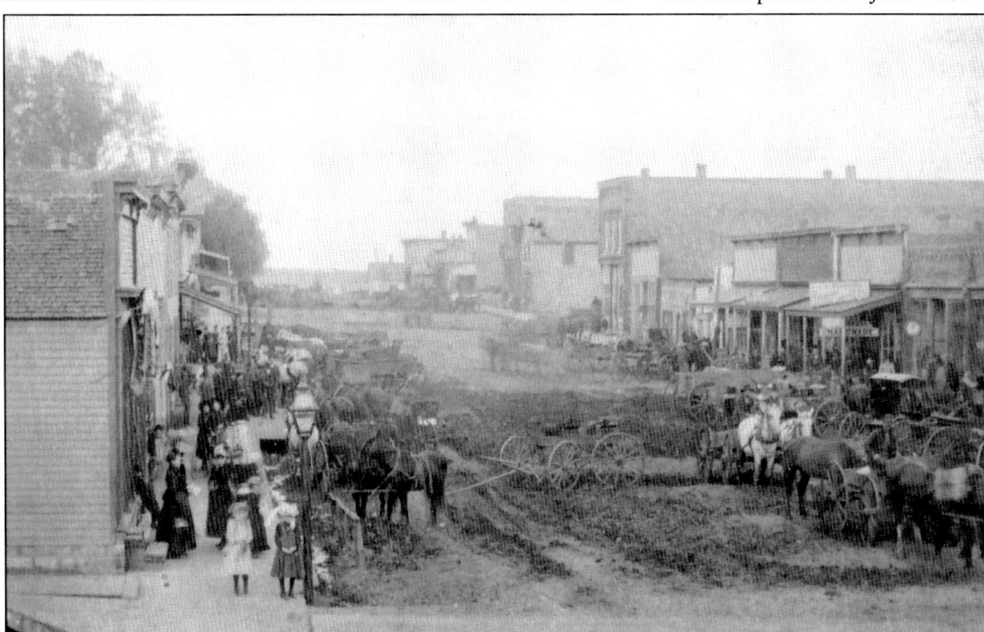

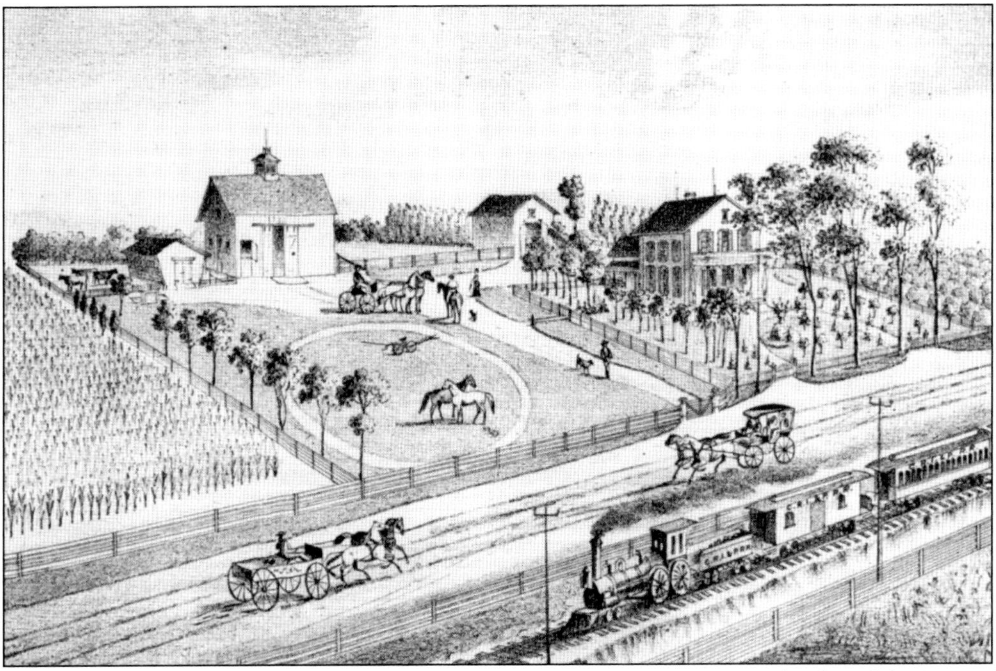

The farm of Lewis Beason, seen here in *A.T. Andreas' Illustrated Historical Atlas of the State of Iowa*, reflects his success as a gentleman farmer. Heading to California in 1856, Beason passed through Cass County and decided to remain. The land he purchased became the townsite for Anita. In 1869, railroad officials, while dining at Beason's home, discussed a name for the town. Beason's wife Augusta's suggestion that it be named after her niece Anita was accepted.

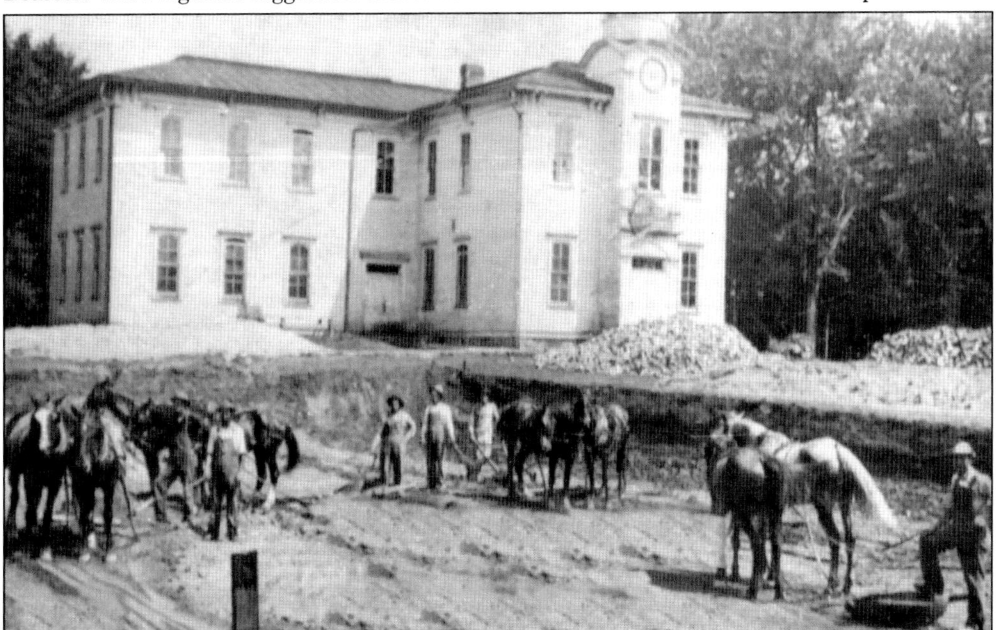

Anita's first high school was built in 1882. This photograph shows the construction crew digging the basement for a new school in 1913. The old school still stands in the background awaiting demolition. Included in the photograph are Tim Knowlton, Earl Knowlton, and Charlie Exline.

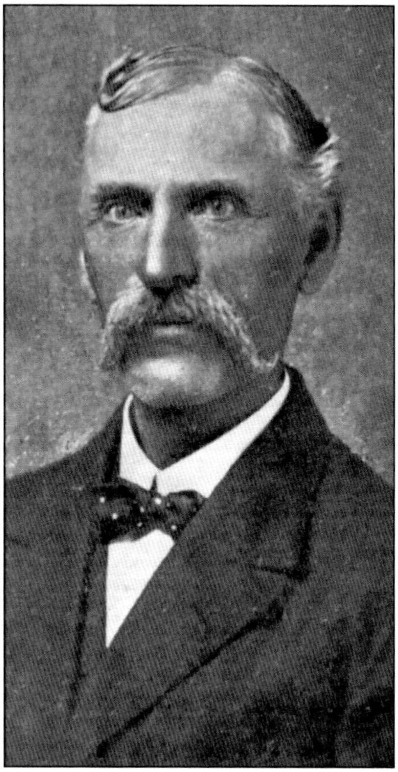

Anita personalities John David Peterson and his wife, Mary Jane, typified the independent character of Cass County residents. Peterson, pictured left, served as a legislator in the Iowa House of Representatives. Mary Jane was the grandchild of Jane Rutledge, a sister of Ann Rutledge, said to be Abraham Lincoln's first love. Another Jane Rutledge connection in Cass County is the fact that Atlantic druggist J.B. Jones was also a Rutledge grandchild.

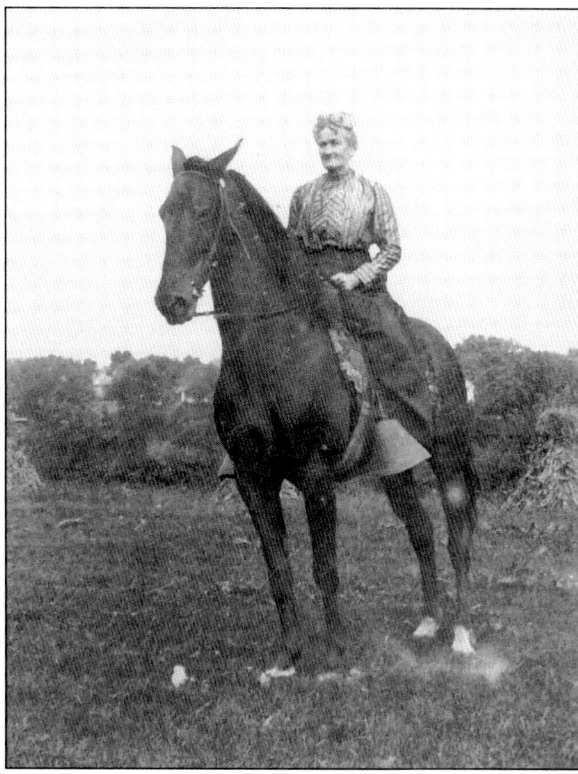

The Petersons were married December 23, 1880, at the home of her parents, Mr. and Mrs. John W. Berry, in Marne. Mary Jane is shown here on her 75th birthday in 1936 astride her horse Bart. To celebrate the occasion, she rode Bart from Anita to Atlantic, a distance of 13 miles.

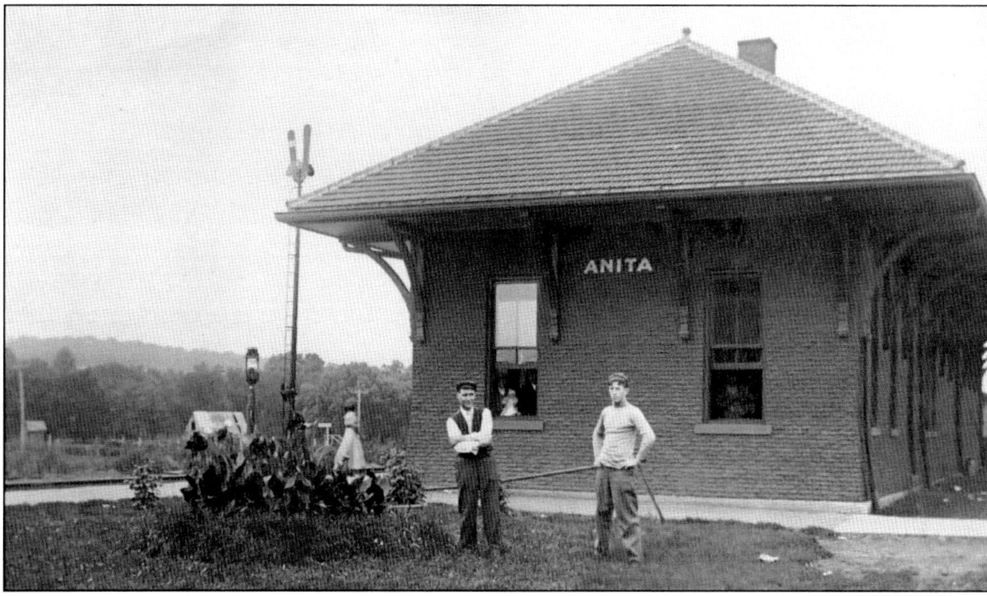

The Chicago, Rock Island & Pacific Railroad route crossed Grant Township in a diagonal path from northeast to southwest. The railroad line was established in Anita in 1868. A brick depot was built in 1899 after Anita residents remarked that they needed a "decent depot" if they were to "keep up" with neighboring communities. They were rightfully proud of the new structure. This photograph, taken in 1925, shows Leland Hubbel on the right.

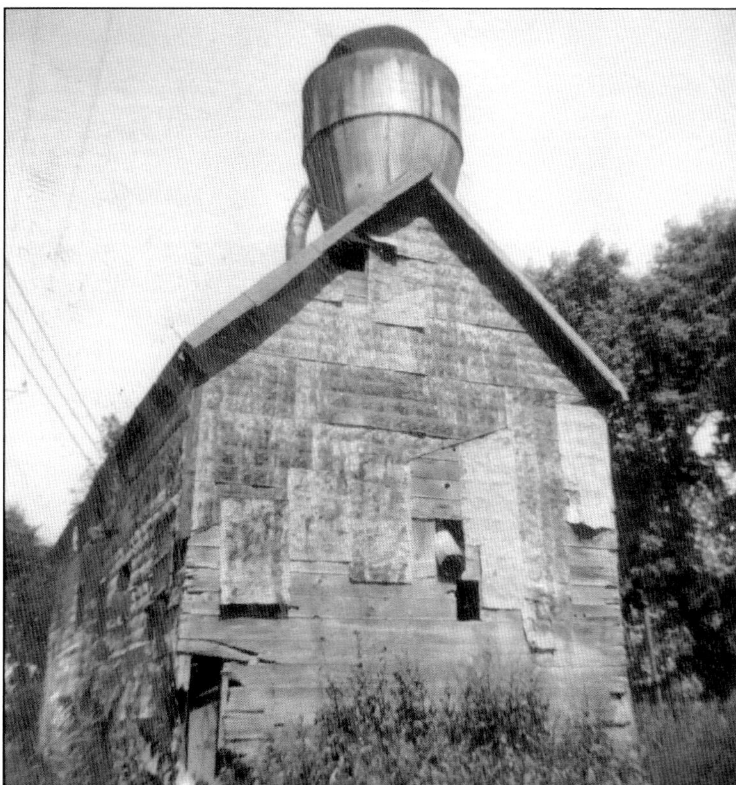

Farmers would bring teams of horses to Anita and leave them at the Ten Cent Feed Barn for the day. When the livery stable provided feed, it cost 10¢, hence the name of the business. Bob Wilson purchased the livery in 1910 and operated it for 10 years with his brother Charles. Wilson had to hire a man to sleep in the barn because the local doctors kept their horses there and could be called out on emergencies at any time of day or night.

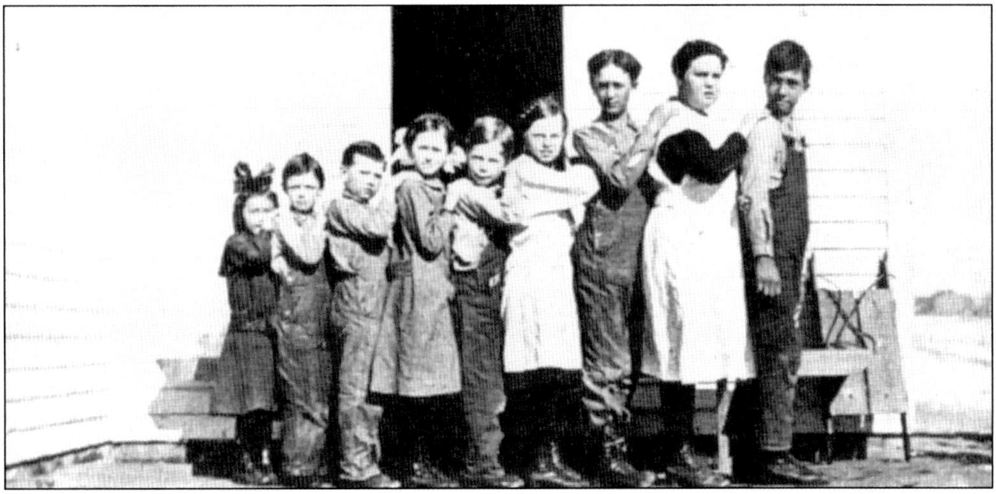

The families of Lincoln Township controlled four school buildings. The White Cloud School was built on land owned by William White. The story is told that while erecting the building, White looked up at the blue sky with its fleecy white clouds and suggested the school be named White Cloud. It was also used as the social center for the surrounding rural community.

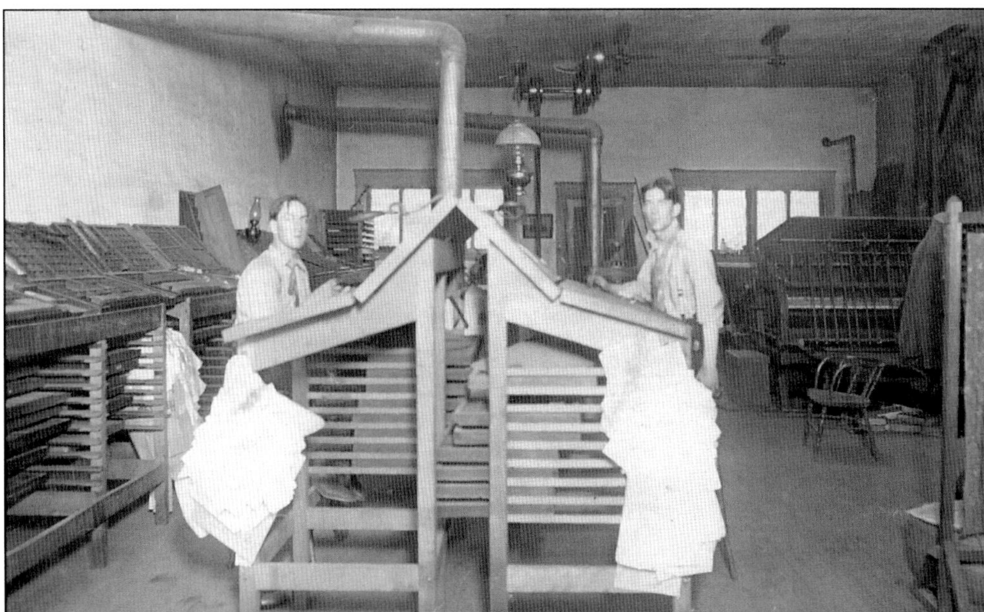

In 1877, Charles Chase and Claude Faust established the *Anita Times*. The inaugural issue, dated November 14, was auctioned off to the highest bidder, Mayor Edwin Cate, for $25. Sherm Myers learned the trade from Chase and Faust and established the *Anita Tribune* in 1883. He served as its editor until August 1911, when he sold out to H.L. Bell and Walter Budd. This 1916 photograph of the Tribune office shows Walter Budd, on the left, and Sherm Meyers.

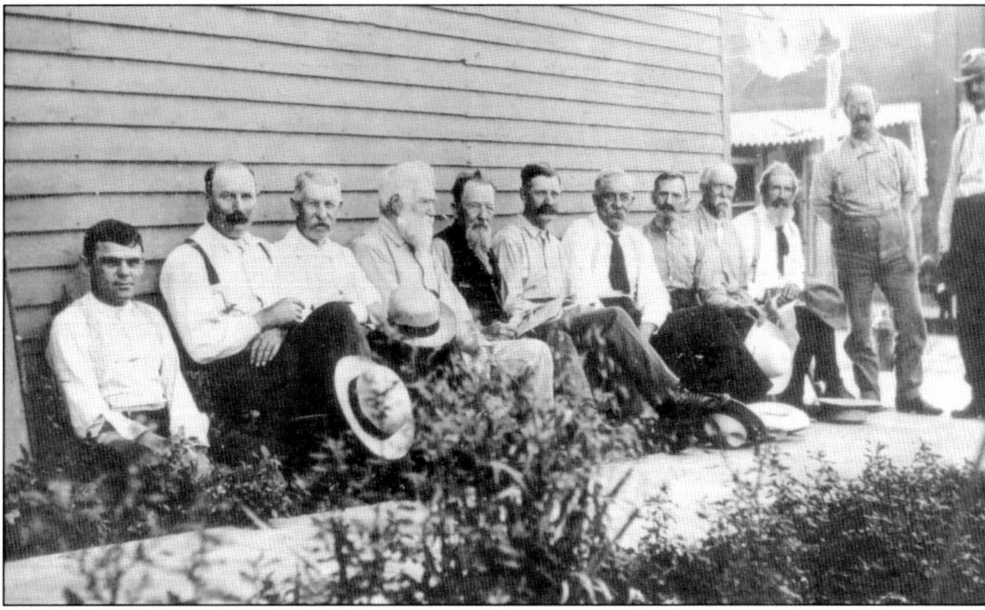

The modern-day advertisement that suggests one should "never let them see you sweat" had nothing on these Anita residents in the early 1900s. This group of well-dressed men spent part of the day sitting on Anita city benches and watching the local scenery. They soon earned the name "Never Sweats" because it is obvious that they did not intend to expend much energy on working.

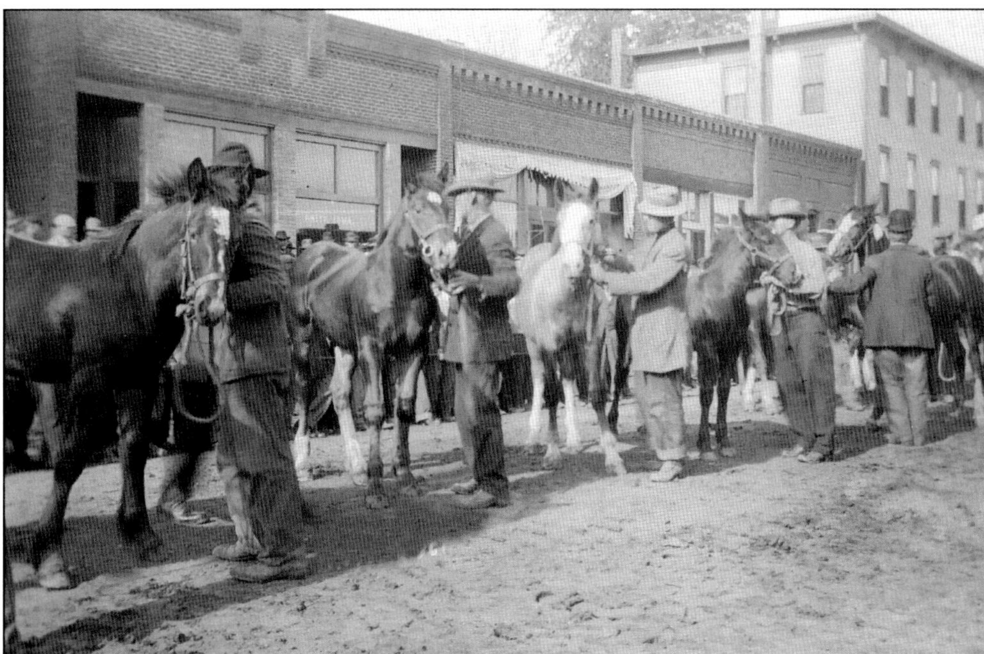

Before the age of the automobile, the horse provided the power needed for farming and transportation. A good horse was a necessary asset, and men placed a high value on their horses. In this October 1, 1913, photograph, men are displaying their prize colts for judging at the colt show on Anita's Main Street.

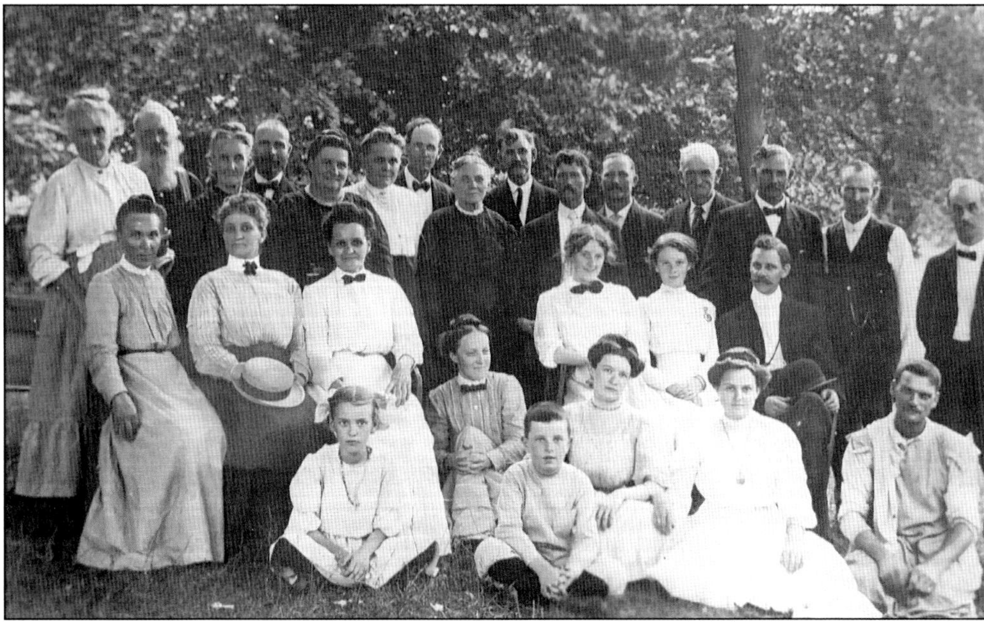

This 1910 photograph was taken at a religious camp meeting in Anita's Keystone Park. Traveling ministers would conduct these events. The land for the park was given to the city of Anita in a rather unusual manner. In June 1912, about 25 men pledged $160 each to purchase the property that was then turned over to the city fathers for the establishment of a city park. Ethel Parker Stager is identified as being second from the right in the first row.

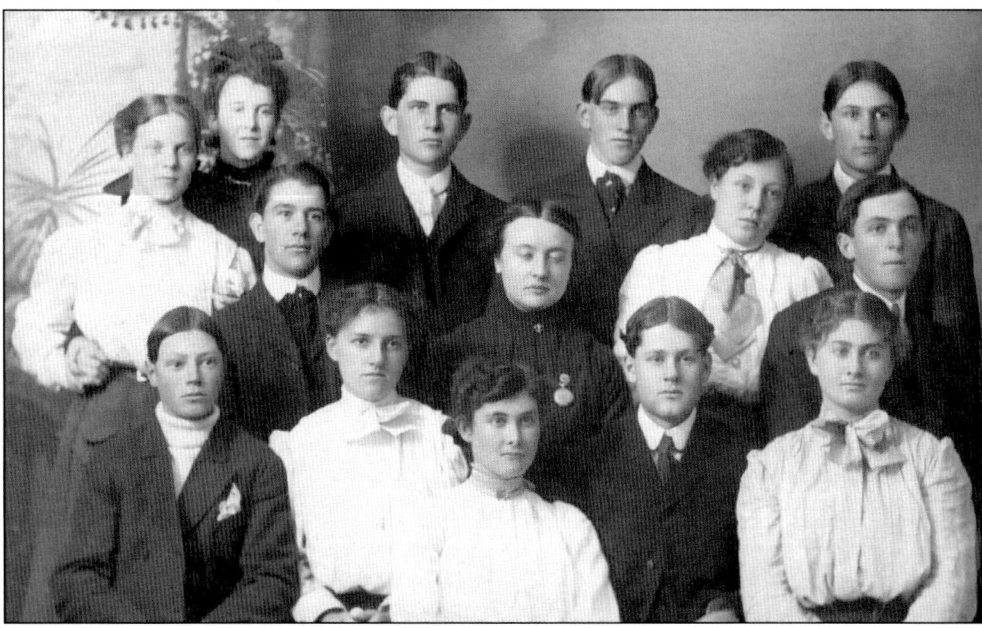

As was usually the case in the early settlements, the education of children was of prime importance. The first school in Anita was established in 1869, with Dr. E.E. Major as teacher. In 1876, the Independent School District of Anita was established, with L.P. Frost serving as president of the first school board. The first schoolhouse was erected in 1882. This photograph shows an Anita graduating class from the turn of the century.

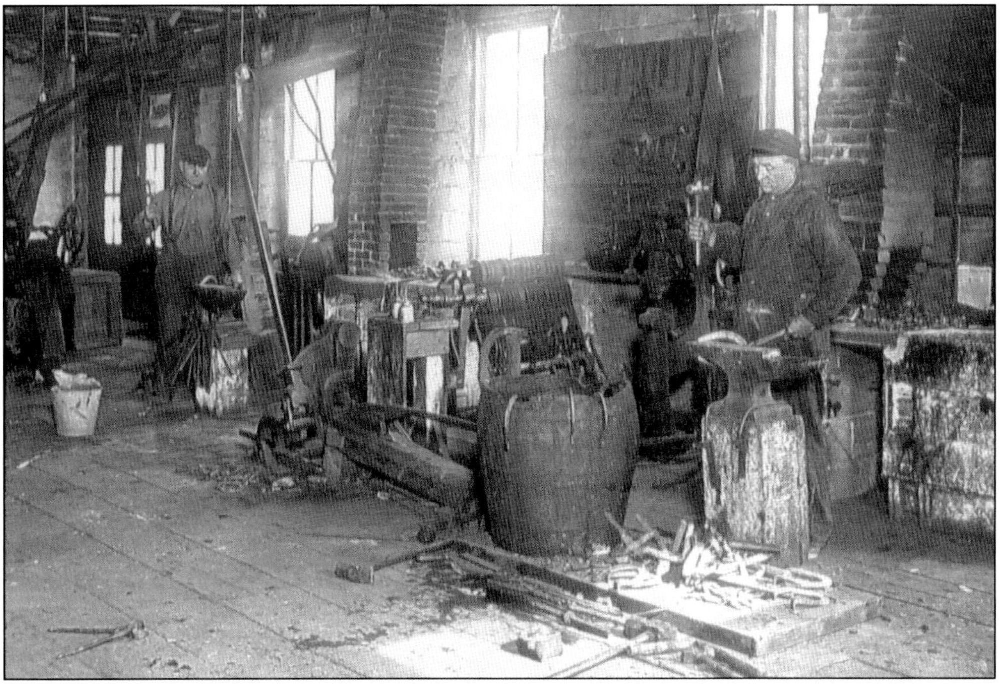

No early Midwestern Iowa town could long exist without a blacksmith. The second building that was erected in Anita was the blacksmith shop opened by H.C. Saunders in 1869. The Anita establishment was located north of Concert Park. Along with many other businesses, it was a member of the Anita Commercial Club. This 1910 photograph shows William H. Wagner, on the left, and Chet Winder.

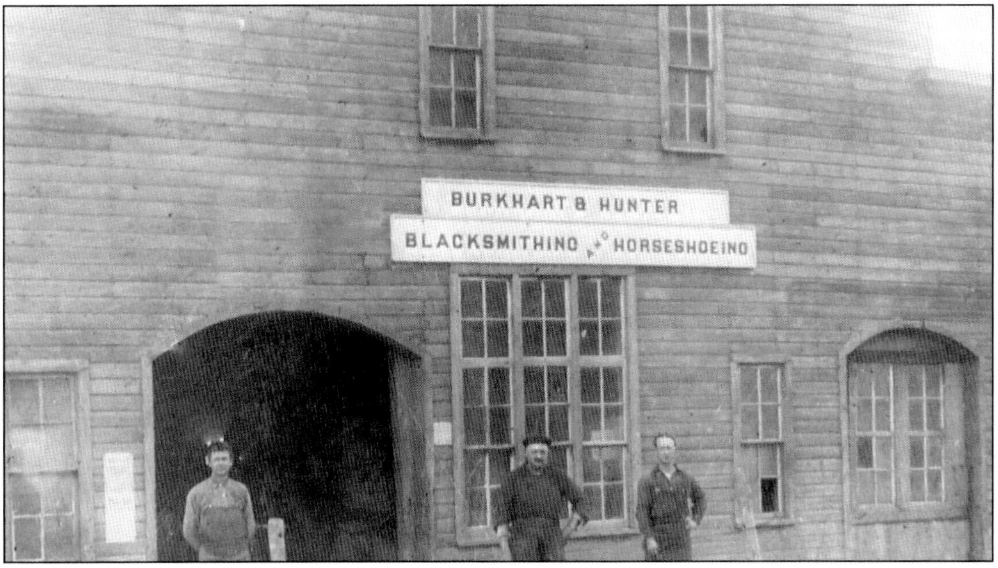

One prominent business in early Anita was the Burkhart and Hunter blacksmith shop. Gus and Bill Burkhart taught the trade of blacksmithing to several apprentices. One such man was Carl Millard. Millard eventually owned his own shop in Anita. His workday started at 6:00 a.m. and ended at 6:00 p.m., six days a week. During harvest time, when farmers needed many repairs, his workdays frequently extended well beyond the usual 12 hours.

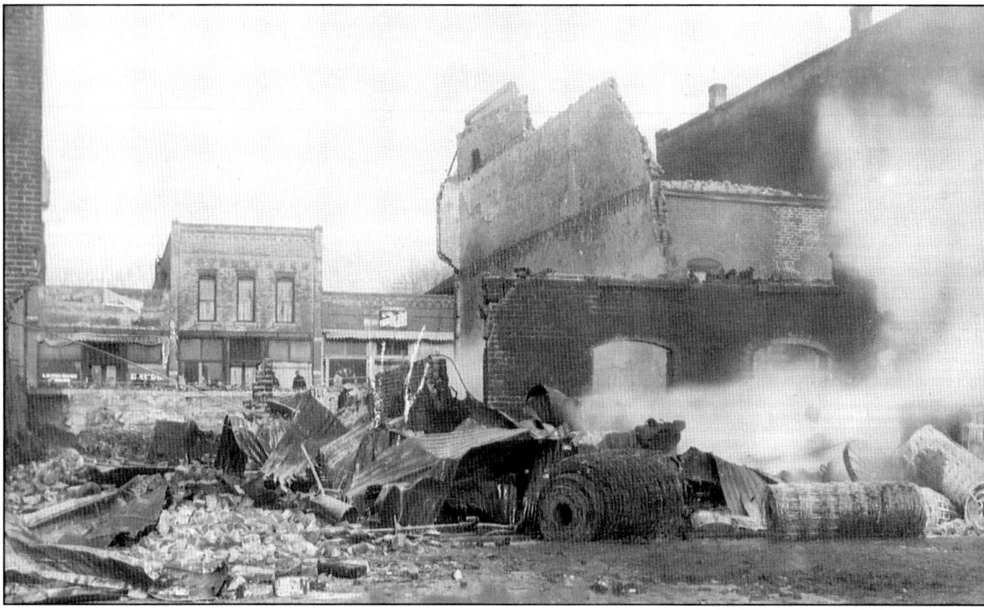

In January 1911, the local hardware store was demolished in one of Anita's most destructive fires. An employee, Fred Chinn, detected the blaze. The heat from the fire was so intense that every plate-glass window on the north side of the street was broken. Gunpowder exploded, and stray bullets from shells and cartridges created a dangerous scene. Built in 1898 at a cost of $14,000, the value of the store was set at $50,000 at the time of the fire.

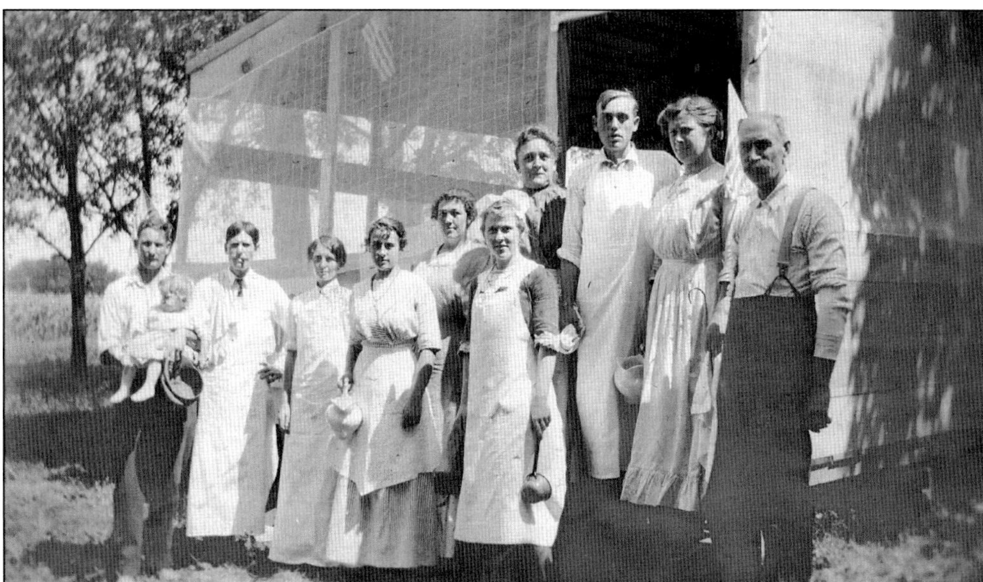

Jesse Deeming, an 1899 graduate of Anita High School, went through four years of high school being the lone male in a class of 13. Deeming attended Drake University in Des Moines and became fluent in Spanish, Greek, and German. From left to right are (first row) Guy Deeming, holding baby Fay Deeming (Nelsen), Jesse Deeming, Eva Atwood, Erma Glynes Deeming, and Nellie Worm; (second row) Lena Schaake, Clara Angell, Fred Angell, Laura Deeming, and William Angell.

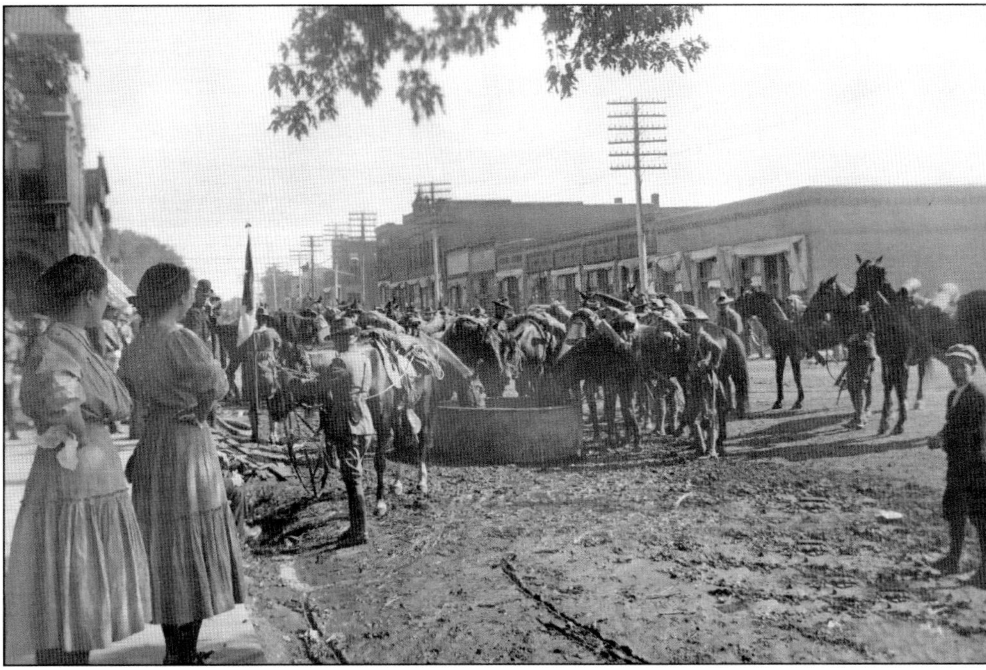

In September 1909, Anita residents welcomed the men of the 14th Cavalry Unit as they stopped to water their horses on Main Street. The group included 1,500 soldiers and 800 horses. They were on their way to Atlantic, where they camped overnight at the Cass County Fairgrounds. The unit from Des Moines was headed to Omaha to take part in an Ak-Sar-Ben gala. The Knights of Ak-Sar-Ben (Nebraska spelled backwards) is a non-profit civic organization founded in Omaha in 1890.

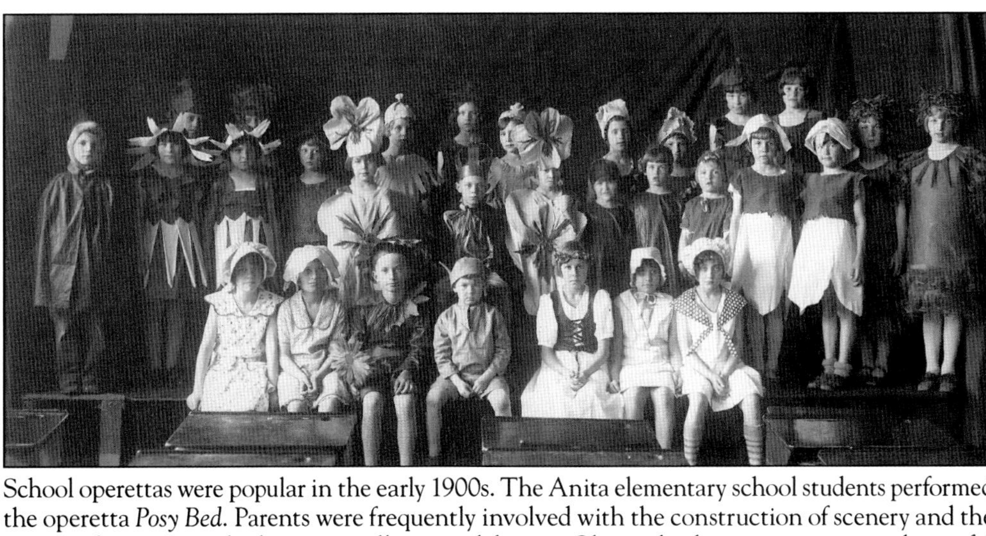

School operettas were popular in the early 1900s. The Anita elementary school students performed the operetta *Posy Bed*. Parents were frequently involved with the construction of scenery and the sewing of costumes, which were usually quite elaborate. Obviously, there were some very beautiful "posies" involved in the production, as can be seen in this 1931 photograph.

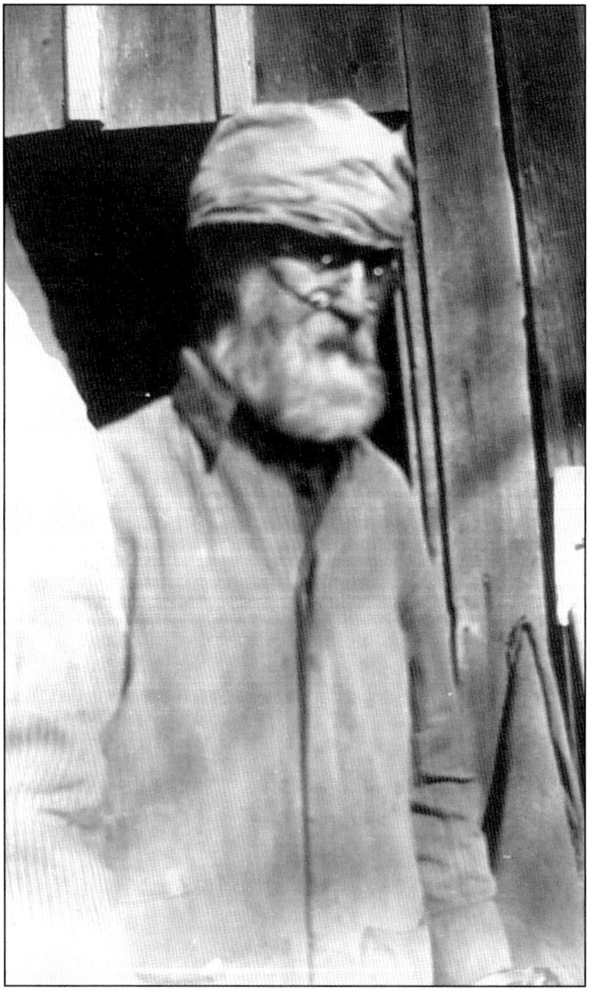

Frederick A. Kauer lived out his simple life in a small cabin in the southern part of Anita. He came to America from Germany when he was 25 and moved to Anita in 1895. Kauer was better known as "Dutch Fred." He had been a traveling Lutheran preacher but had to change his vocation due to a throat affliction. He held a series of menial jobs, saving most of his wages, spending little on himself, and living frugally in the tiny cabin shown in the photograph below. He gave his money to the needy, to churches, and to charities. Kauer received national publicity with his announcement that he intended to will his savings of $7,000 to the government because this country had given him the opportunity to earn an honest living. He died October 29, 1940, at the age of 88.

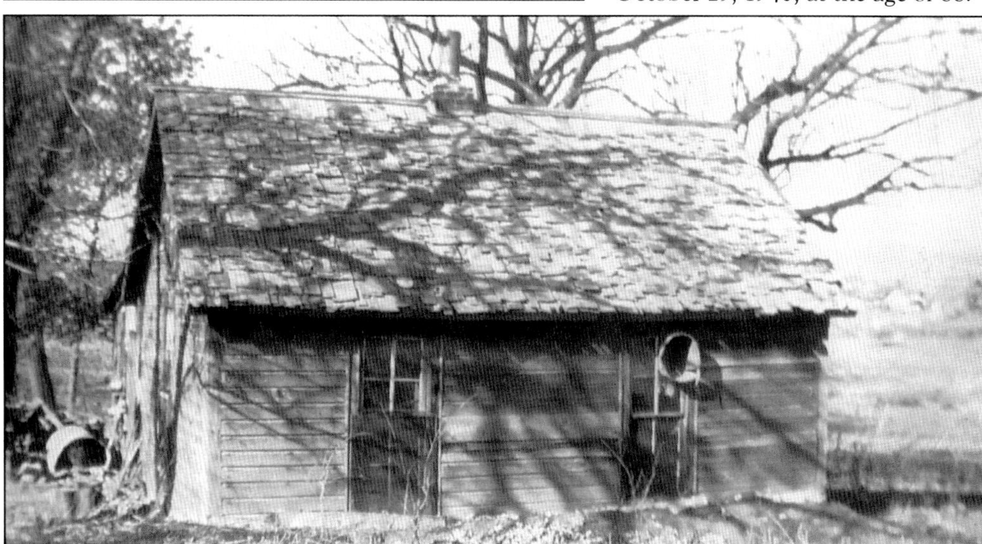

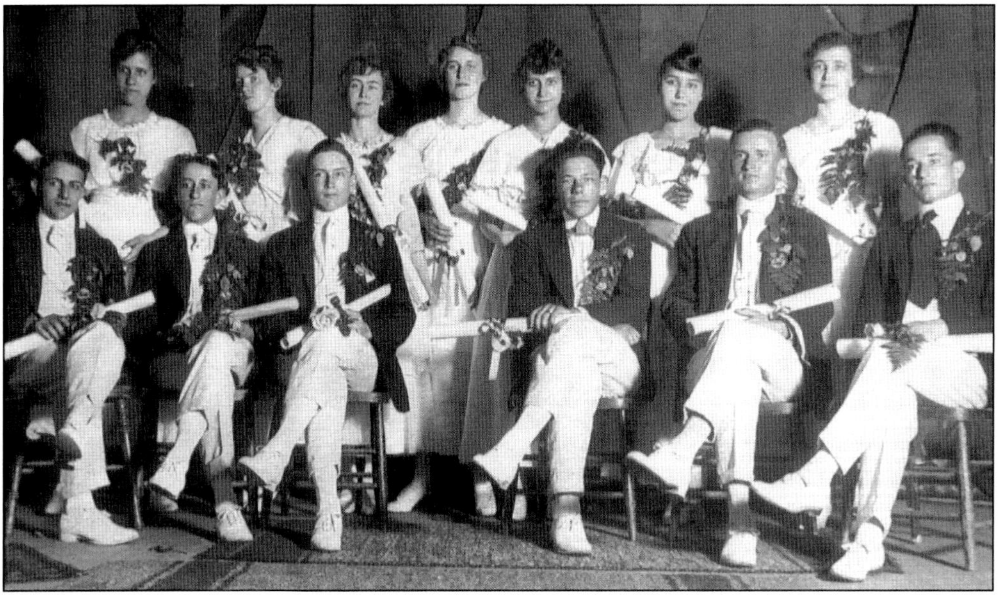

High school graduation was a major event, as shown in this 1916 Anita photograph. The girls are elegantly dressed, and young men wear black jackets and white trousers. All graduates hold their diplomas proudly. The graduates are, from left to right, (first row) Charlie Wagner, Raymond Wagner, Tom Burns, Hobart Newton, Raymond Peterson, and Edwin Burkhart; (second row) Mildred Walker, Wilma Wagner, Lenore Walker, Alta King, Gladys Rickel, Katherine Galiher, and Mary Denne.

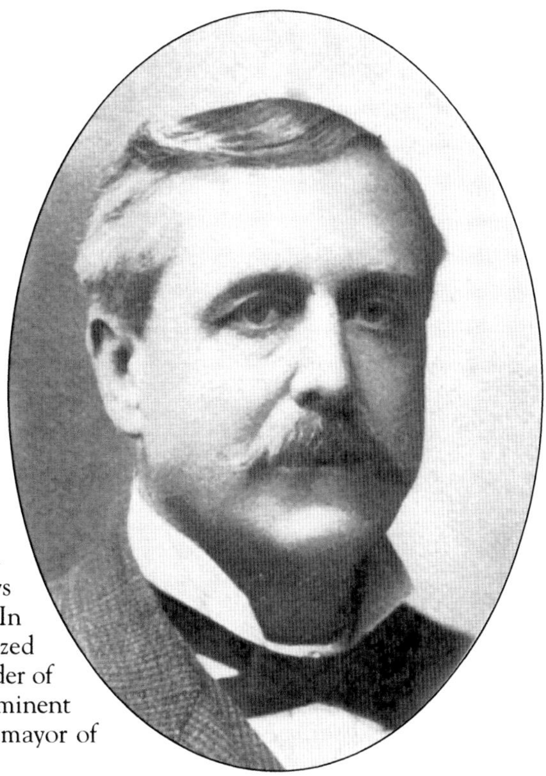

Fraternal orders and lodges played a very important role in many emerging towns. As early as 1884, Anita had five thriving lodges, the Masonic, Grand Army of the Republic (GAR), Independent Order of Odd Fellows (IOOF), Knights of Honor, and Workmen. In 1879, Dr. J.M. Emmert of Atlantic organized Emmert Lodge No. 192 of the Ancient Order of United Workmen. The lodge had many prominent Anita citizens as members. Edwin Cate, mayor of Anita, served as its first president.

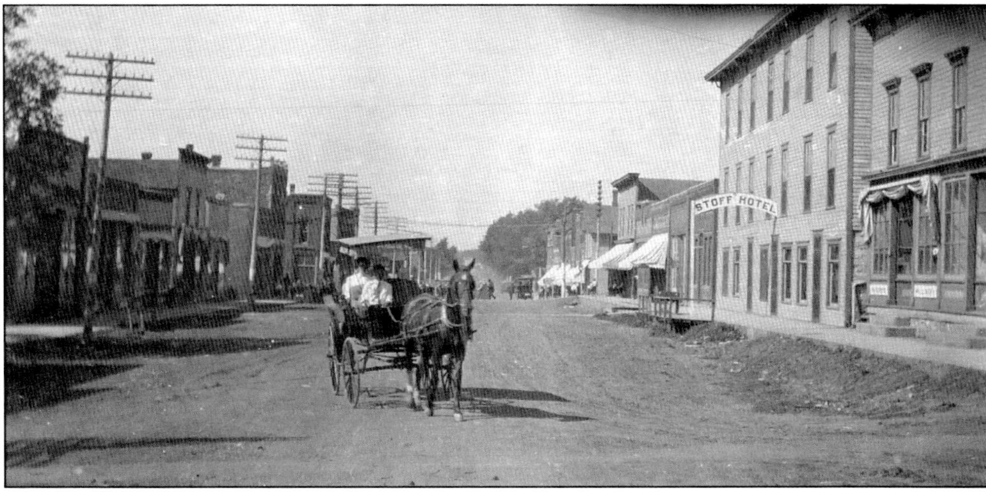

In 1896, amenities were in short supply. An issue of the *Anita Times* from that year states, "There are several streets in Anita that know not what a sidewalk is . . . There are also new crossings needed and we think that property owners and the city fathers should combine and furnish goods for substantial sidewalks and crossings where they are actually needed. Little one-horse towns all around Anita are organizing fire companies. Anita, wake up."

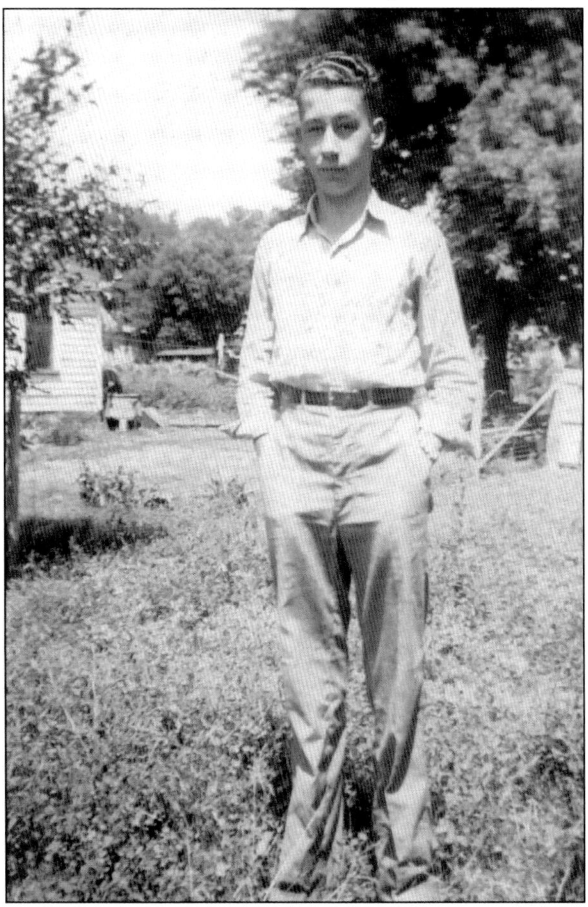

In 1936, 14-year-old Carl E. Benson of Anita was awarded the Carnegie Hero Medal for risking his life while attempting to save his friend John Davey. Davey fell into the deep, icy water of Turkey Creek. Fully clothed and wearing heavy boots, Benson dived into the stream. Pushing away chunks of drifting ice, he reached his friend, but both boys sank beneath the water. Benson was able to make it back to the surface but could not save his friend's life.

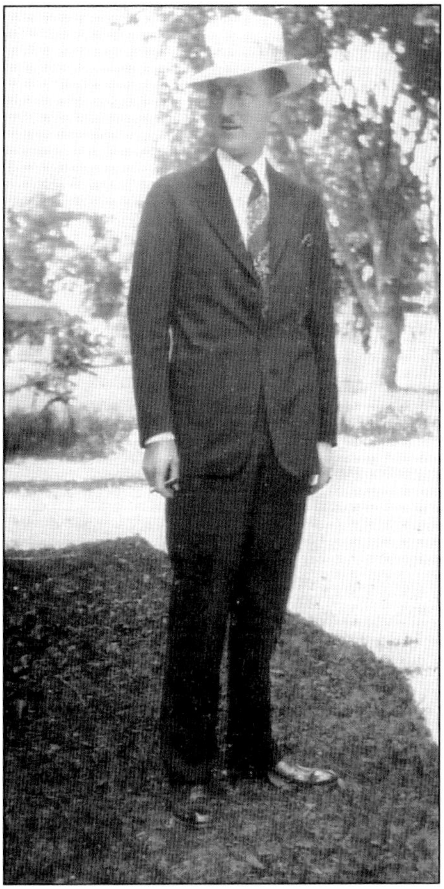

Dr. Gail M. Adair received his medical degree in 1909 and opened a practice in Anita. He did not own a horse and buggy, so Tom Reed drove him on his rural rounds. Later, Adair purchased a Ford roadster. However, driving the roadster must have been a bit frustrating because there was an Iowa law declaring that all cars must stop and drivers had to turn off their motors when meeting a horse. To make matters worse, the driver was to get out of the car and lead the horse past the parked car. Dr. Adair delivered hundreds of babies during his time in Anita. In 1944, as president of the Anita School Board, he presented 42 diplomas to seniors, 29 of whom he had brought into this world. The photograph below shows the Citizens Bank Building in Anita. Dr. Adair kept his office above the bank until his death in 1952.

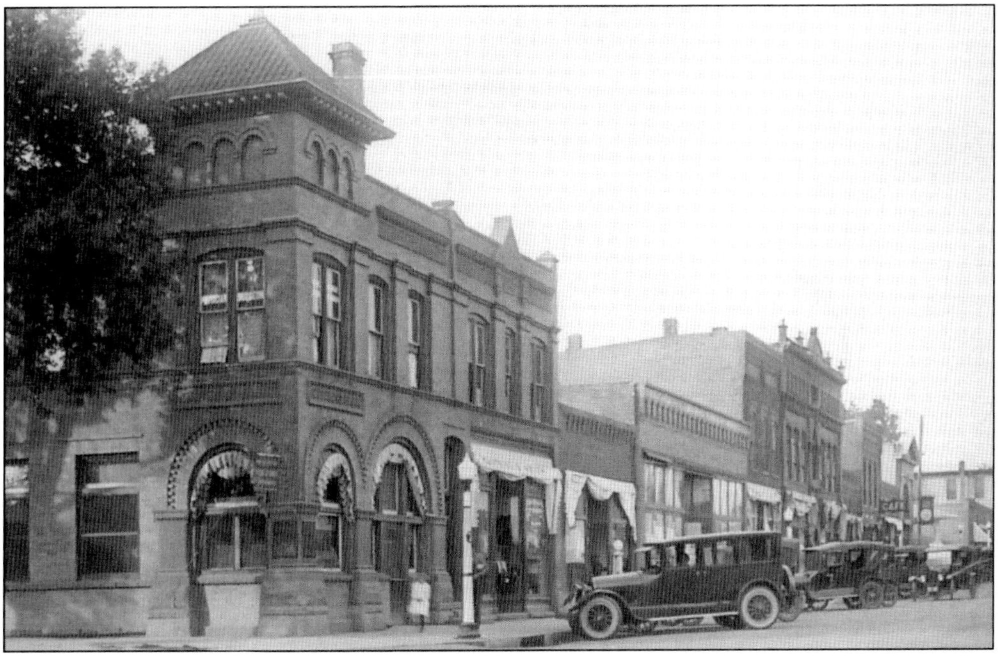

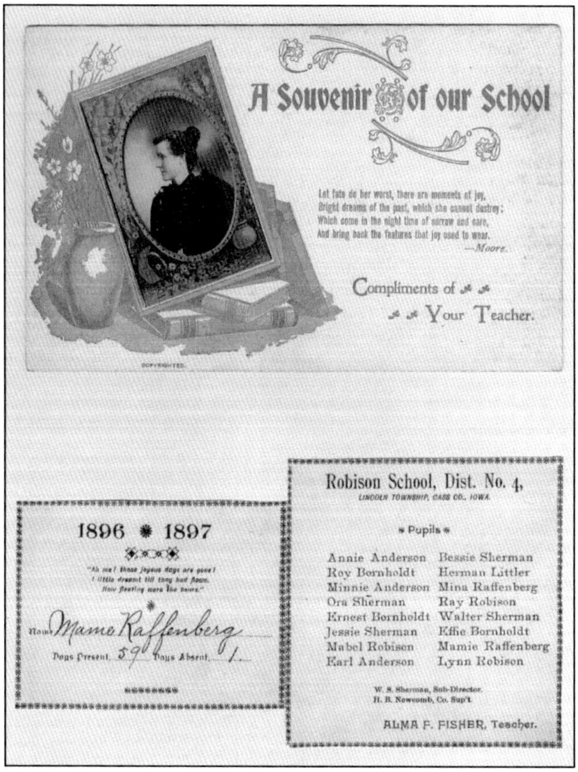

Mina and Mame Raffenberg attended Robinson School District No. 4 in Lincoln Township. J.F. Robinson served as the director in 1884. The schoolhouse was situated on the northeast corner of Section 19. This was a typical country school, comprising the first through the eighth grades. The photograph at left shows the list of pupils attending in 1896. Teachers often presented their students with a gift at the close of the year. Teacher Alma F. Fisher chose a card with her photograph and a Moore poem as her gift.

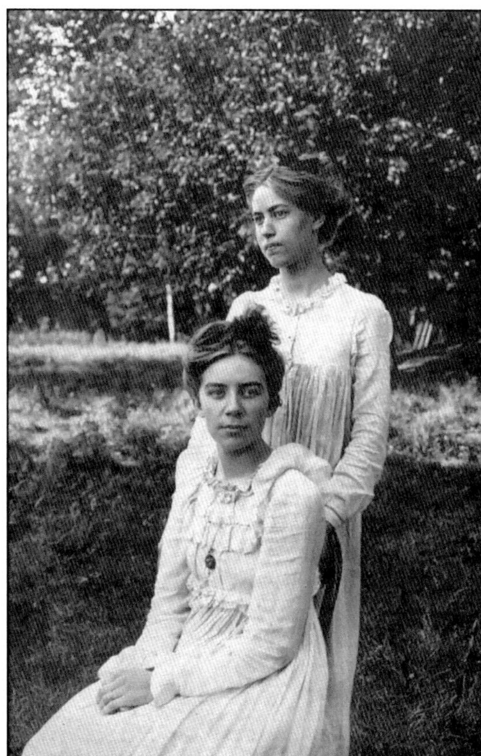

The photograph at right shows Mina Raffenberg, seated, and Pluma McDermott. In 1896, the Robinson School District had 16 students: Annie Anderson, Roy Bornholdt, Minnie Anderson, Ora Sherman, Ernest Bornholdt, Jessie Sherman, Mark Robinson, Earl Anderson, Bessie Sherman, Herman Littler, Mina Raffenberg, Ray Robinson, Walter Sherman, Effie Bornholdt, Mamie Raffenberg, and Lynn Robinson.

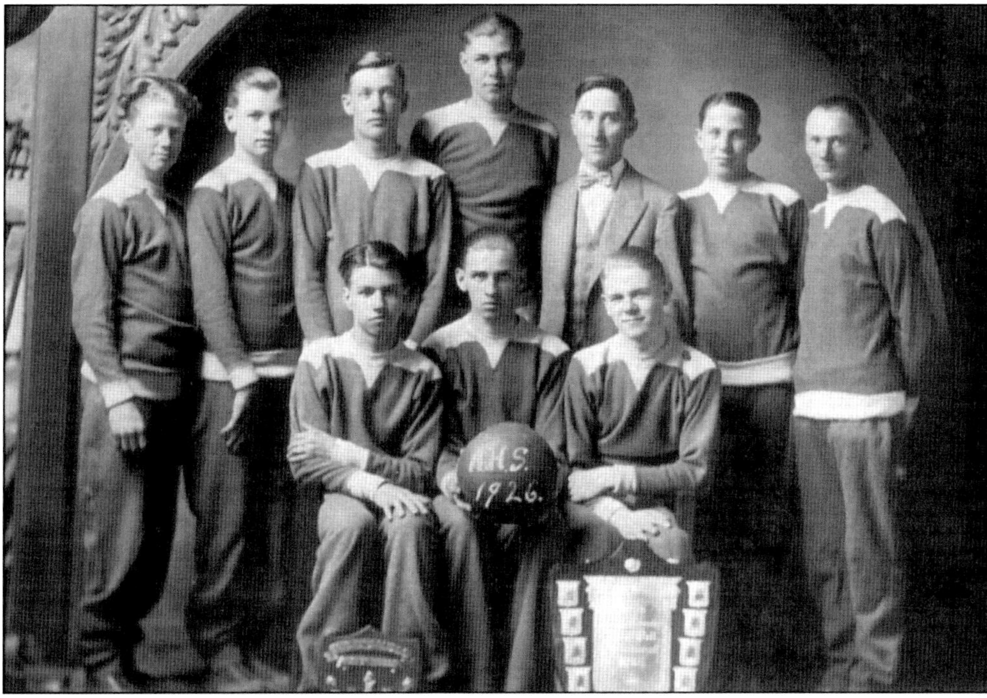

Basketball is considered the one sport that is uniquely American. It was invented in December 1891 by Dr. James Naismith and rapidly became a standard sport in high schools and colleges across the country. This photograph shows the 1926 Anita High School team. From left to right are (first row) Max Walker, Archie Worm, and Laurence Jewett; (second row) Merle Robison, Bill Forshay, Byron Turner, Glen Lindblom, Coach Horsewell, Olaf Hansen, and Shorty Lowden.

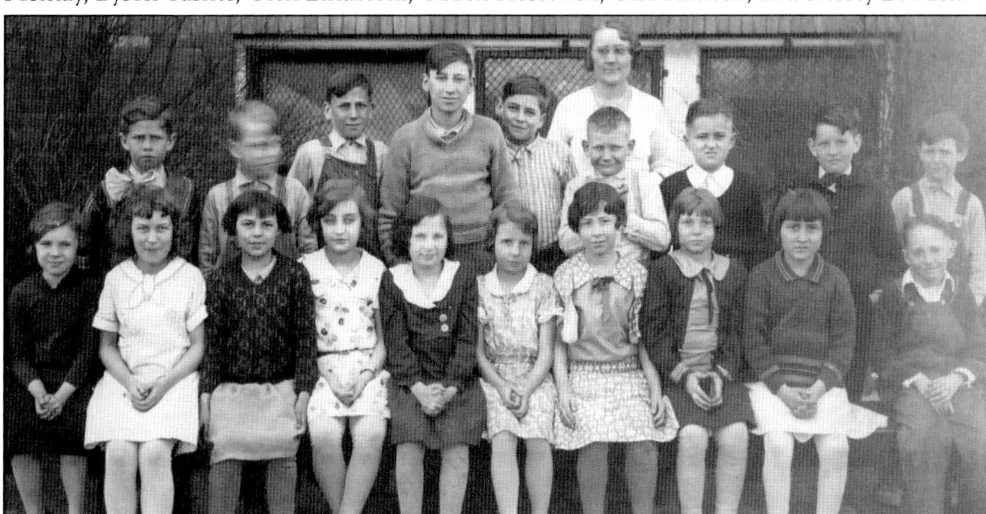

This photograph of the 1931 fourth graders at Anita Public School is typical of the annual class photographs. Pictured are, from left to right, (first row) Margaret Kopp, Lita Knudsen, Ruth Johnson, Marilyn Kohl, Mary Lou Bell, Virginia Nichols, Marion Bartley, Marilynn Biggs, Rose Boehme, and Coryell Bell; (second row) Harry Noblits, Gordon Hansen, Ralph Lett, Arthur Lett, Howard Karns, Eugene Daubendick, Frank Budd, Leo Bongers, and Jesse Miller. In the back is their teacher, Lillie Lentfer.

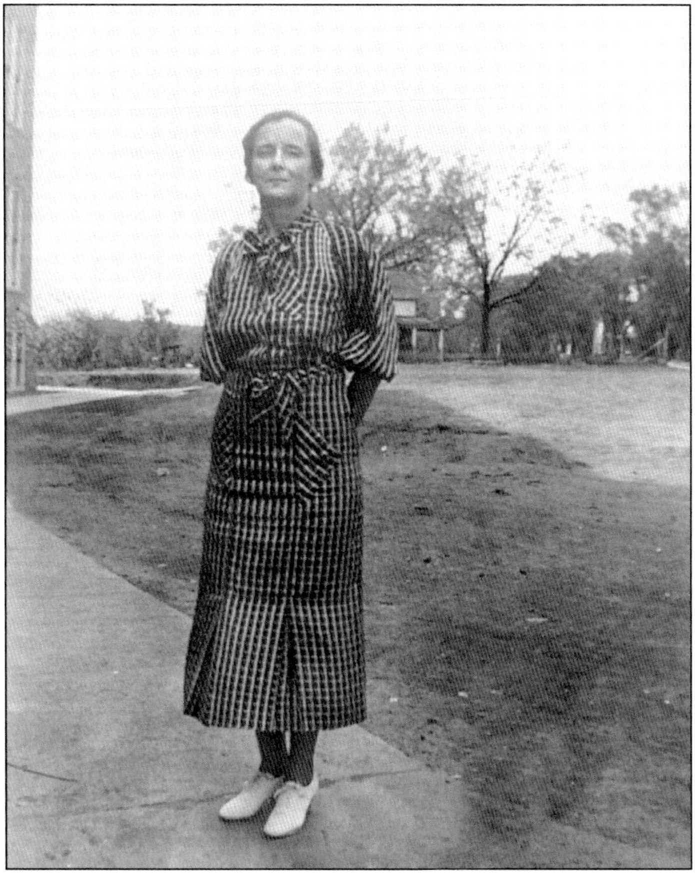

In Des Moines in 1933, 12-year-old Betty Burns of Anita won the *Des Moines Register and Tribune* statewide spelling bee. Christina Hollen was her teacher, and she accompanied her student to the contest. After the win, both were welcomed home by hundreds of county residents, the high school band, and Burns's proud parents, Tom and Wilma Burns. Pictured left is Christina Hollen. The *Des Moines Register and Tribune* sent Burns and Hollen to the national spelling bee in Washington, DC, where Burns placed fourth in the nation. She missed the word *vinaigrette*, leaving out the letter *a*. Burns, pictured below, received $75 for her efforts.

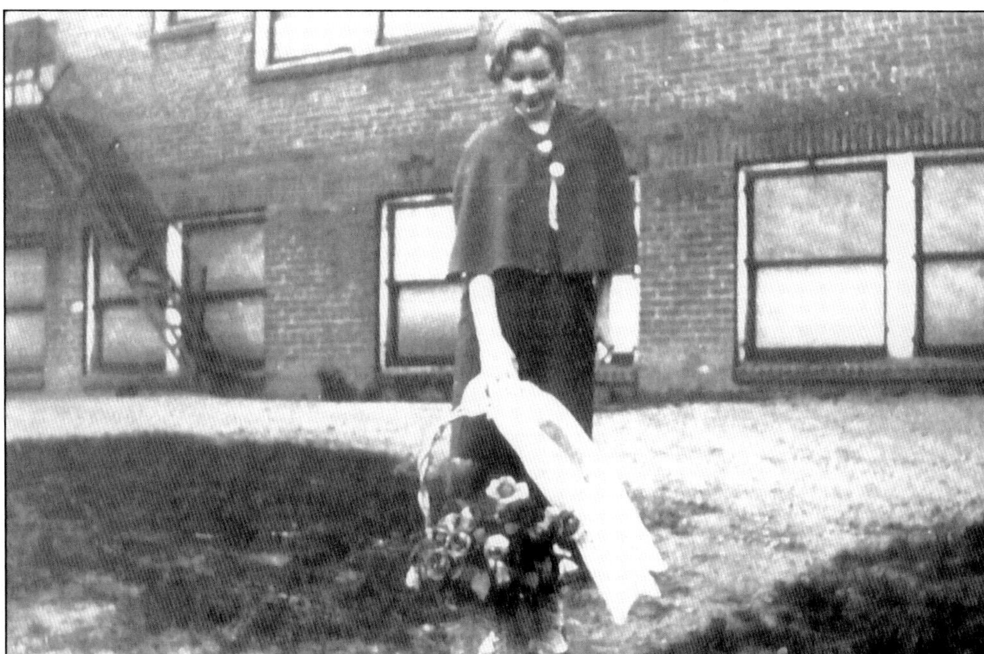

Seven

Pleasant Township

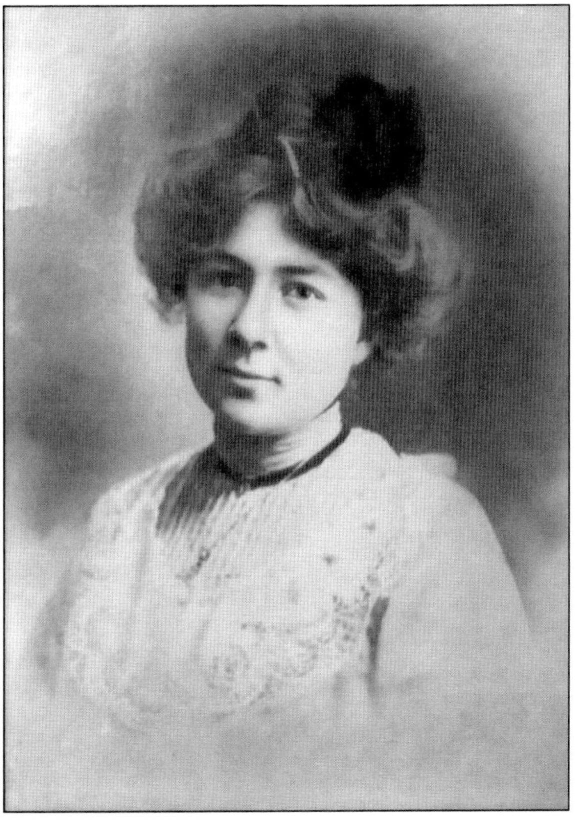

Ethel May Jones, the first girl born in the new town of Griswold, arrived March 16, 1880. For this distinction, she received a free town lot from the city fathers. She married Vernon Clements, and they were parents of three sons—Dale, born in February 1907, along with a twin brother who did not survive, and Donald, born in May 1908. Ethel died in 1916 at the age of 36.

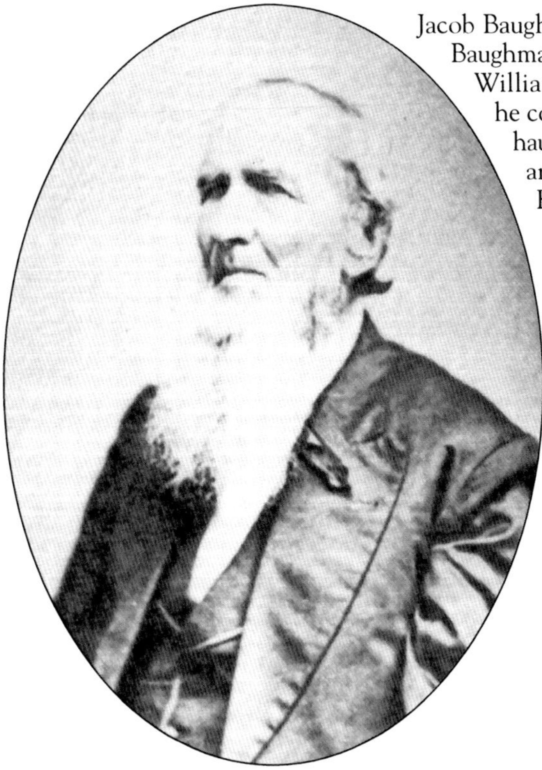

Jacob Baughman, pictured, was the father of William Baughman who came to Pleasant Township in 1856. William settled his family at Indiantown while he constructed a home. Jacob cut rough timber, hauled it to the sawmill at Lewis, brought it back, and built the first house in Pleasant Township. He was well respected and served as a member of the General Assembly of Iowa. Baughman Creek, which flows through the township, is named in his honor.

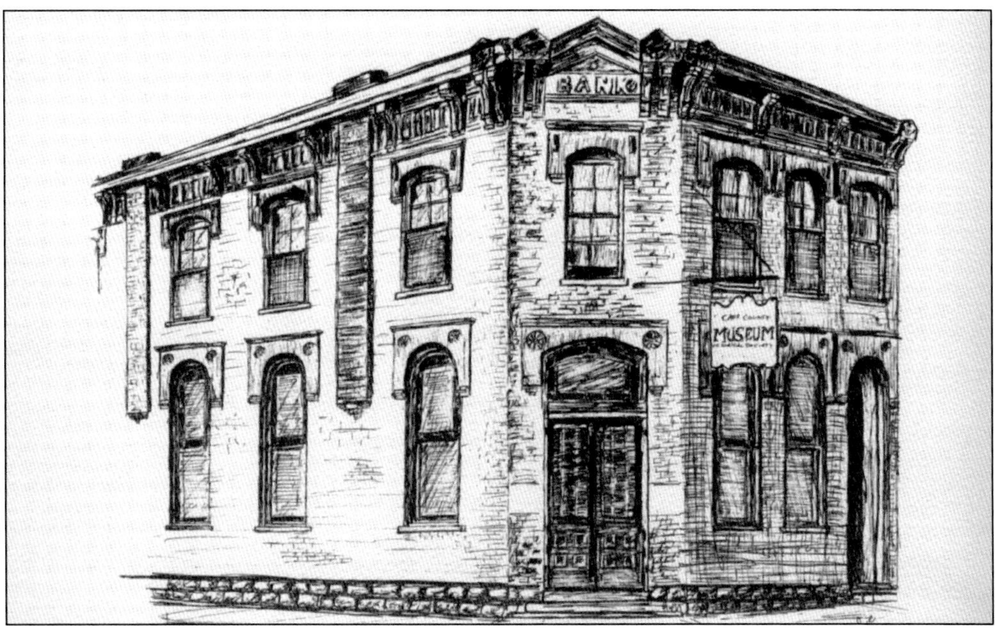

In 1880, Franklin H. Whitney, Cass County's indefatigable entrepreneur, established the first bank in the newly established town of Griswold, the Bank of Griswold. He was in partnership with Theodore H. Brown, and the partnership lasted until 1883, when the bank was reorganized as the First National Bank. This building on the corner of Main and Cass Streets is the only one in Griswold in the National Register of Historic Places. It appropriately houses the Cass County Museum.

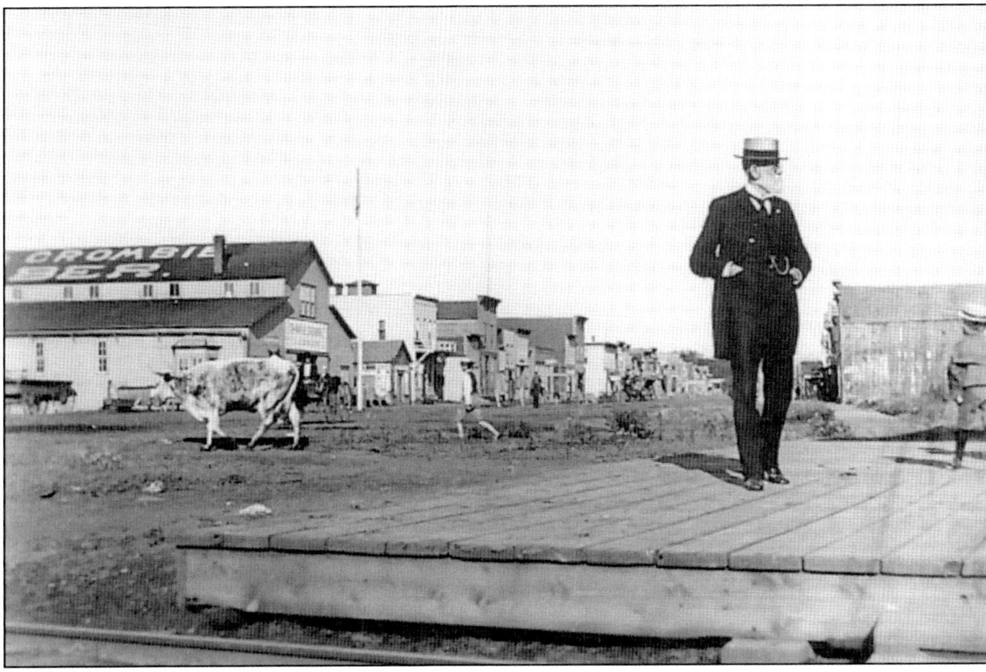

The 1900 photograph of Griswold's Main Street is a study in contrasts: from the primitive, rutted, dirt street to the impressive new lumber company, Crombie and Shaw, and from the elegantly dressed gentleman and child to the cow strolling leisurely across the street. When the Civil War started in 1861, emigration stopped, and settlers in Cass County had no market for their farm products. In 1868, the scene changed with the Rock Island & Pacific Railroad building program that brought people and money to Cass County. The first train of the Rock Island Railroad arrived at Griswold's Union Depot, shown below, on September 13, 1880. That day, bands from Atlantic and Lewis, along with several dignitaries, arrived in Griswold to cheering crowds. Oliver Mills of Lewis spoke and, along with conductor Bradbrook, led a parade up Main Street. An evening dance ended this gala celebration.

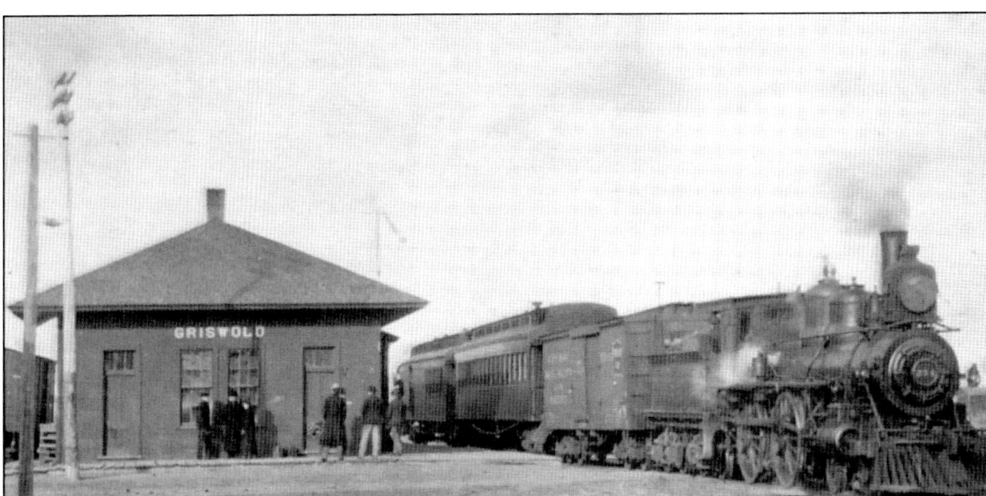

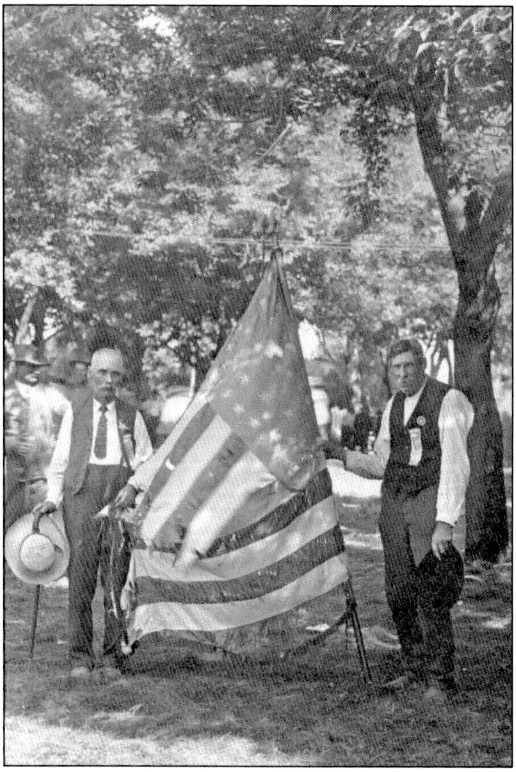

Jasper M. Quick served in the Union army during the Civil War, was taken prisoner, and was incarcerated in the infamous prison at Andersonville, Georgia. During the last 18 months of the war, nearly 1,300 men died there. After the war, the camp commander, Maj. Henry Wirz, was convicted of murdering prisoners and was hanged. Quick survived the war and became a very active member of the GAR. Several Quick artifacts are on display in the Cass County Museum. The photograph at left shows E.W. Headlee on the left and Quick holding an 1865 Civil War flag. The first GAR reunion in southwest Iowa was held at the farm of John R. Schofield, near Griswold. Later reunions were held at the city park in Griswold. The 1895 reunion is shown below. The Old Soldiers' Reunion remains an annual event in Griswold.

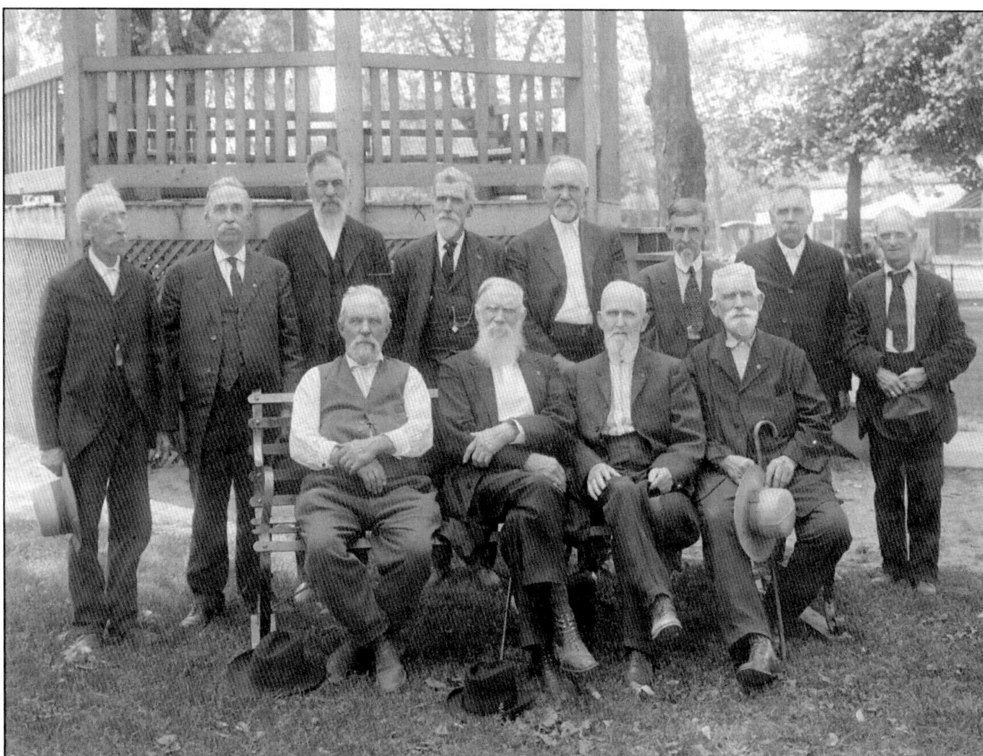

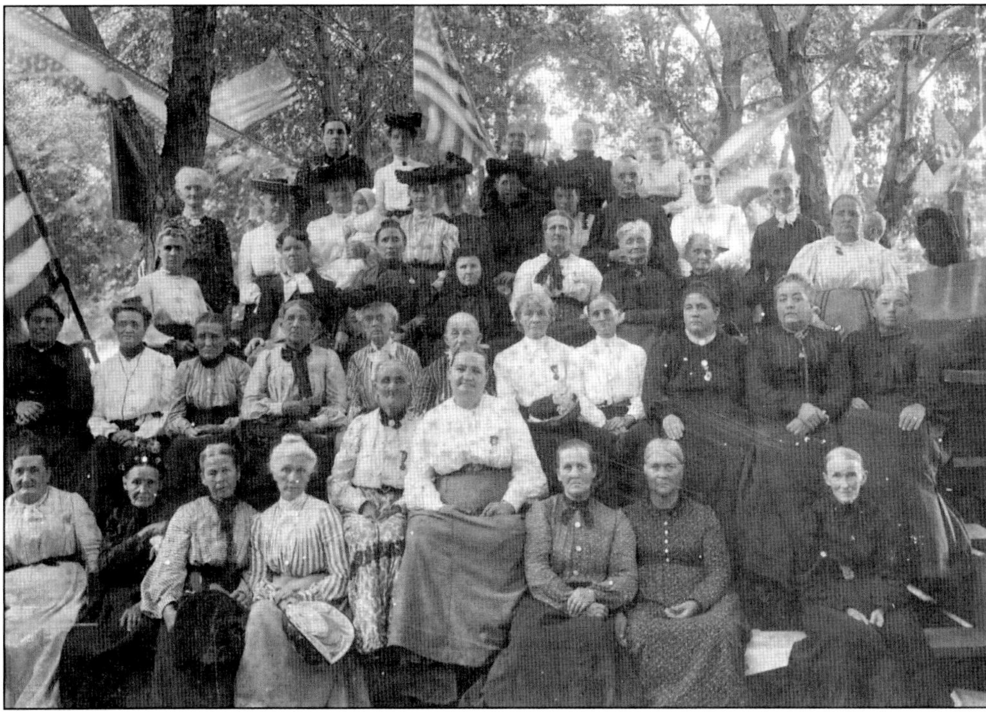

After the close of the Civil War, Northern veterans, wanting to preserve their camaraderie, banded together to organize the GAR. That was all well and good, but the wives, adhering staunchly to the adage, "They also serve who only stand and wait," formed auxiliary groups. This photograph features the wives of Civil War veterans. Emma Cunningham Schultz, former missionary to the Yankton, Sisseton, and Wahpeton Sioux, is seated fourth from the right in the second row.

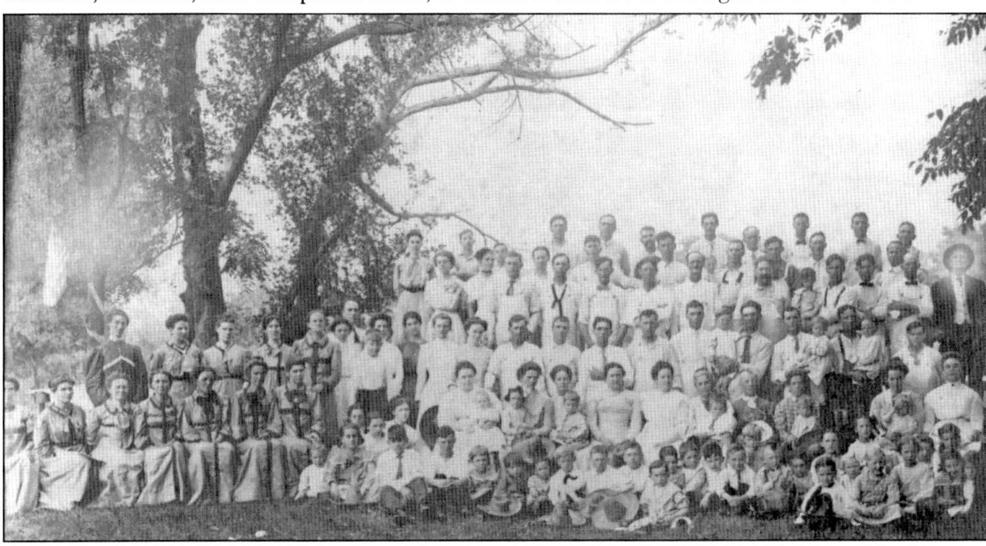

On April 25, 1898, Congress declared war on Spain. Iowa was asked to supply three regiments of infantry. One Iowa regiment left Des Moines on June 5, 1898, for the Philippines, saw action, and returned to the United States on October 22, 1899. About 200 Iowans lost their lives in this war, with the majority dying of disease due to poor food and improper sanitation. The photograph shows the wives with the Spanish American War veterans at the 1901 gathering north of Griswold.

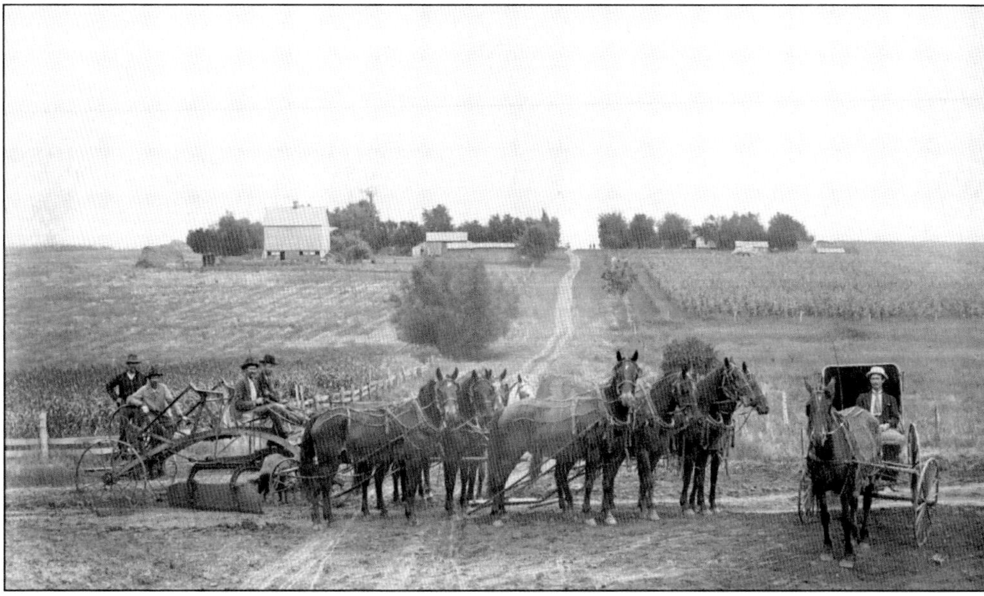

This September 1898 photograph, taken at the George Senholz farm east of Griswold, shows the prosperous farm of a typical successful gentleman farmer. The era of improved farm machinery was well under way, and the farmer's life was no longer dawn-to-dusk drudgery. Visiting with the local road crew, Senholz is identified as the man in the buggy at the far right. He was a member of the Griswold Town Band.

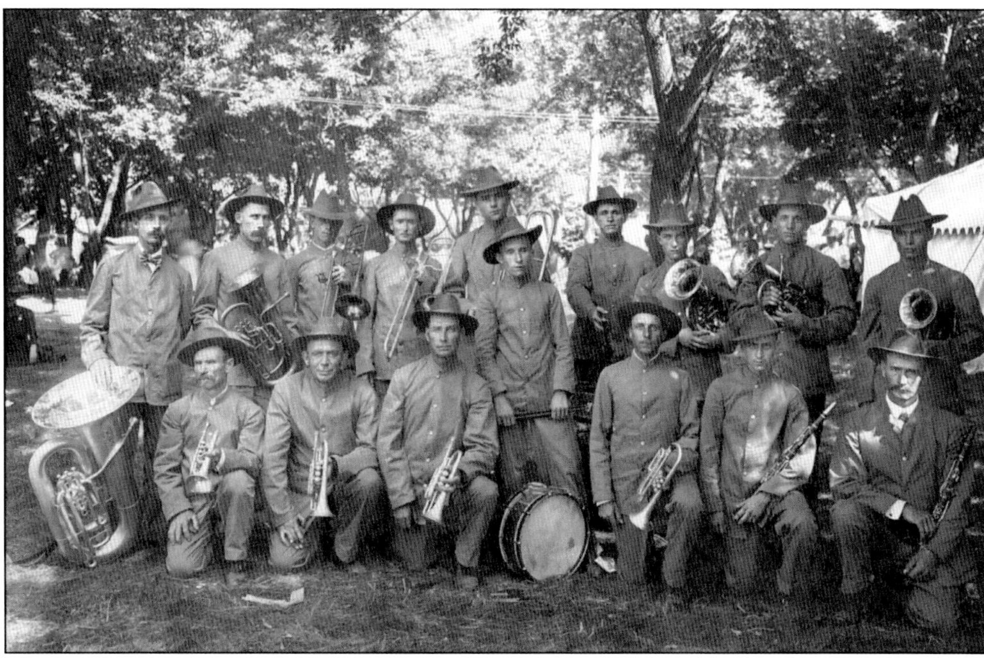

In 1898, the Griswold Town Band poses for this photograph in the city park. The early city bands consisted of men only. They held weekly concerts and played for many special celebrations. It was an honor to be a part of these groups, and the members took great pride in maintaining their uniforms and instruments. George Senholz is identified as the man at the right end of the first row.

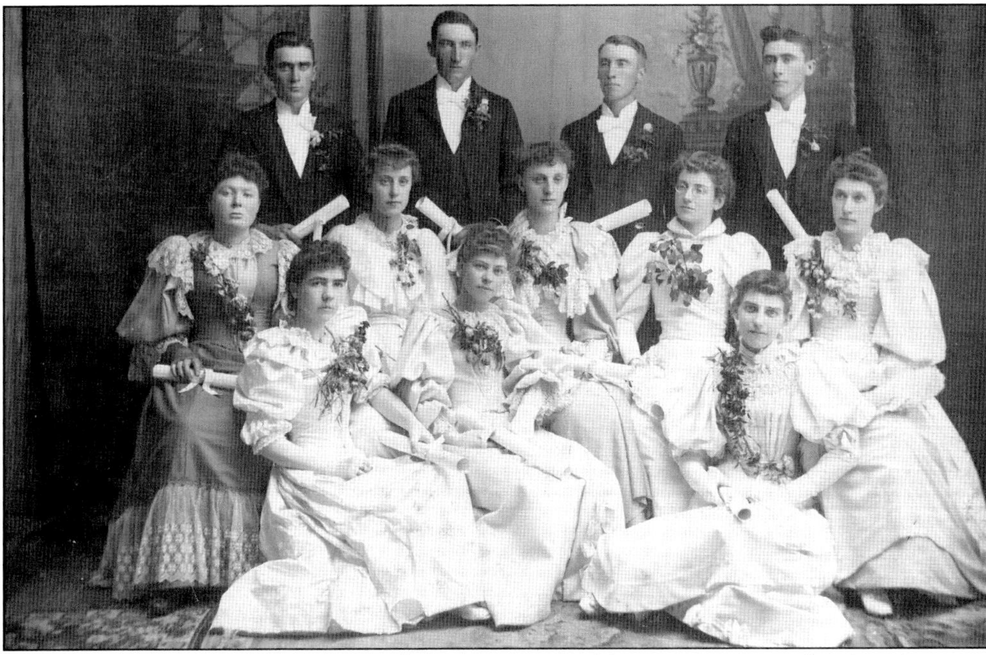

High school graduation was a formal event in Griswold in 1894, as seen by the white ties, boutonnieres, and black suits worn by the men and the lovely gowns and elegant corsages worn by the young ladies. From left to right are (first row) Lulu Mackerell, Nellie Van Scyoc, and Della Clovis; (second row) Carrie Morgan, Georgia Cook, Anna Baughman, Gertrude Van Scyoc, and Minnie Moulton; (third row) Willard Salisbury, Lew Adams, George Knight, and Leonard Salisbury.

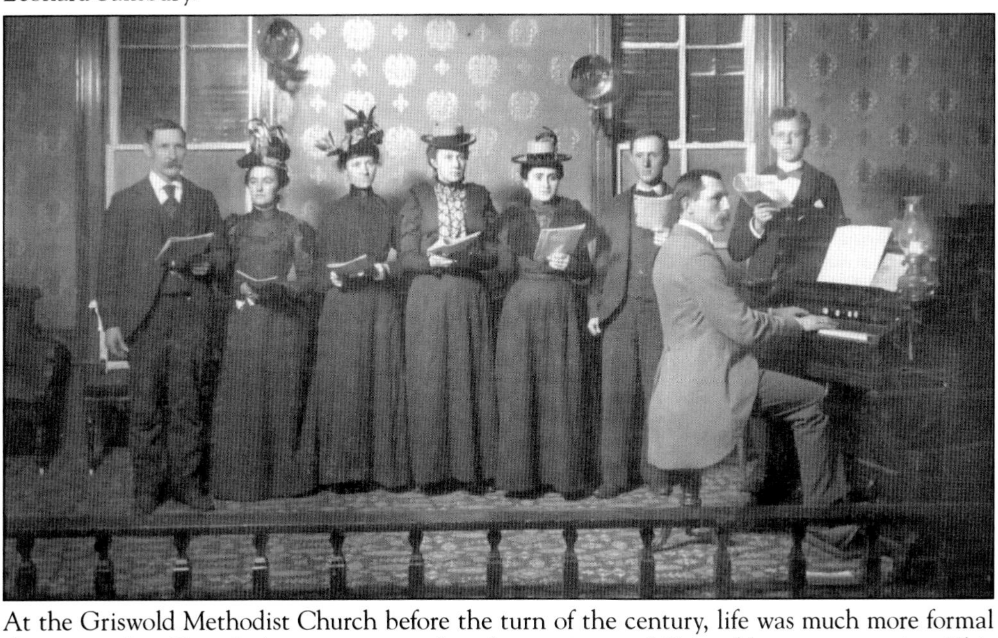

At the Griswold Methodist Church before the turn of the century, life was much more formal than it is today. Church choirs were part of regular services, and Griswold was no exception. This photograph of the Griswold Methodist Church choir depicts this formality. Parishioners would always wear their Sunday best. Obviously, milliners did a great business.

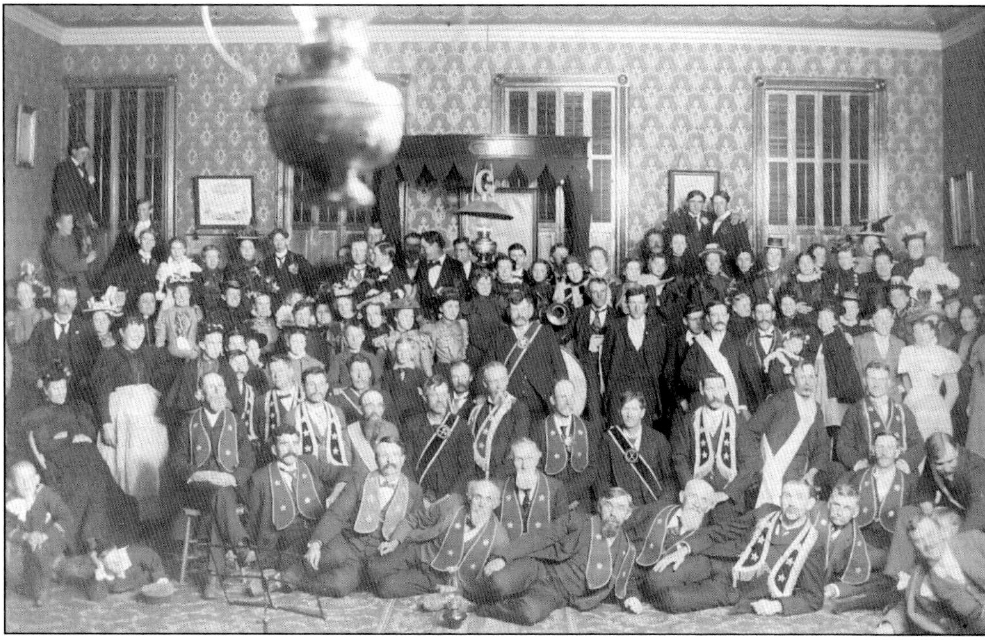

The IOOF (Independent Order of Odd Fellows) can trace its origins to the 17th century. Lodges were first constituted in England but spread to the United States by 1819. The women of the organization are called Rebekahs. This 1900 photograph is of a joint IOOF and Rebekah meeting held in the IOOF Hall located on Griswold's Main Street. The imposing lodge hall was built in 1891 and is currently undergoing renovation.

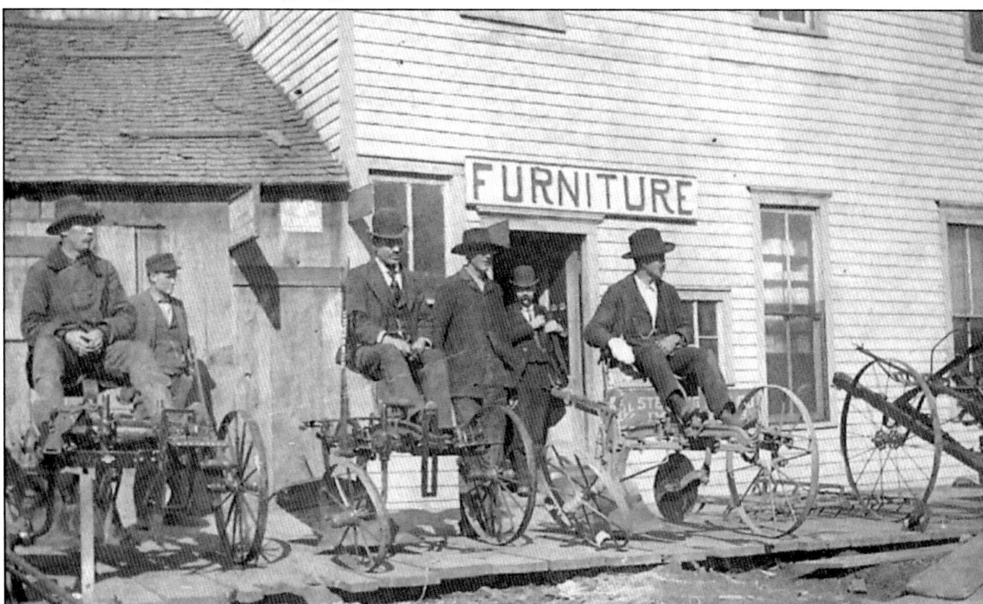

These Griswold men are posed on implements outside the Wheeler and Schuler store. In the early 1900s, the business encompassed an equipment, furniture, and hardware store as well as a mortuary. After the store was remodeled, Finny Wyman held dances in the upper story that was appropriately called the Playmor. The store was located on Main Street in Griswold.

Goldie G. Brown, age 16, was obviously a fashion plate in Pleasant Township in the late 1890s. It was unusual for a young woman to wear spectacles when having her photograph taken, but Brown appears to be completely at ease breaking with convention. No well-dressed woman was without her hat, and this one features elegant ostrich plumes. At this time, nearly every town, large or small, had a flourishing millinery business.

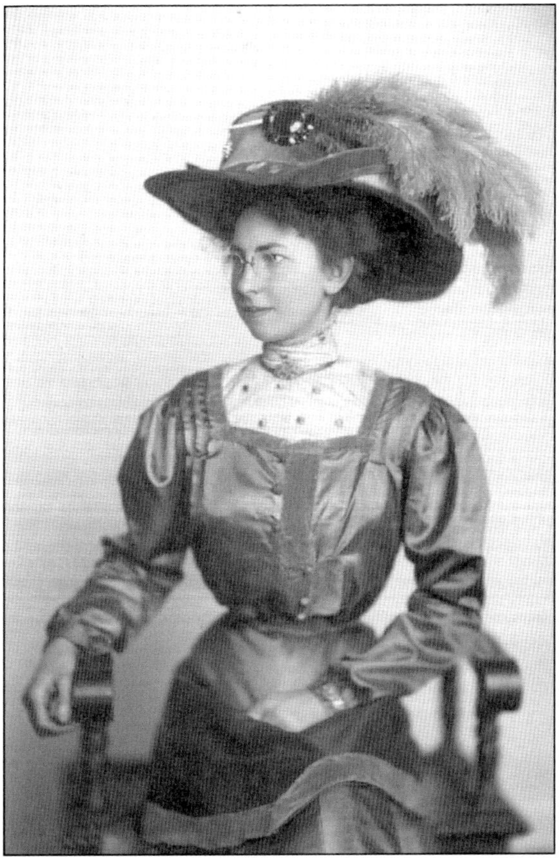

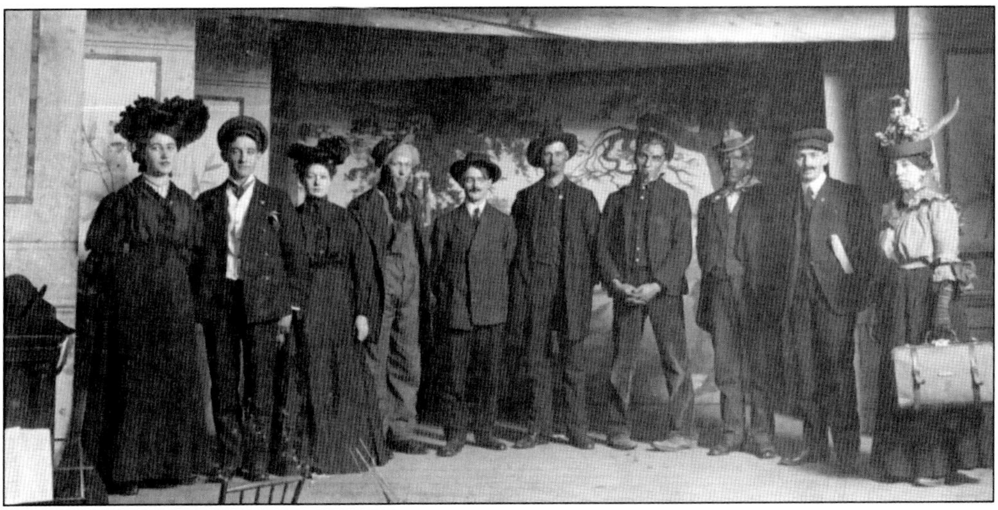

In 1883, Joseph Cullen Root founded the fraternal organization known as Modern Woodmen of America in Lyons, Iowa. This cast presented a play at the Griswold Opera House in the early 1900s for the Modern Woodmen. The Boston Opera Company managed the opera house in 1892. Cast members are, from left to right, Ethil Roberts, unidentified, Neva Kimball, Rolla Huchisen, John Carlton, Bill Lukembill, Sher Croghan, Harry Hawley, Clarence Moyer, and Maude Chauassen.

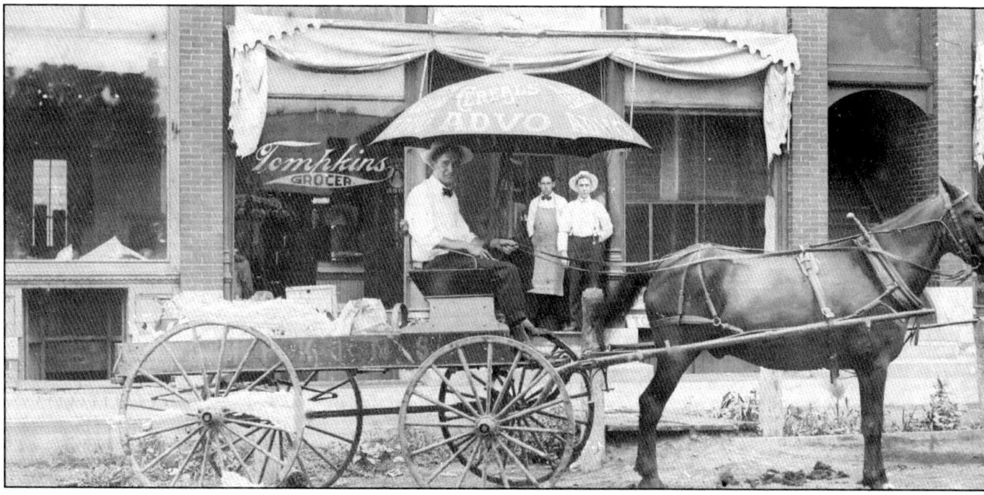

At the turn of the century, C.S. Tompkins owned and operated a thriving grocery business on Main Street in Griswold. Some of the typical prices at that time included the following: sugar, 21¢ per pound; corn, 20¢ a bushel; 8 bars of soap, 25¢; and 100 strawberry plants for $3.

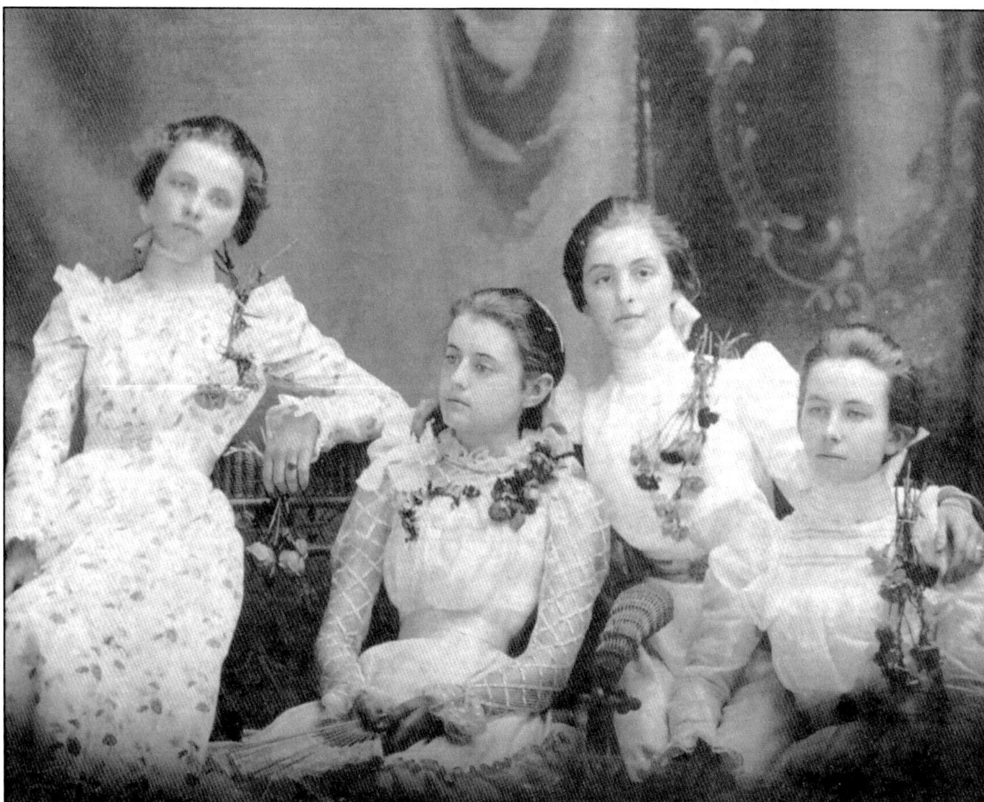
Eighth-grade graduation ceremonies were very important occasions because many students finished their formal educations at this level. The boys had to help with farming as it was very labor-intensive, and the girls were expected to assist with household chores and learn domestic skills. This photograph is of the 1898 eighth-grade graduates at Griswold. They are, from left to right, Edna Boggs, Alma Garvin, Lucile Boggs, and Ina Tompkins.

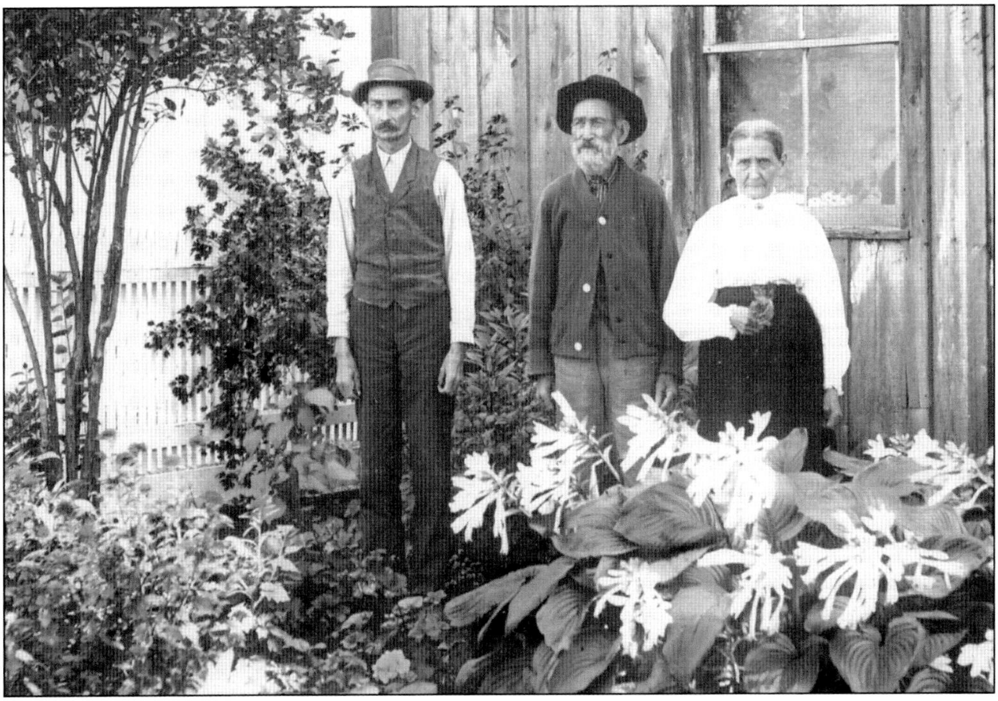

George Truax, his wife, and their son Charley are shown in this 1916 photograph taken in the flower garden outside their home in Pleasant Township. Mrs. Truax, standing behind her hosta bed, obviously had the luxury of using part of the family gardening plot to grow flowers instead of the usual utilitarian vegetable garden, where the produce of her labor could be used to enhance the winter food supply.

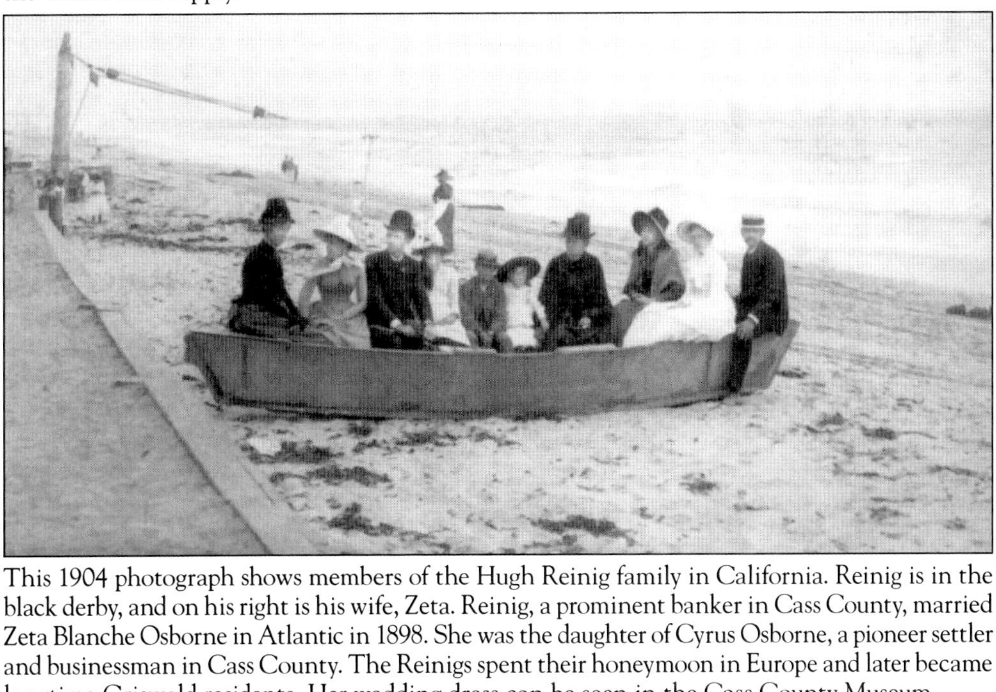

This 1904 photograph shows members of the Hugh Reinig family in California. Reinig is in the black derby, and on his right is his wife, Zeta. Reinig, a prominent banker in Cass County, married Zeta Blanche Osborne in Atlantic in 1898. She was the daughter of Cyrus Osborne, a pioneer settler and businessman in Cass County. The Reinigs spent their honeymoon in Europe and later became longtime Griswold residents. Her wedding dress can be seen in the Cass County Museum.

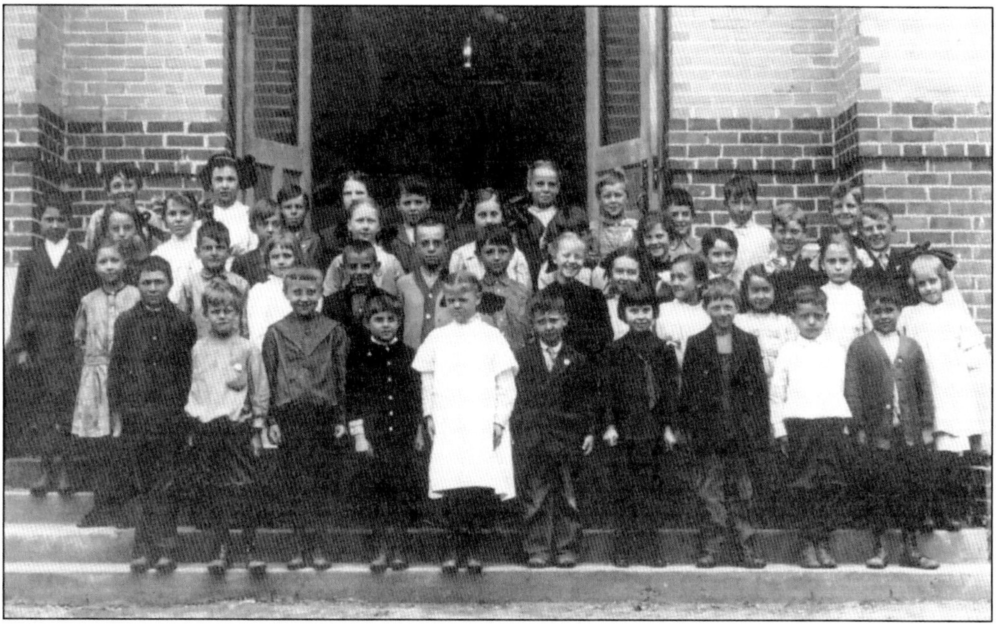

This 1905 photograph shows Pleasant No. 2 Pioneer School, more commonly called the Baughman School, located two miles east of Griswold. The teacher was Anna Walters. Some of the pupils enrolled at that time were Austin, Clarence, Mabel, Ethel, Lucille, and Irene Baughman; Albert, Roy, Harry, Esther, Emily, Alma, Elmer, and Cordelia Bierbaum; Jessie, Max, Walter, and Garold Brown; Katie and Roland Miller; Emma, Myrtle, Zaola, and Martha Wright.

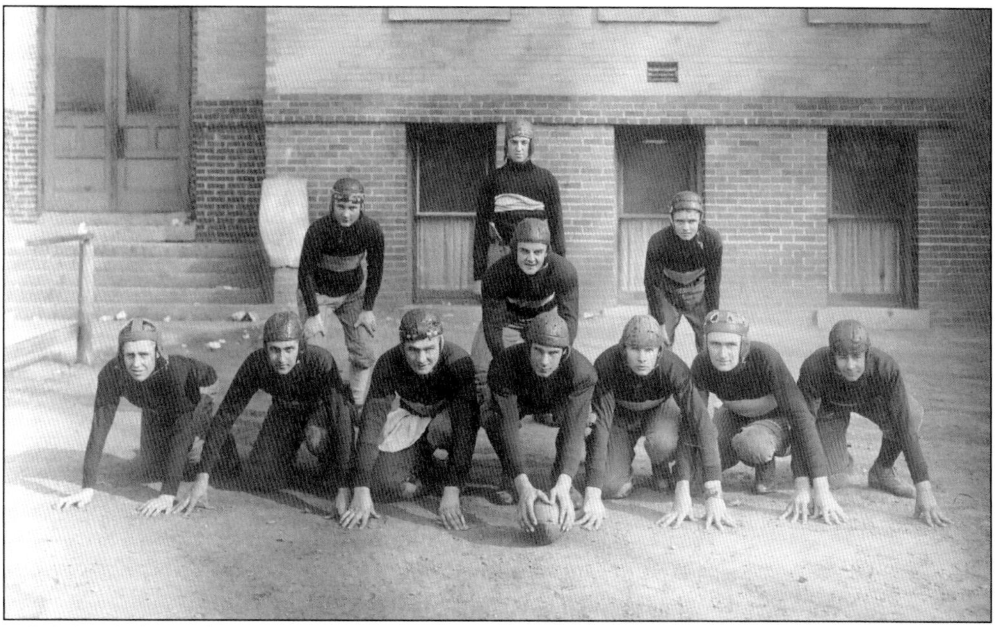

While baseball was the quintessential American sport, football was not far behind. In many schools in America, the strength and skill displayed by the football team was a source of considerable local pride and gave the town's citizens important bragging rights. This 1917 photograph shows the Griswold High School football team. While most are unidentified, Roy C. Bierbaum is second from the right in the front row.

Advertisements, such as the one at right, were common around 1900. The country was in a depression, and many people in the East could not afford to care for their families; children had to be abandoned. The Children's Aid Society and the New York Foundling Hospital established the Orphan Train. Children were placed on trains headed west, and when they stopped, people who wanted children selected one or more from the train and took them home. Over 100,000 children arrived in Iowa in this way.

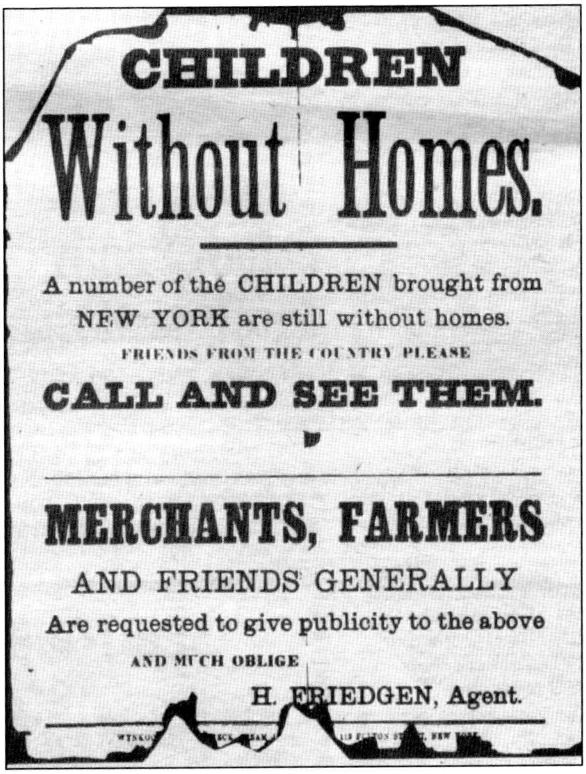

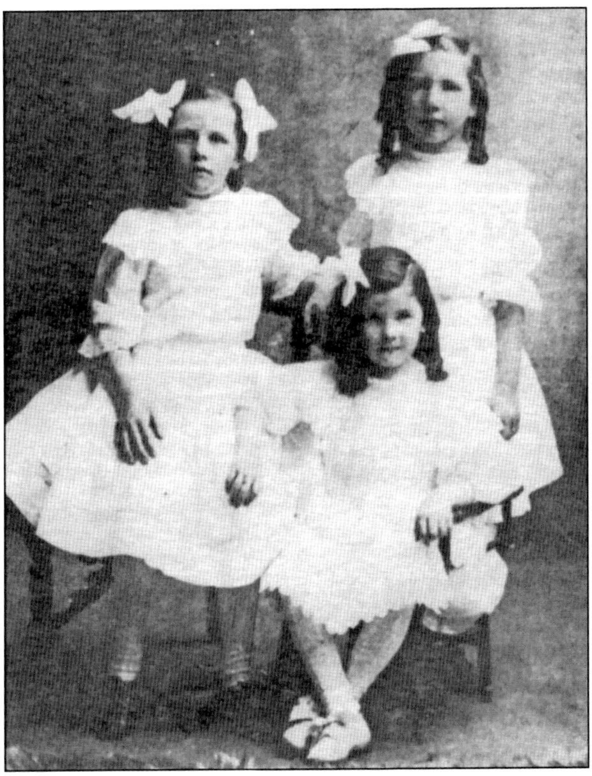

The photograph at left depicts three sisters who arrived in Griswold in 1904 on the Orphan Train. They are, from left to right, Maggie, Jennie, and Nellie ?. Johnny Johnson arrived in Griswold on such a train in 1906 when he was eight years old. The Chris Taylor family of Grant took him. Pieces of his Orphan Train clothing are on display at the Cass County Museum.

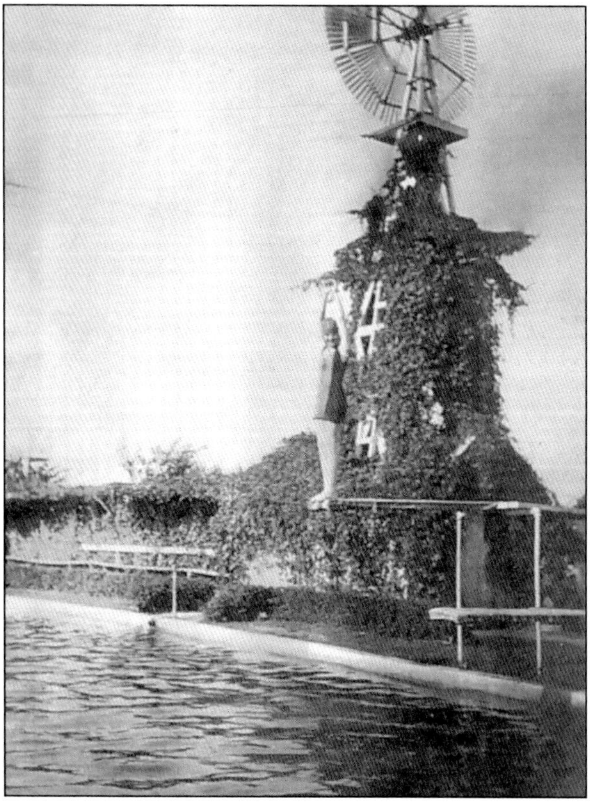

Knop Arbor was a favorite place for families to picnic, relax, and socialize with friends while swimming, skating, or playing on the nine-hole golf course. Dances were held during the summer, and Lawrence Welk's band played there as well as at several Old Soldiers' Reunion street dances. Otto Knop started building this recreation park in the early 1900s, and it thrived until the mid-1930s.

In 1913, construction was underway on the new Methodist church in Griswold. The men in this photograph are taking a break from pouring the footings and foundation. From left to right are (first row) Louis Scharf, W.T. O'Conell, Martin Dean, Charles Brown, David Lindvall, Charles Miller, Lyle Hendle, and Dell Burnham; (second row) Grover Small, Jack Adams, and Milo Cook.

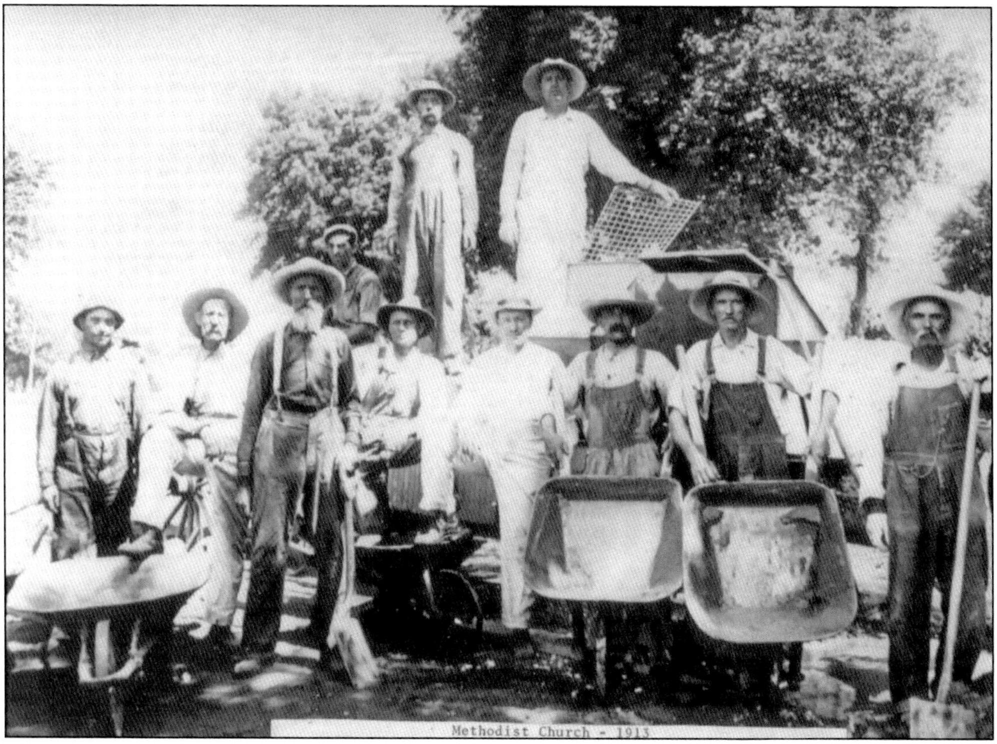

The words "Griswold High School" and "the principal" are synonymous with the name Winifred Bromelkamp. This bigger-than-life personage was the principal at Griswold High School from 1917 to 1946. In 1923, the Griswold annual was dedicated to her. In the yearbook, students state that she had won their love and esteem by being ever ready to lend a helping hand. She shared their failures as well as the honor of their achievements. She was loved, feared, and revered.

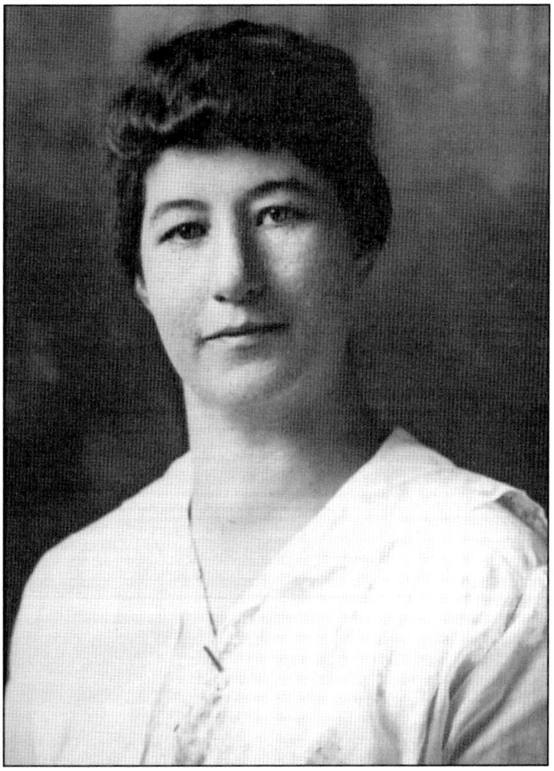

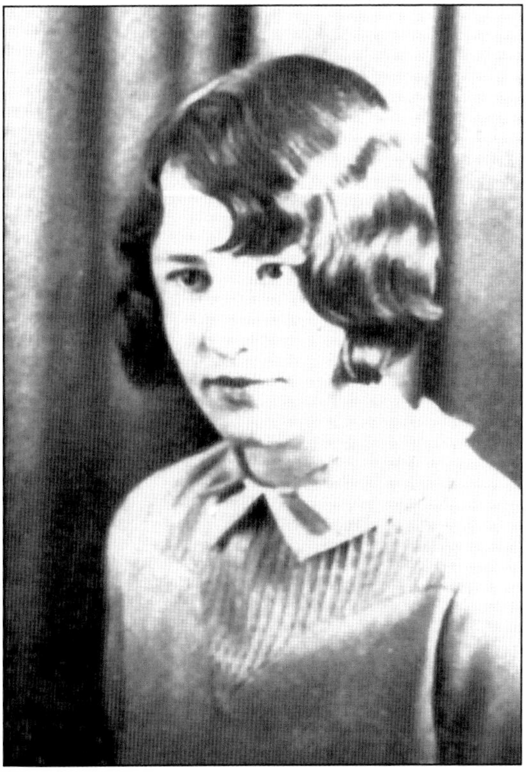

Alice Buckman, a Griswold graduate, was voted the outstanding athlete in soccer, basketball, baseball, and track. She was also the star player on the boys' baseball team in 1928. In one game held at Sunnyside Park in Atlantic, Alice was pulled due to an injury, and Griswold lost to Atlantic, 109-0. This set a national record that still stands for the most runs scored in a high school game. Following graduation, Buckman became a member of the Georgie-Porgie Kittenball Team in Chicago.

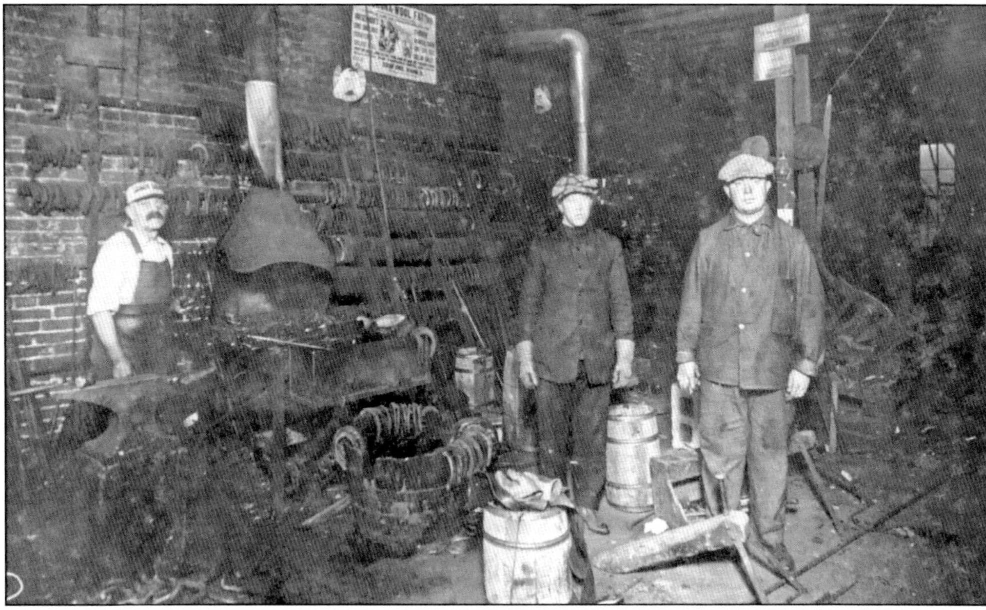

The Scharf Brothers Blacksmith Shop was located in Griswold. When the first towns in Cass County were established, success would depend on whether or not the services of a reputable blacksmith could be secured. Horses had to be shod, harnesses made and repaired, and tools had to be forged and kept in working condition. Pictured above are, from left to right, Robert Scharf, unidentified, and Louie Scharf. The Scharf Brothers Blacksmith Shop was a hive of activity on Main Street in the 1920s and 1930s. The business sold farm implements and received the first threshing machine shipped to Griswold in February 1920. It was a Racine Special. When a new shipment of machinery arrived, the local men took the opportunity to try the devices out, as shown below in this early 1930 photograph.

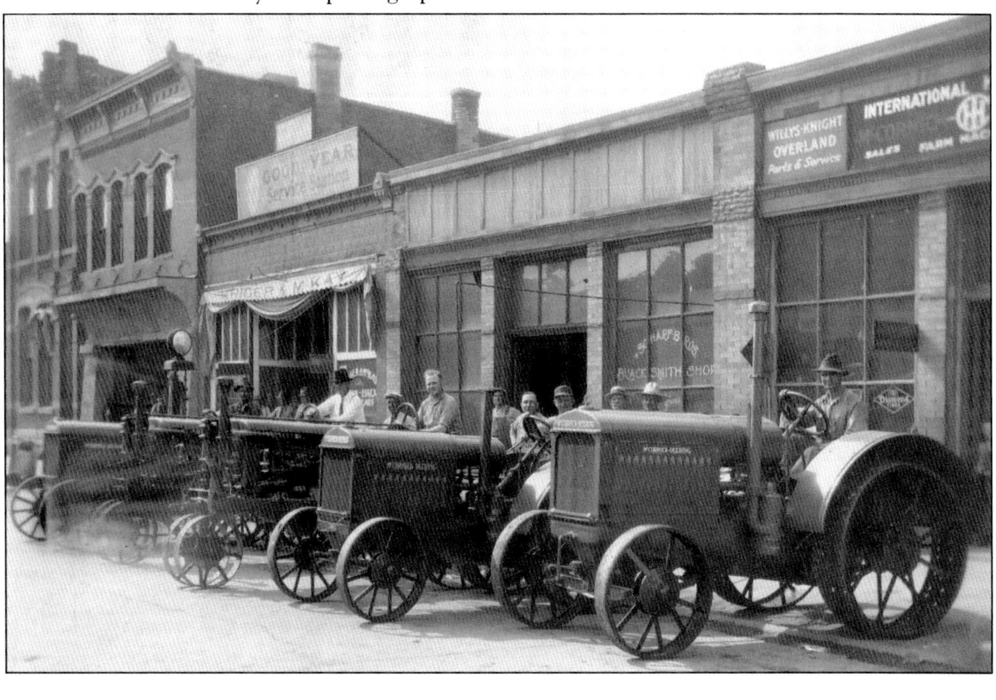

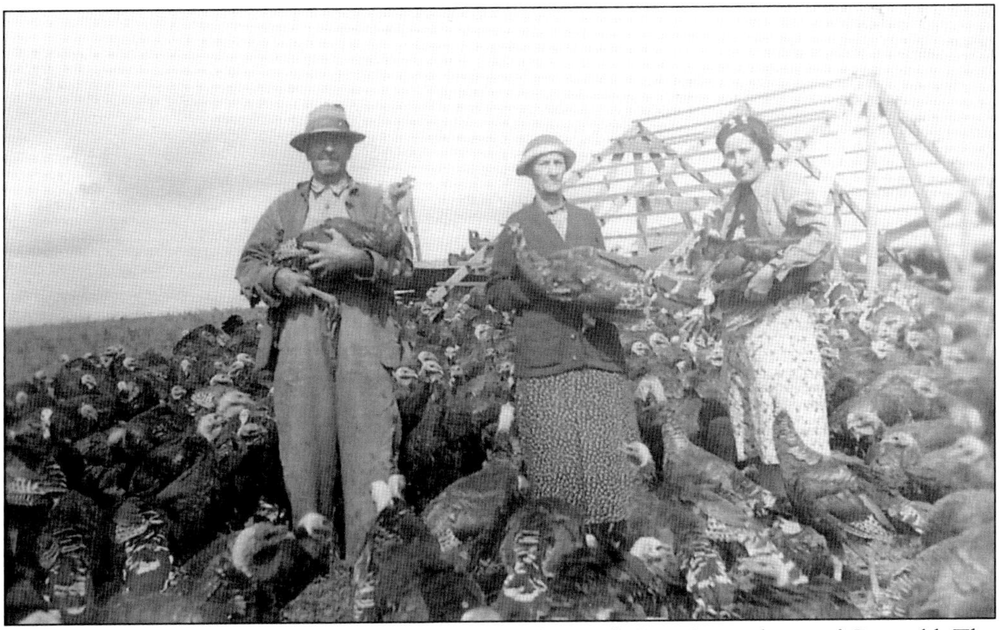

This 1930s photograph was taken at the Yarger Turkey Hill Farm located east of Griswold. The turkey is indigenous to the Western Hemisphere. The bird was readily adapted to domestication, and by the 1930s, many farms like Yarger's came into existence. Commercial breeding is now found around the world, and all varieties are descendants of the North American wild turkey. Pictured are, from left to right, J.W. "Cap" Yarger, Charlotte Yarger, and Nellie Yarger Hamilton.

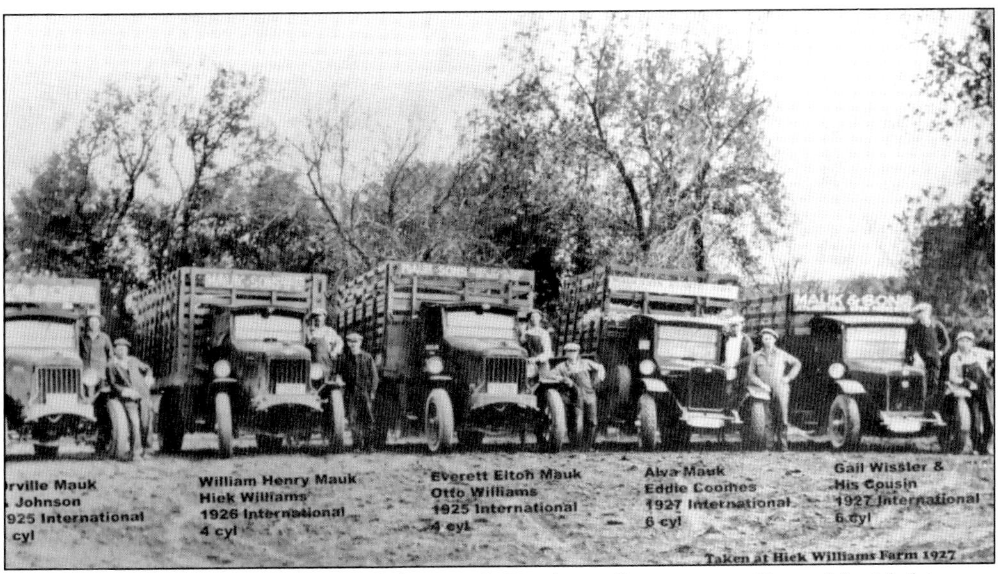

In 1925, William Mauk established the Mauk Trucking Company in Griswold with his sons Orville, Alva, Everett, and Wilbert. They trucked stock to Omaha, the largest stockyard in the nation. When the weather was bad, Highway 100 to Omaha would be almost impassable, so the trucks would leave town hooked to one another by a 10-foot rod allowing for a "push-pull" effect. Before arriving in Omaha, sometimes 20 trucks would be hooked on to the caravan.

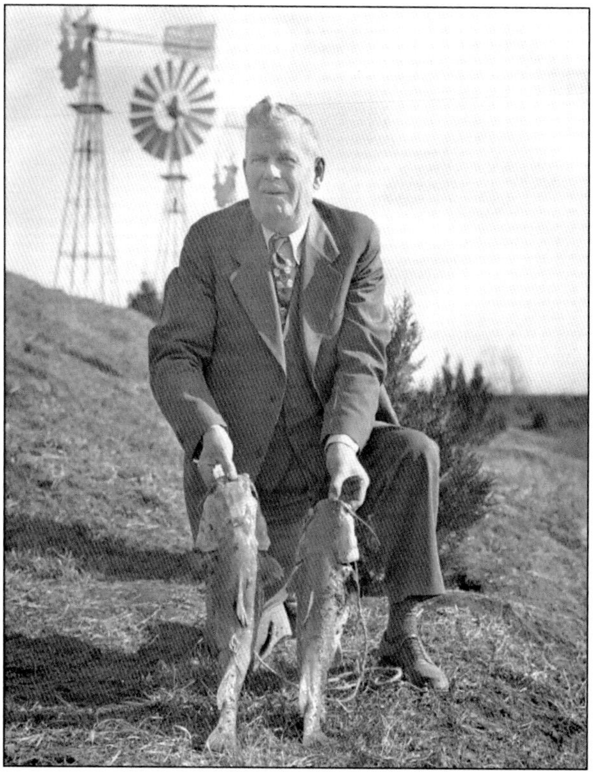

In 1926, L.A. Cocklin, pictured left, built Griswold's largest factory, the Laco Company. It was internationally known for its burners and oil heaters. In 1936, Cocklin built the Fish Farm, a 40-acre recreation area. In 1940, that land was deeded to the city of Griswold. During World War II, portable Laco heaters were used in the field by the military. Recently, a church in the Netherlands inquired about the Laco factory, as they had a Laco furnace that had been in use since 1942. The Laco plant closed in 1961.

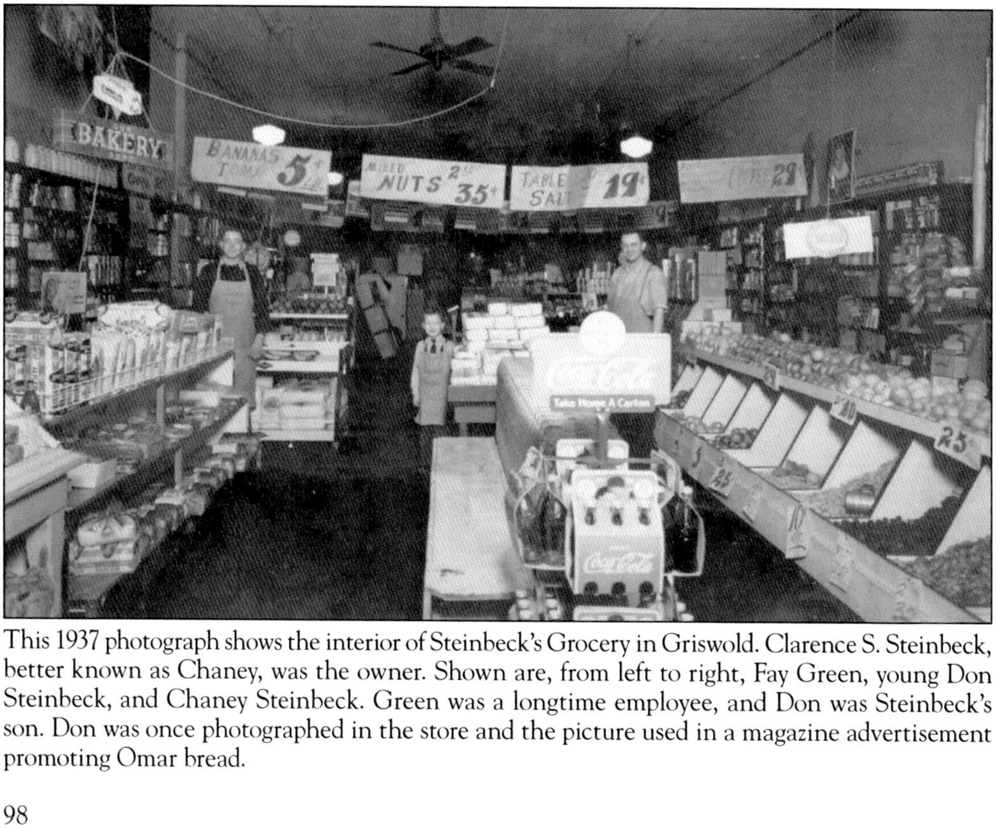

This 1937 photograph shows the interior of Steinbeck's Grocery in Griswold. Clarence S. Steinbeck, better known as Chaney, was the owner. Shown are, from left to right, Fay Green, young Don Steinbeck, and Chaney Steinbeck. Green was a longtime employee, and Don was Steinbeck's son. Don was once photographed in the store and the picture used in a magazine advertisement promoting Omar bread.

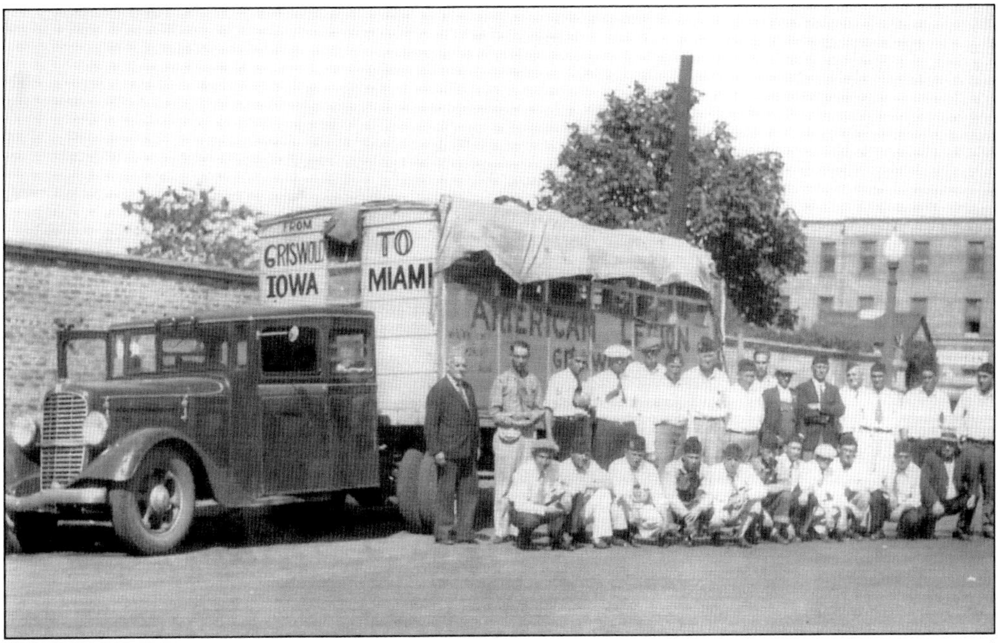

On October 25, 1934, at 9:00 p.m., a group of American Legionnaires was given a rousing send off to the national convention in Miami, Florida. Their home-away-from-home was a remodeled truck that was converted into a Pullman-style conveyance. The trip was an exhilarating adventure with stops at Civil War monuments, cotton fields, and at mini-conventions of other posts headed to Miami. They were greeted in Miami to the sound of the "Iowa Corn Song." Shown in the photograph below, those making the trip are, from left to right, (first row) Leroy Spiker, Ross Reynolds, Harry Greene, Millard Wallace, Malcolm Reynolds, Ernest Harris, William Smith, Carl Burnham, William Linfor, Charles Robinson, and Hugh Reinig; (second row) Doc Ryder, Robert Boseck, Virgil Boseck, Herman Russman, Tony Hansen, Frank Kuester, Clarence Bradow, Roy Bierbaum, Frank Hardenberg, and Leon Talbott; (third row) Frank Wyman, ? Miller, Dave Porter, and Doc Chalmers.

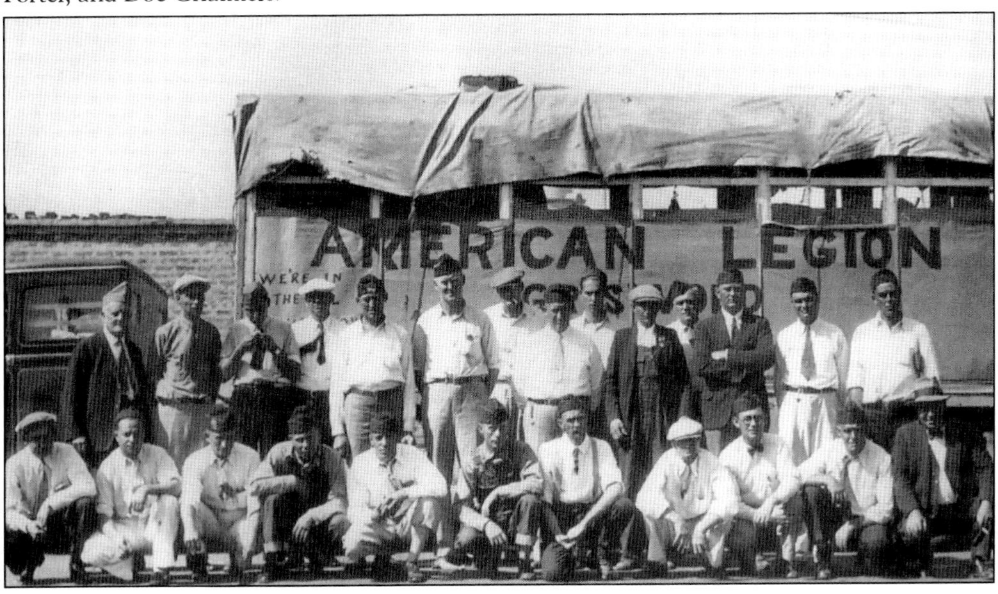

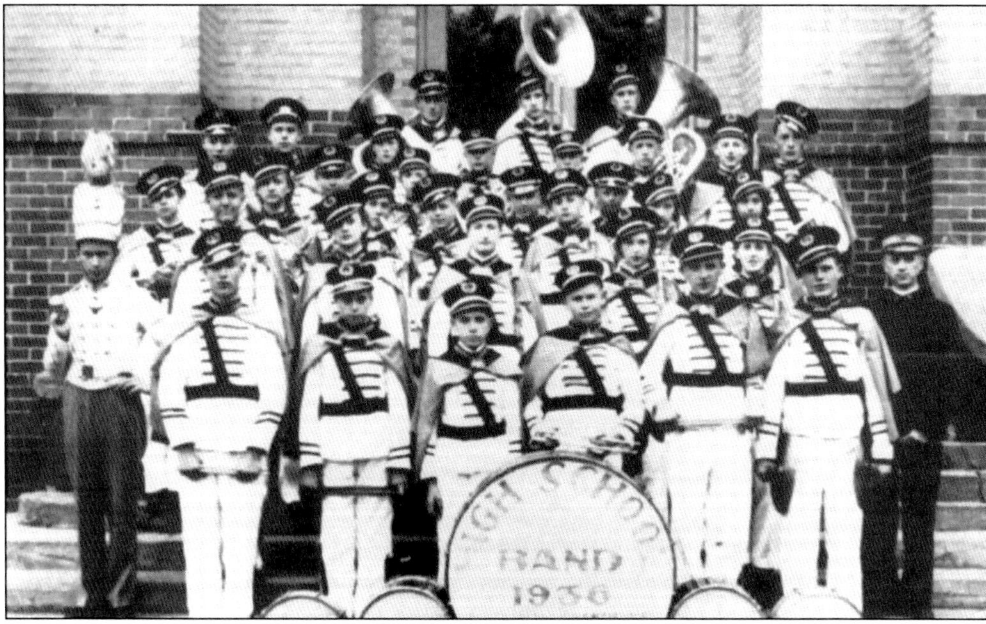

Members of the 1936 Griswold High School band are pictured above in the homemade uniforms sewn by their mothers. Members pictured include Ray Green, Junior Hendricks, Paul Peebles, Chuck Seeley, Bill Hanton, Fred Wheeler, Dale Knoke, Shirley Woodward, Gilbert Cook, Pearle Perdue, Gene Rogers, Helen Perdue, Elmer Wall, Dale Peebles, Stanley Braden, Annette Jenkins, Boyd Carlton, Cleo Wohlenhaus, Norman Engle, James Perry, Orlo Perdue, Dessamore Dickey, Ruby Patton, Harold Foy, Mary Briscoe, Lucille Kirk, Roland Frank, Dale Swanson, Irene Foy, Edward Crawford, Junior Christian, Junior Seastrom, Harold Dickey, and Quentin Shultz. Director John Dickey is on the right side in the dark uniform. For three consecutive years, the band was the National Champion. The band traveled to Cleveland, Ohio, in 1936, to Jackson, Mississippi, in 1937, and to Omaha, Nebraska, in 1938. The photograph below shows the 1938 band.

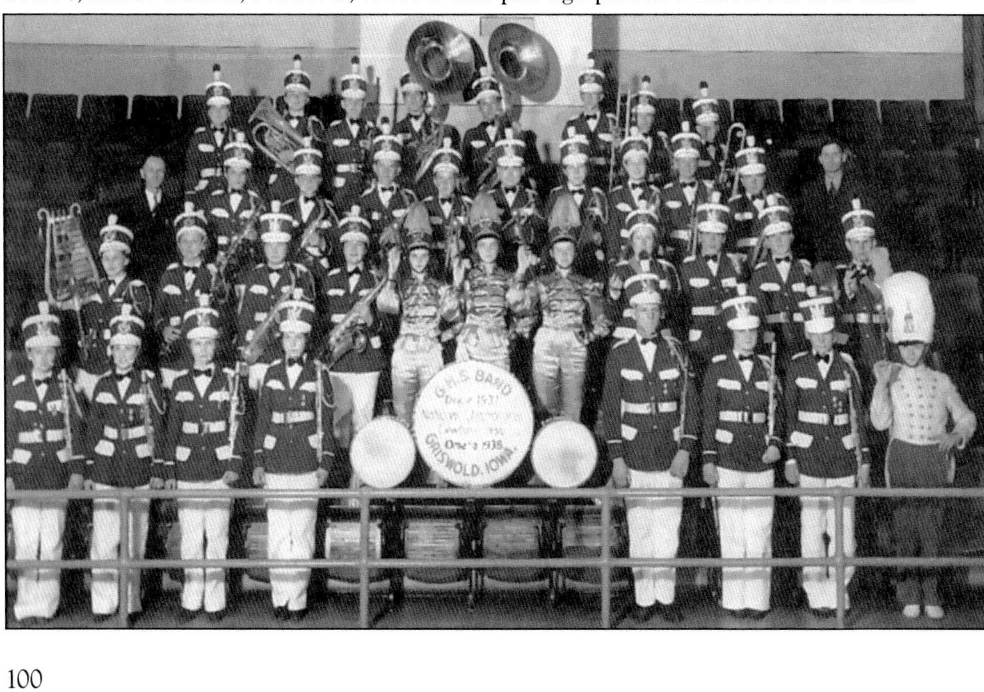

Eight

Bear Grove and Noble Townships

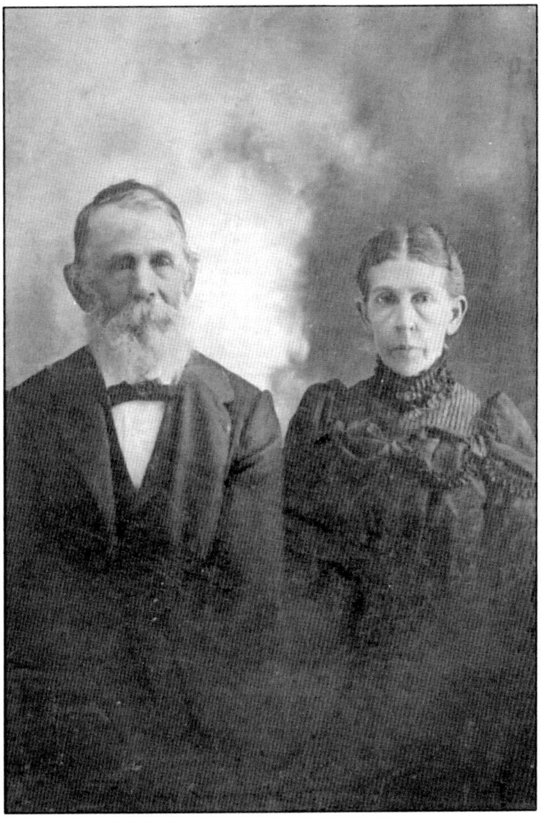

John Baughman Schultz and his wife, Emma Cunningham Schultz, were very progressive pioneers. Schultz began with 40 acres of wild prairie and increased his holding to 308 productive acres. He served in the Civil War and took part in many battles, including Shiloh, Vicksburg, and Sherman's March to the Sea. After returning from the war, he married Emma Cunningham in August 1867. She also had a brave and adventurous spirit.

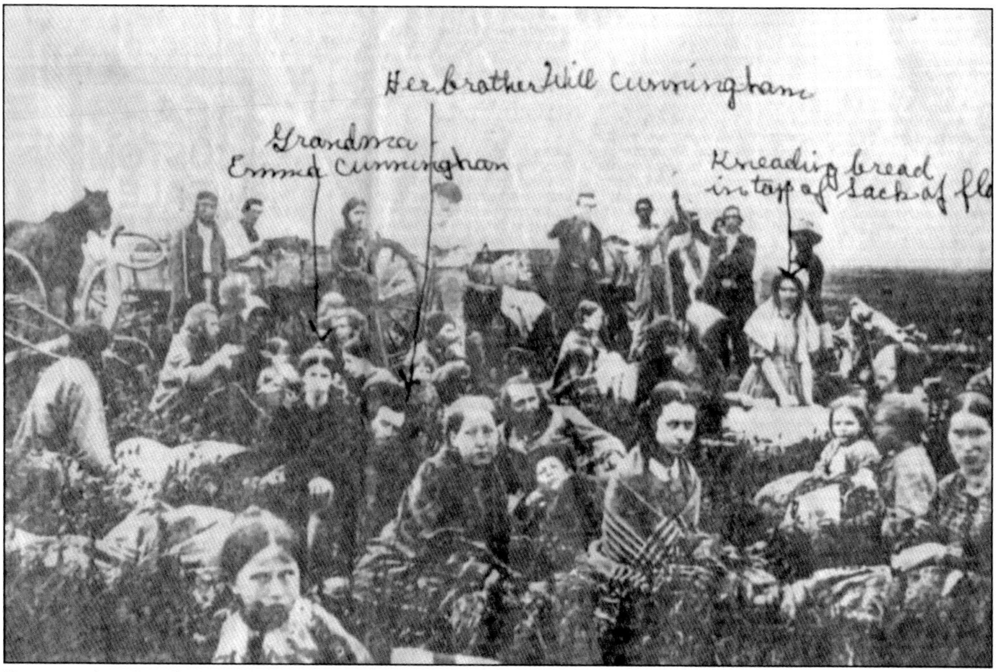

During the Civil War, Emma Cunningham served as a missionary teacher near Granite Falls, Minnesota. When the Dakota Sioux, who were angered at broken promises, went on a rampage in August 1862, killing over 500 men, women, and children, she was forced to flee. John Other Day, a friendly Sioux, saved Emma's party by leading them on a four-day trip to safety at Henderson, Minnesota. It seems a real oddity that Emma's party, fleeing from the rampaging Sioux, could look so relaxed in this photograph, taken by Adrian J. Ebel. In the above photograph, Emma Cunningham and her brother Will are identified. In the photograph below, another of Emma's brothers, Hugh Doak Cunningham, is identified at the lower left front wearing the white shirt. He also served as a missionary to the Indians.

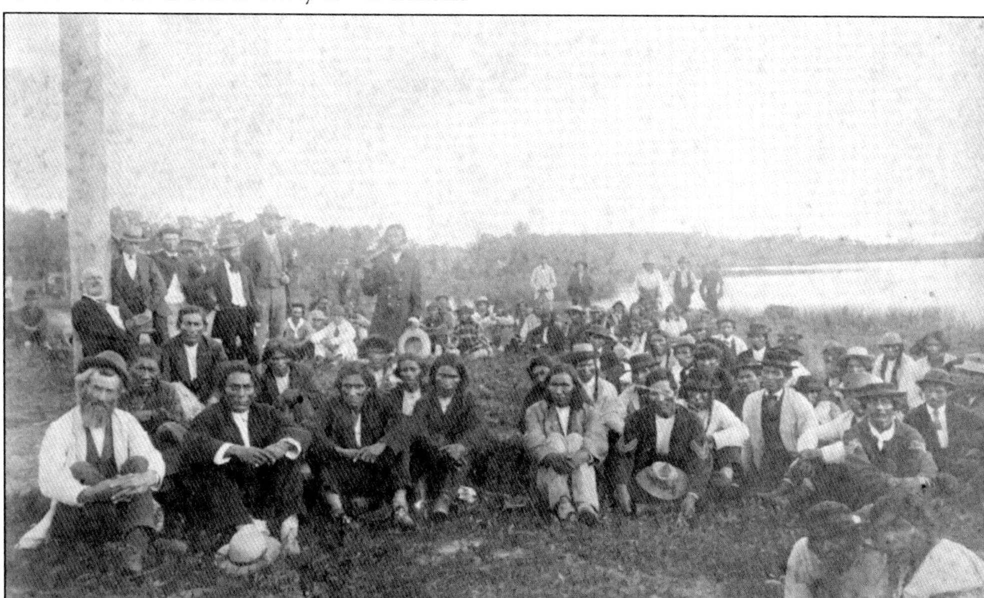

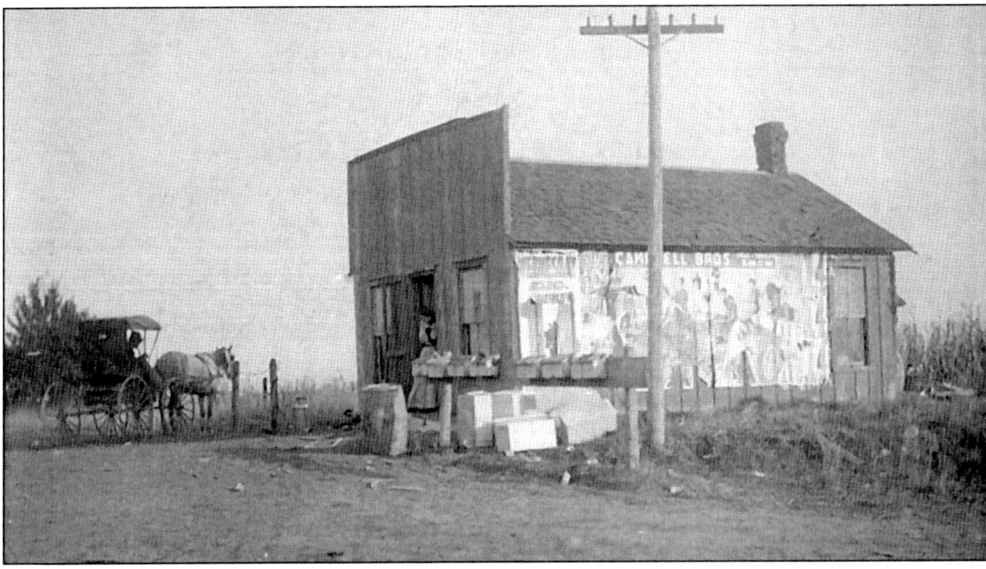

In this 1909 photograph, George Gerloch and his wife, Tillie, are standing in the doorway of their store visiting with Lyman Nettz, who is sitting in his buggy. The sign on the side of the barn is advertising the Campbell Brothers Bicycle Show coming to Griswold. Gerloch relocated his business many times, including a move to New Lyman with the coming of the ANSR (Atlantic Northern & Southern Railroad). He spent his last years in Old Lyman.

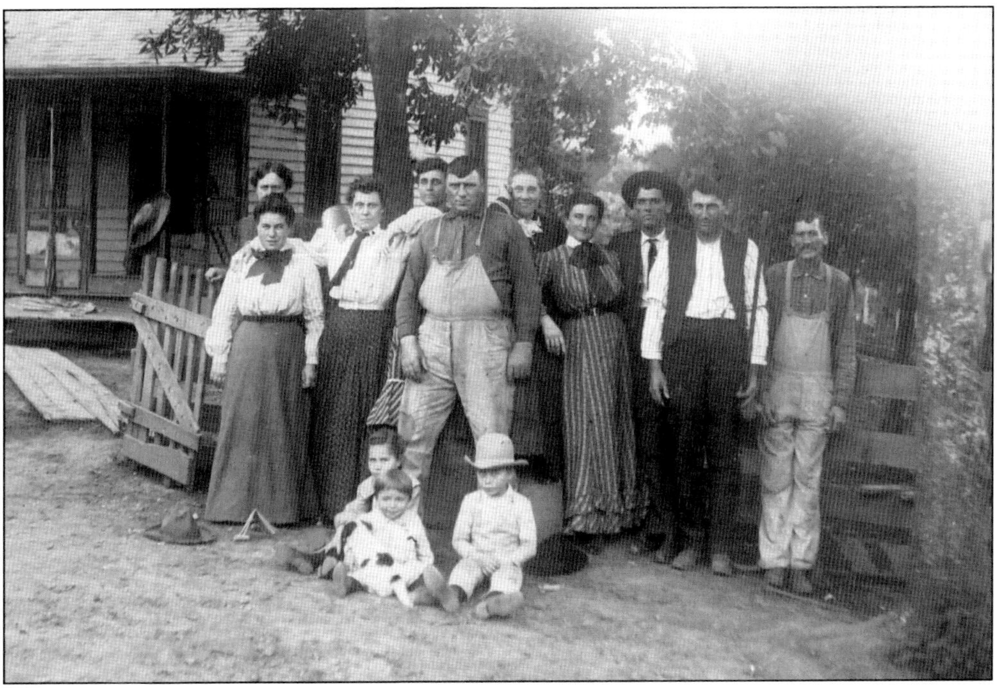

This photograph was taken in front of the Simon Sunderman farmhouse. When the railroad established its new route, the town of Lyman relocated onto a section of his property. The children are not identified. Pictured are, from left to right, (first row) Fannie Gibson, Jennie Winebrenner, Simon Sunderman, Frances Adams, Lyman Nettz, John Adams, and William Gibson; (second row) unidentified, Alice Adams Sunderman, and Molly Adams Brenner.

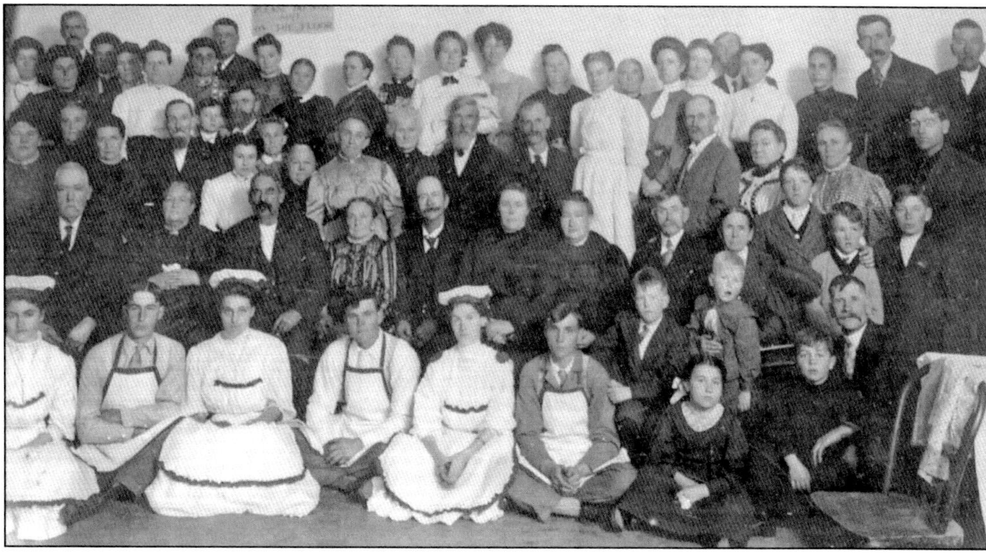

In 1909, Adam and Frances Adams celebrated their 50th wedding anniversary at the opera house in Griswold that Adams owned and operated. This gala affair featured M.H. Funk of Atlantic as master of ceremonies. There were 175 guests, tables were decorated in golden colors, and monogrammed napkins were used. After a program and gift exchange, a sumptuous meal was served. P.D. Gordon, a popular Griswold photographer at the time, took pictures at the party. Following the meal, the celebration continued with everyone invited to attend the rest of the festivities. In the image below, members of the wait staff include, from left to right, (first row) Cora Nettz, Ruth Rose, and Etta Sunderman; (second row) Walt Sunderman, Bert Sunderman, George Rose, and Jess Adams.

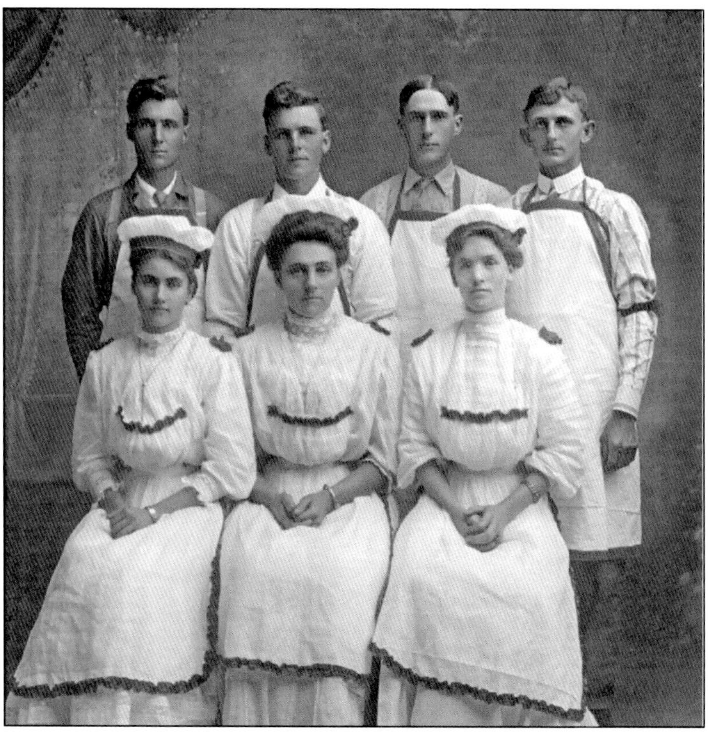

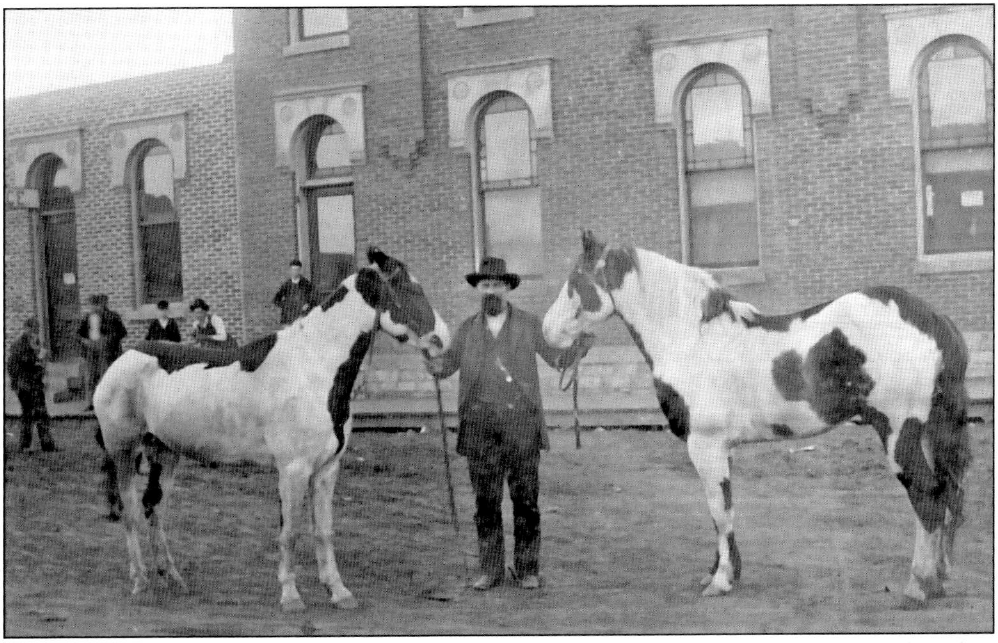

In 1870, Adam and Frances Adams had put into practice the advice popularly attributed to Horace Greeley: " Go west, young man, and grow up with the country." At their 50th wedding anniversary, they told the story of coming to Cass County and Noble Township in two covered wagons. The photograph shows Adams with two of his prize horses.

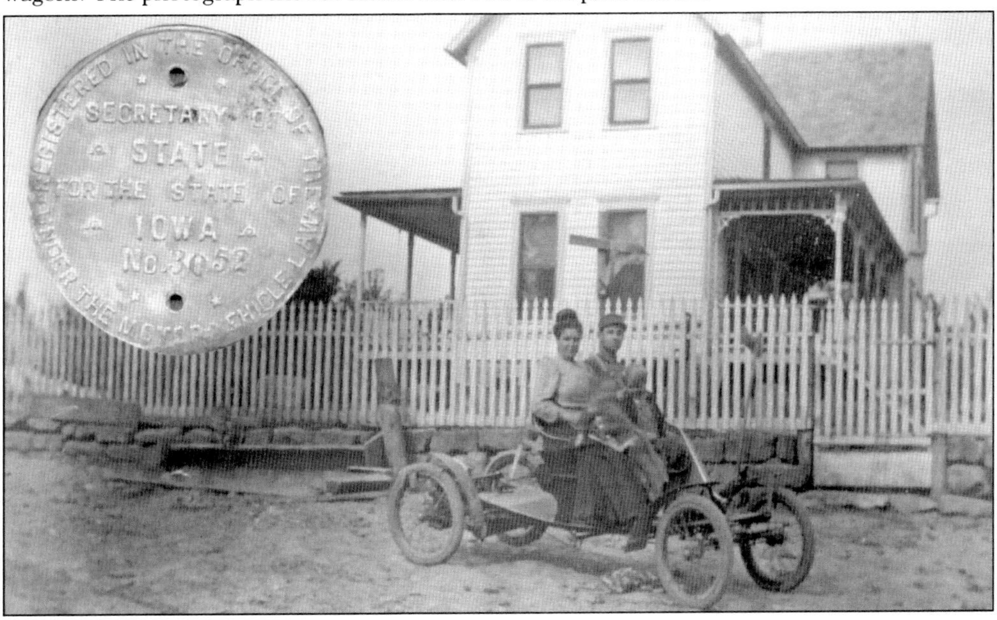

This Orient-Buckboard was equipped with a one-cylinder engine; it had two speeds forward and one reverse and a top speed of 30 miles per hour. It weighed 350 pounds. Shown are Cass Lindeman Heckman and Wilbur Heckman with their sons William and Lester. This 1907 photograph was taken at William Lindeman's in Lyman. Heckman remembered coming to Cass County in a covered wagon in 1882. The aluminum tag superimposed on the photograph is the first Iowa license purchased for this car.

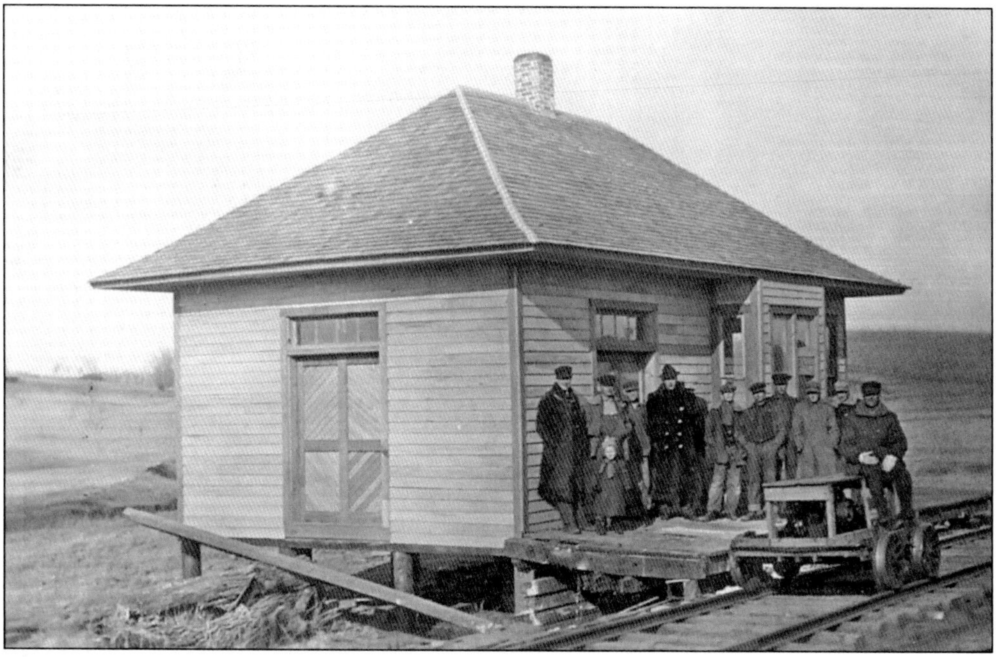

The ANSR was referred to as the "Awful Noisy and Slow Railroad" by locals. Built in 1911, it ran from Atlantic to Villisca. Lyman residents, seeing an opportunity for a more progressive town, moved everything to the Simon Sunderman farm, about a mile south of the original site, placing the town on the new rail line where this depot was built. The town was then named New Lyman. When the railroad discontinued service in 1917, the town moved back to its original site.

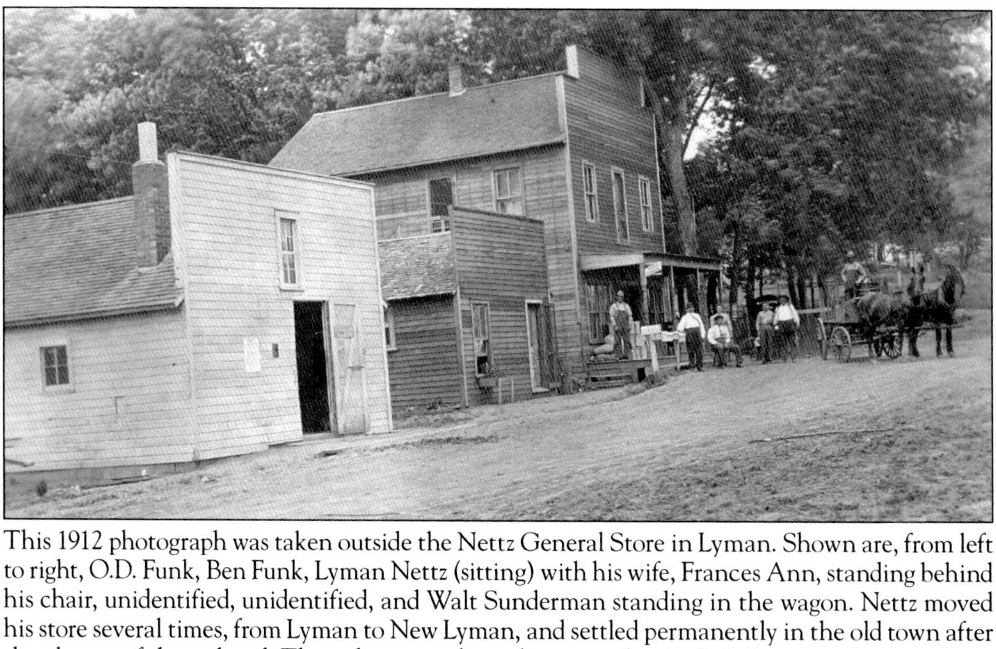

This 1912 photograph was taken outside the Nettz General Store in Lyman. Shown are, from left to right, O.D. Funk, Ben Funk, Lyman Nettz (sitting) with his wife, Frances Ann, standing behind his chair, unidentified, unidentified, and Walt Sunderman standing in the wagon. Nettz moved his store several times, from Lyman to New Lyman, and settled permanently in the old town after the closure of the railroad. There, he opened another store that included a service station.

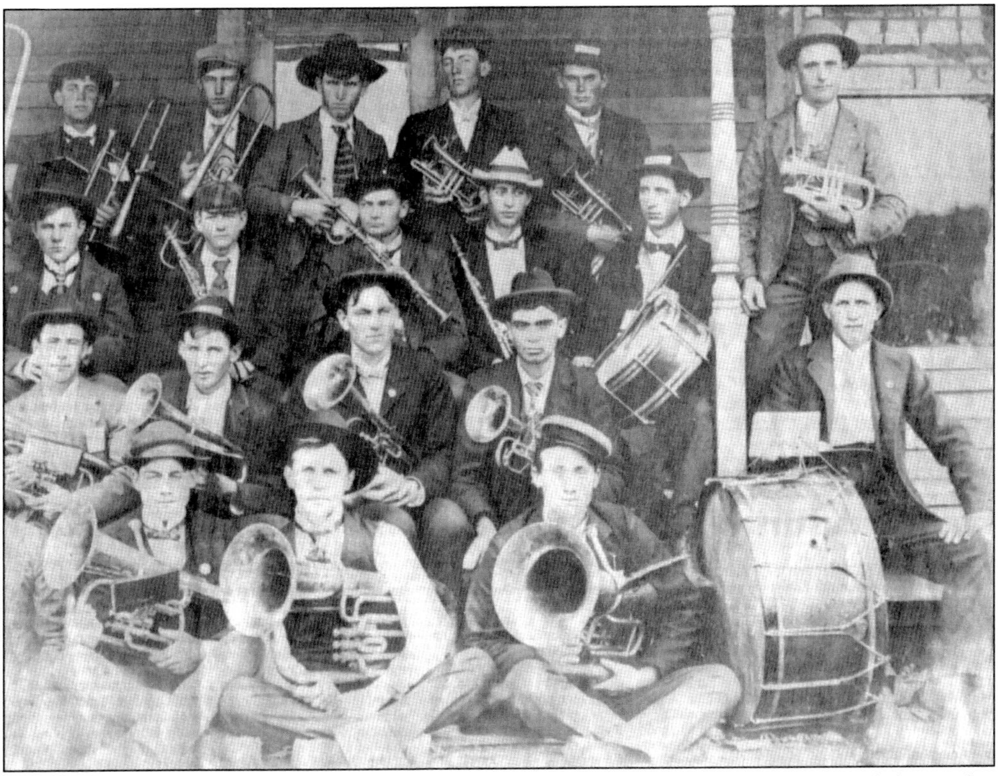

The Lyman Town Band poses for this photograph in 1899. Those pictured are, from left to right, (first row) Edwin Mueller, Lou Riedeman, and Henry Wohlenhaus; (second row) ? Martin, Phil Tanner, John Mueller, Chris Boseck, and unidentified; (third row) Walt Mueller, Butler Dilch, Fred Boseck, ? Smith, ? Smith, and John Herstein (standing); (fourth row) Wilbur Heckman, Dick Wohlenhaus, Joe Lindeman, Bill Wohlenhaus, and Jack Mueller. Not pictured are Andrew Keiser and George Lindeman.

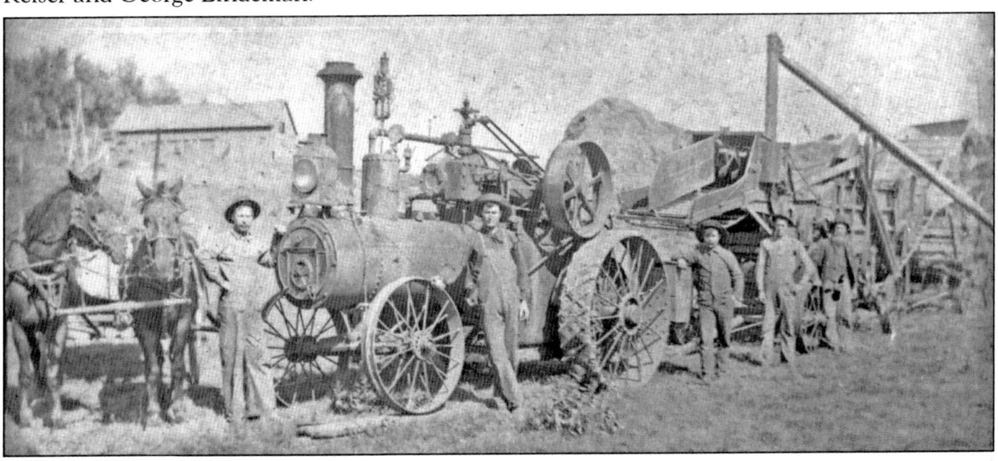

For many years, custom threshing crews were a part of the rural scene. One such crew consisted of Bill, Ernest, and Werner Sothman. This team used steam-powered threshing machines, and by 1906, Sothman owned nine of them. Bill handled the Grant and Griswold area, with Ernest taking care of Lyman and Werner handling Wiota and Massena. When not threshing, the men would shell corn, fill silos, and saw wood to keep busy year-round.

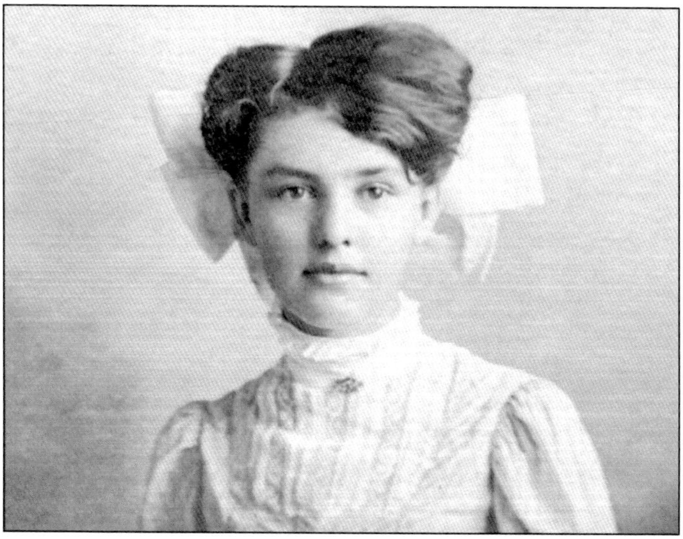

Vera Elizabeth Gerlach, daughter of George and Cora Gerlach, married Eno Schroeder, who had come to America from Germany in 1892 at the age of three. They had one son, Don. Eno Schroeder operated the Schroeder Garage in Lyman, and his son later established the Lyman Oil Company there. For a time in 1943, Don Schroeder worked on building the famous Alcan Highway through Canada to Alaska.

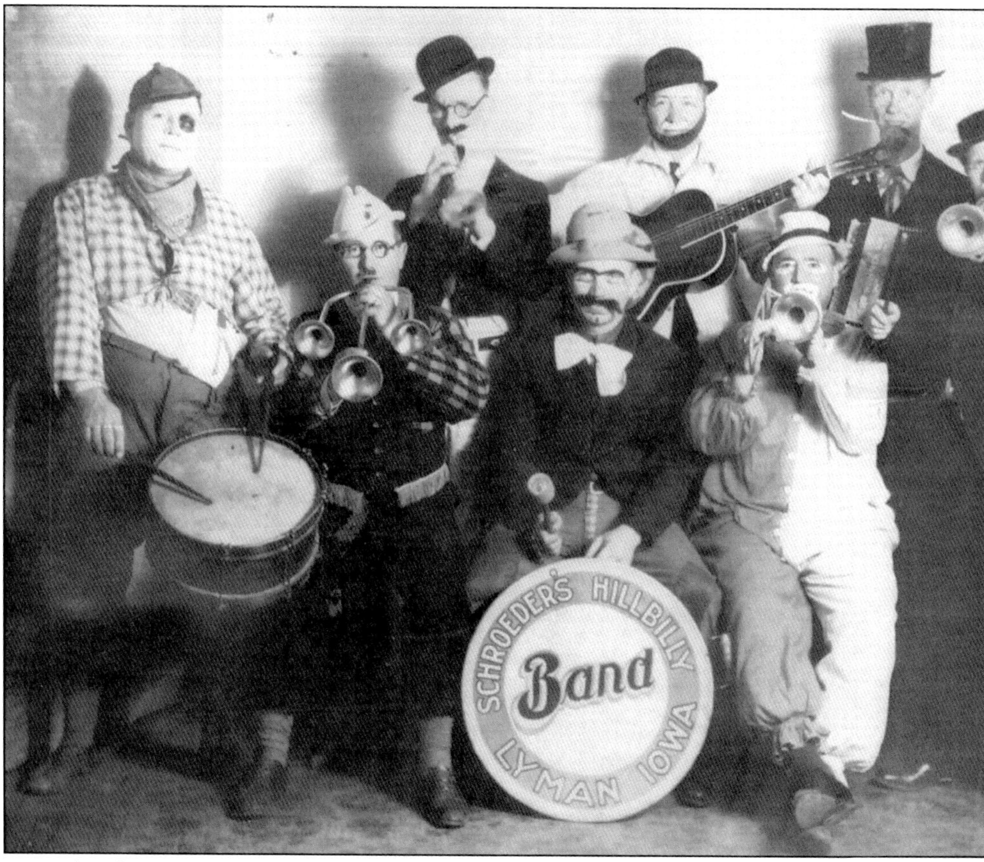

It was hard to tell who was having the most fun, the spectators or the band members, when Schroeder's Hillbilly Band from Lyman was performing. Their theme was the song "I Like Mountain Music." Walt Sunderman was the lead singer. Those pictured in this 1935 photograph are, from left to right, (first row) Bert Sunderman, Carl Dunmire, Alvin Lehmkuhl, and Walt Sunderman; (second row) Lloyd Wohlenhaus, Emil Pelzer, Billy Miller, and Eno Schroeder.

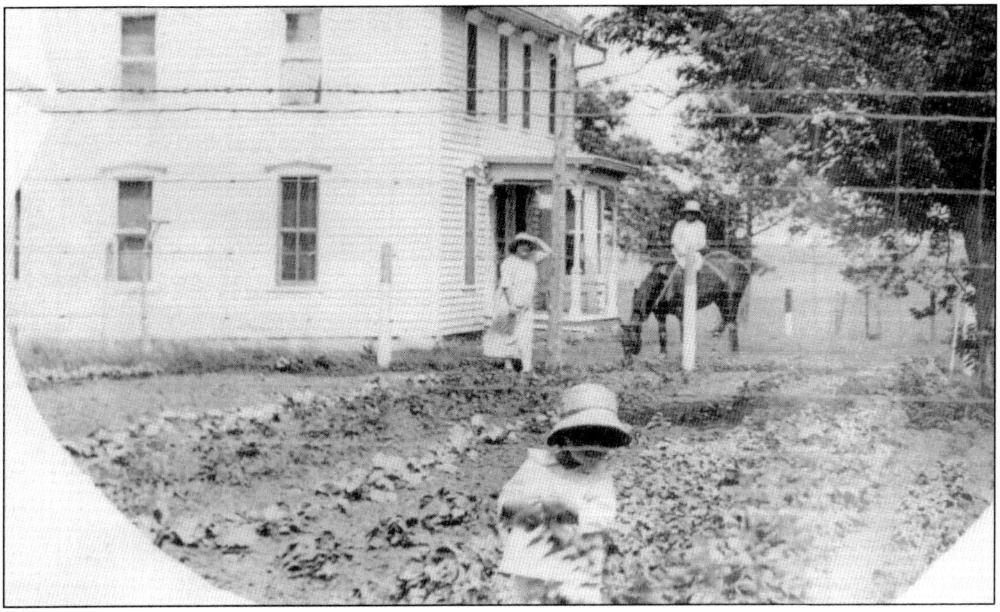

In 1904, at age 16, Gus Kuester took over the family farm, shown above, due to the death of his father. He married Elda Weaver in 1917. Hogs were the mainstay of the farm operation, along with horses, cattle, leghorn chickens, and milk cows. The farm crops were corn, oats, and hay. Always interested in local and civic affairs, Kuester was elected state representative from Cass County in 1932. He was reelected for 11 terms and served as speaker of the Iowa House. In the photograph below, Kuester listens to his constituents as they gather at Nettz's Garage in Lyman. Shown from left to right are (first row) Lyman Nettz, Gus Kuester, and Paul Breeling; (second row) Louie Riedeman, Ben Johnson, and Clarence Rabe. After retiring from the legislature, Kuester returned to his farm to enjoy his orchard and garden.

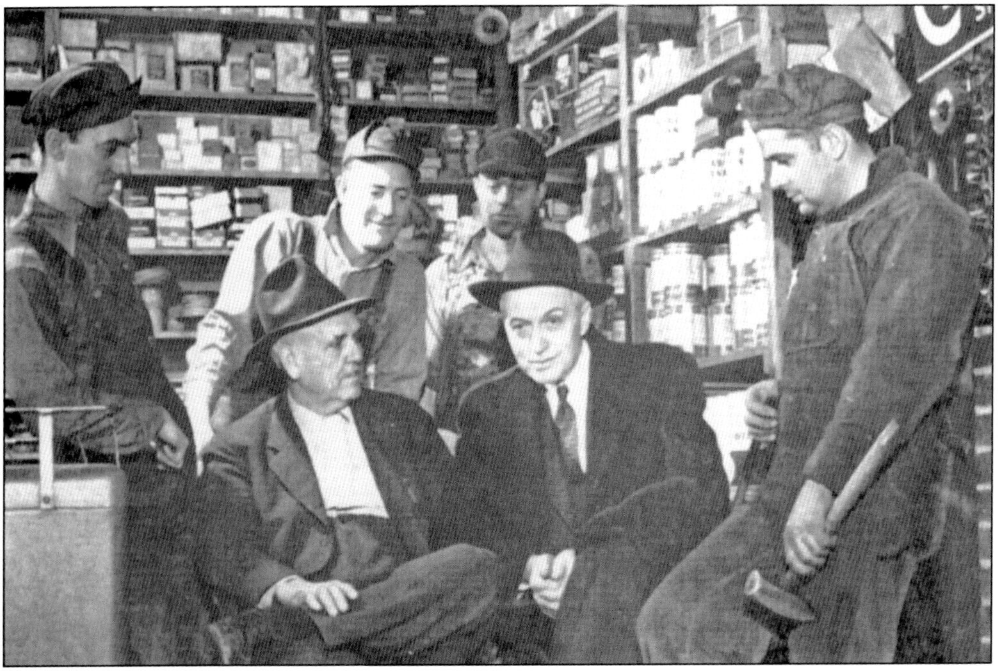

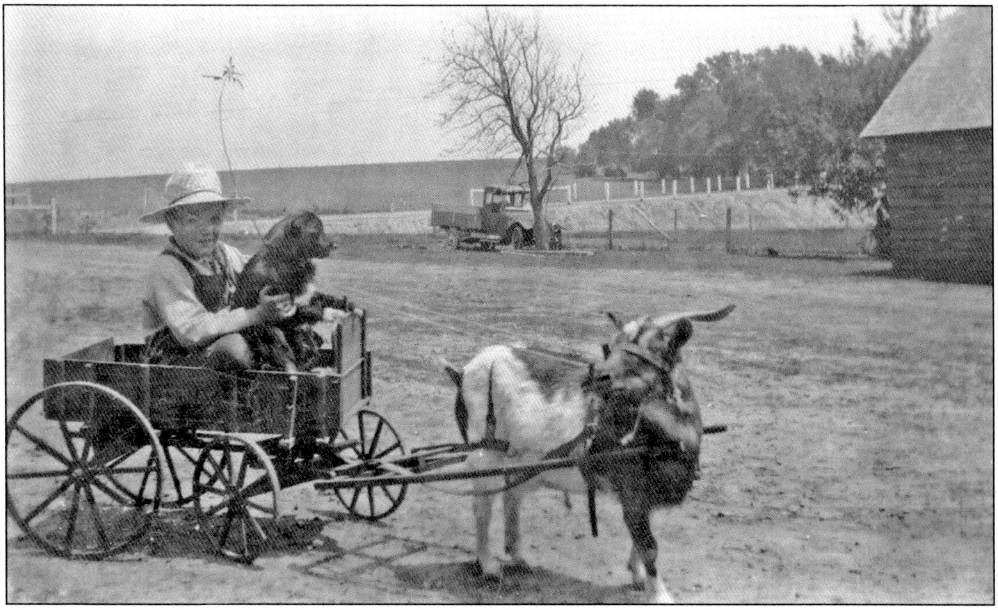

This 1920 photograph shows Clifford Sunderman with his pet goat and puppy. As an adult, Sunderman farmed, purchased and operated the Kemling store, and later owned a greenhouse business. Everyone in the community remembers that before eating or drinking, Sunderman always offered the following blessing: "Jesus bless what thou hast given; feed our souls with bread from heaven; guide and lead us every day in all that we may do and say."

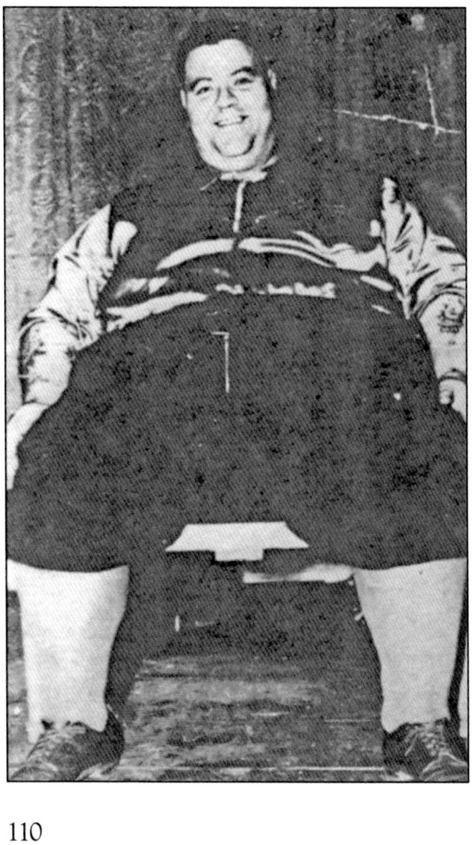

Leander "Tiny" Kistler had a glandular disorder as a result of spinal meningitis. It caused him to gain weight, and at one time, he weighed 495 pounds. Kistler traveled with a circus in the 1930s. The Key Overall Company furnished him with made-to-order overalls that had a 92-inch waist. Kistler had a special chair in the local movie theater. He was frequently seen in county celebrations in the "Bucking Ford," built by Delbert Coon.

Nine

UNION AND EDNA TOWNSHIPS

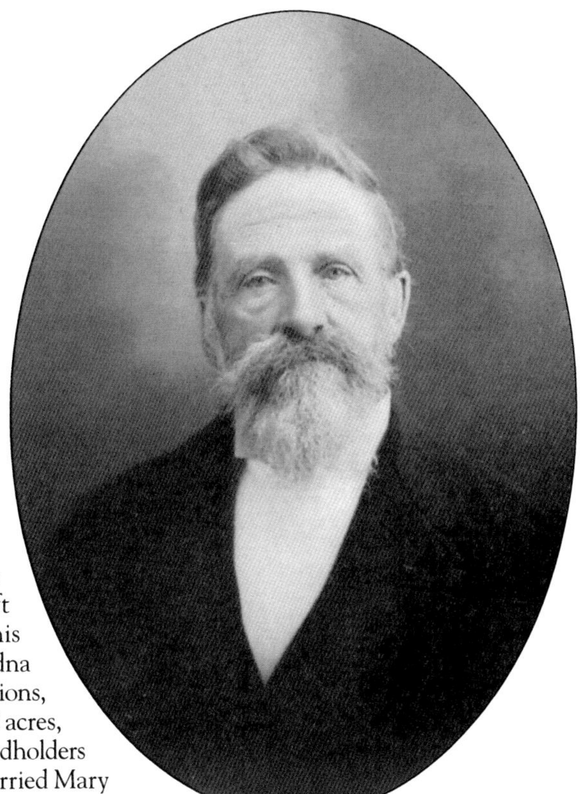

John Leslie was born in Ireland in 1833 to wealthy and cultured parents. Leslie arrived in Cass County in 1856 but left to serve briefly in the Civil War. Upon his return, he purchased 80 acres of land in Edna Township and, through judicious acquisitions, eventually amassed a land holding of 900 acres, which made him one of the wealthiest landholders among the early pioneers. In 1878, he married Mary Cudney of New York.

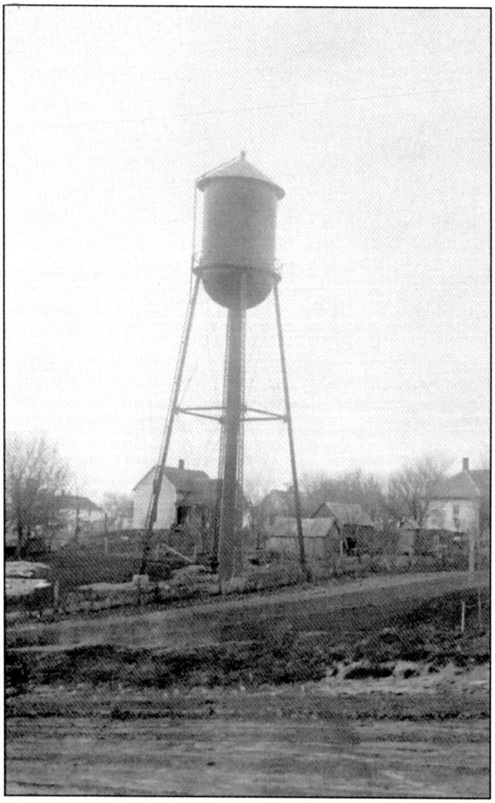

Cumberland, like many early Cass County towns, could trace its beginnings to the railroad. The town was founded in 1884. The public water system was installed in 1902. This photograph of Cumberland's water tower is dated 1916. Two other towers were erected before a 75,000-gallon tank was built in 1979. This newer 140-foot tower so improved the city's water supply that insurance rates were lowered.

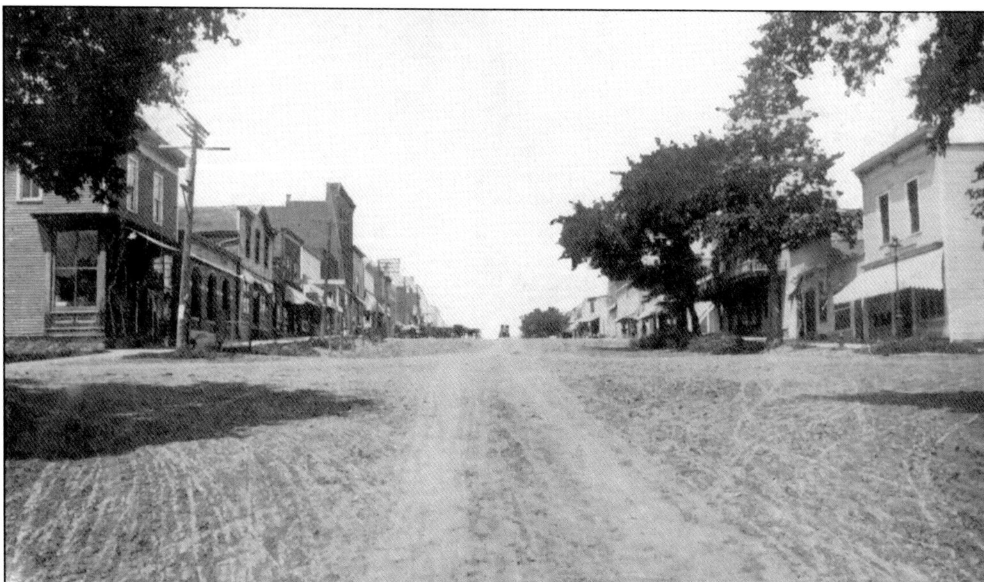

This view of Main Street in Cumberland was taken before the fire in 1920 that destroyed one entire city block on the west side. Before the fire, a three-story opera house stood on Main Street. The community enjoyed plays, home talent shows, and other cultural events as well as the annual outdoor Chautauqua celebration. During the summer, band concerts were held right in the middle of Main Street every Wednesday night.

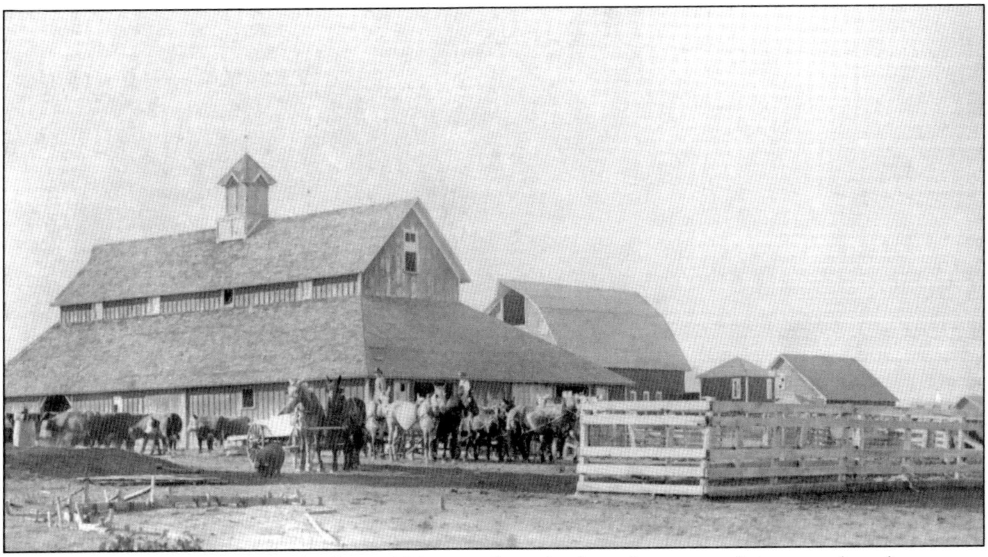

The soil in Cass County in the late 1800s was described as always supplying an abundant crop. Through the years, the land has produced cereals, fruits, grasses, and vegetables. The county is also suitable for the raising of stock due in large part to its many rivers and streams. This photograph shows the beginning of a typical workday on a prosperous Cass County farm.

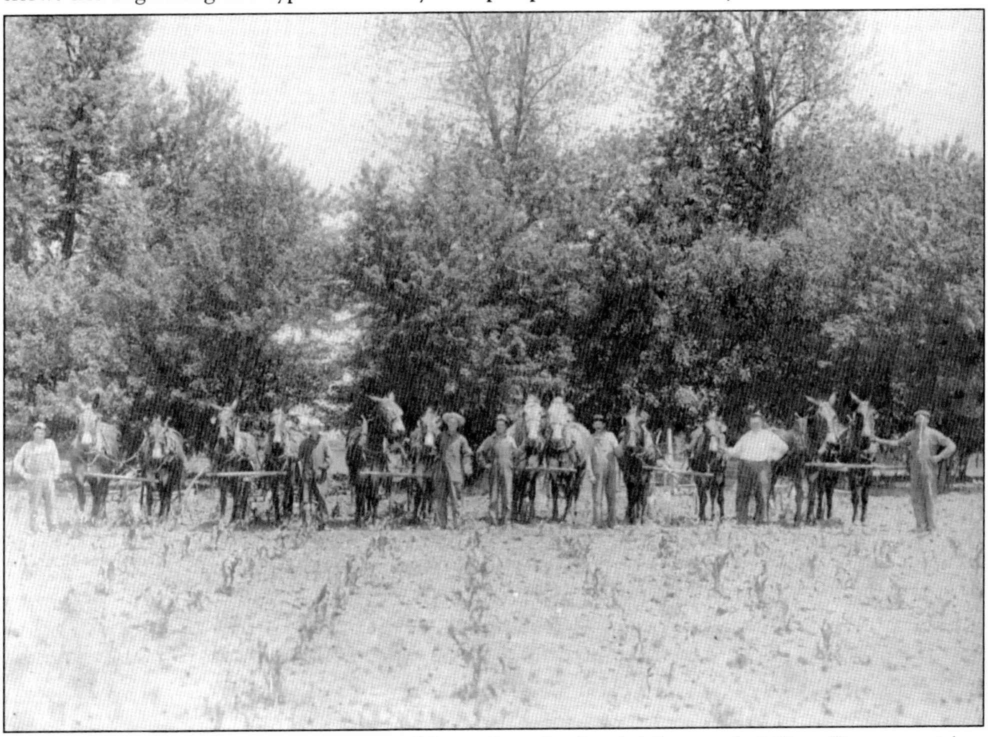

The future of Cass County is inextricably tied to the land. Men settled Cass County with a determination to tame the prairie and to establish a good life based on an agricultural economy. Early Cass County farmers knew how to work together. Note the meager stand of corn. At this time, corn was cultivated in both directions across the field so the hills of corn were spaced about 40 inches apart.

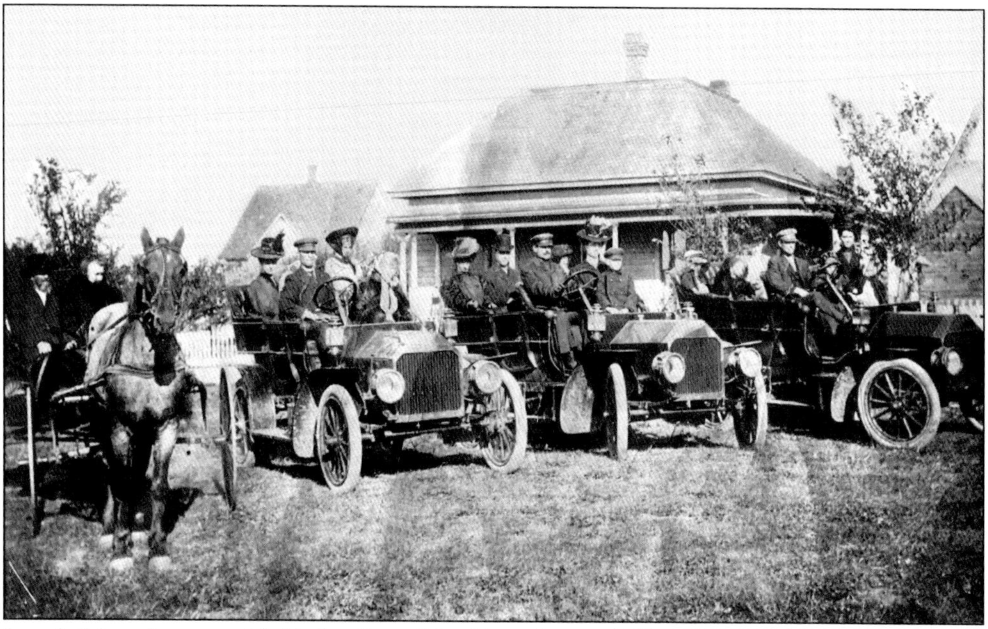

Joseph Edwards came with his family to Edna Township in 1855 and started farming. He erected a small log cabin for his wife and children, worked to improve his land, and became one of the most prosperous farmers in the area. His home was considered the finest in the township. The 1908 photograph shows the Edwards family in Cumberland, with the younger members enjoying a time of leisure in their horseless carriages.

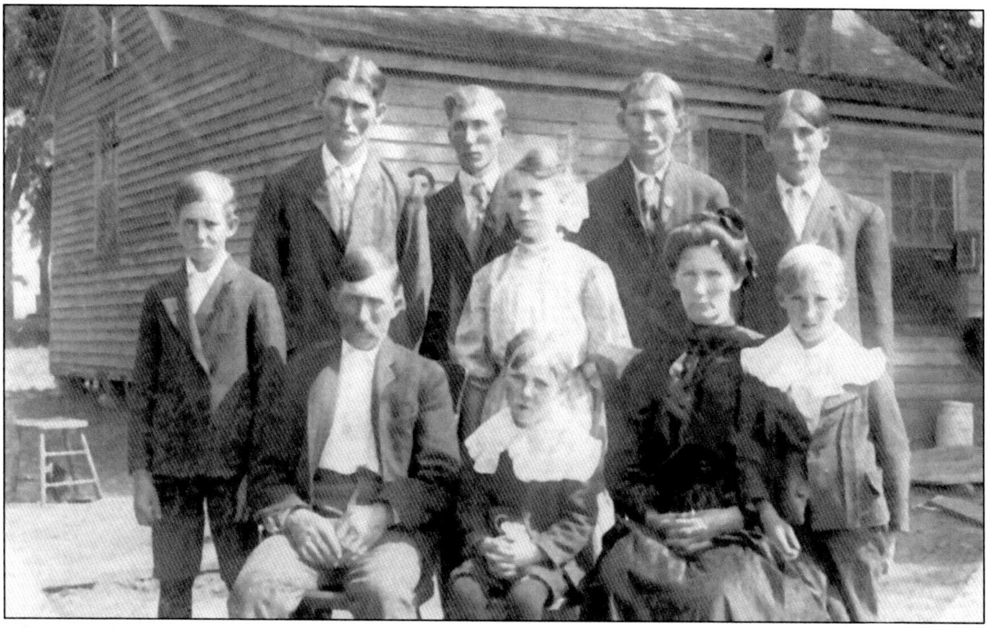

This 1908 family photograph was taken at the farm home of John Milton Landon in Edna Township. Family members are, from left to right, (first row) John Milton Landon, Charles Landon, Susan Eblen Landon, and Frank Landon; (second row) Ralph and May Landon; (third row) Jacob, John, Demas, and Joseph Landon. John Milton Landon was fortunate to have seven sons to help with the farming operation.

While living in a small, rural town at the turn of the century usually required a lot of hard physical labor, education remained a high priority, and music was especially revered. Many a dull workweek was relieved by a square dance that was complete with fiddlers. However, other forms of music were also appreciated. In this 1910 photograph, the promising young musicians are brother and sister Eno and Esther Schroeder.

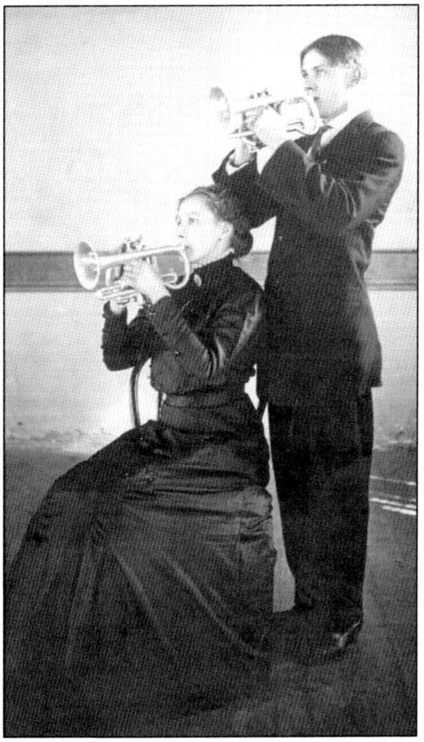

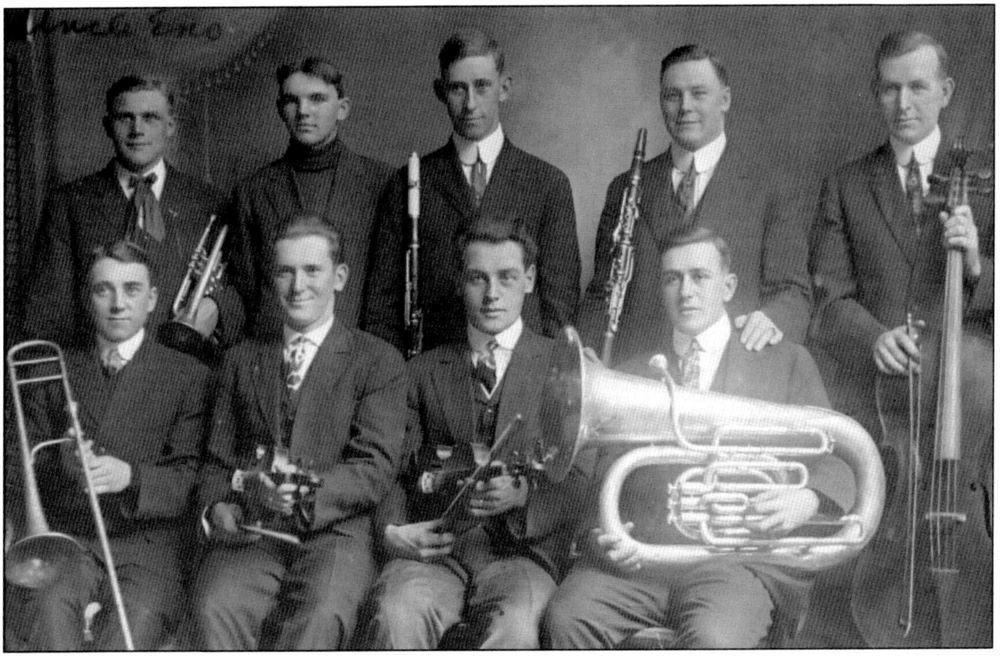

The importance of cultural enlightenment is obvious in the number of plays and musical events that were presented in even the smallest of communities. This photograph is of the Cumberland Chamber Orchestra. From left to right are (first row) Vernon Purvis, Clarence Worthington, John Mattheis, and Clarence Richardson; (second row) Eno Schroeder, Ralph Worthington (pianist), Sam Studley, Bill Waters, and Sam Morgan.

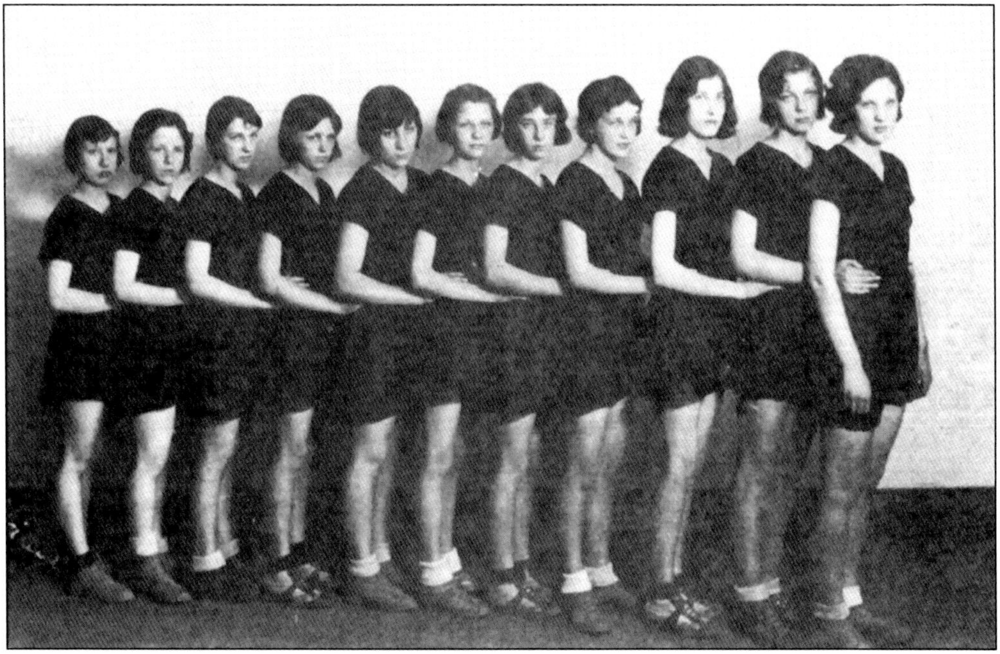

The Cumberland High School girls' basketball team made it to the state championship tournament five times from 1931 to 1936. Members of the squad are, from left to right, Arlene Lattimer, Florence Robinson, Ruth Worthington, Leona Jarvis, Ena Coakley, Dorothy Persels, Clara Martens, Evelyn Eblen, Velma Sothman, Elizabeth Clark, and Arlene White.

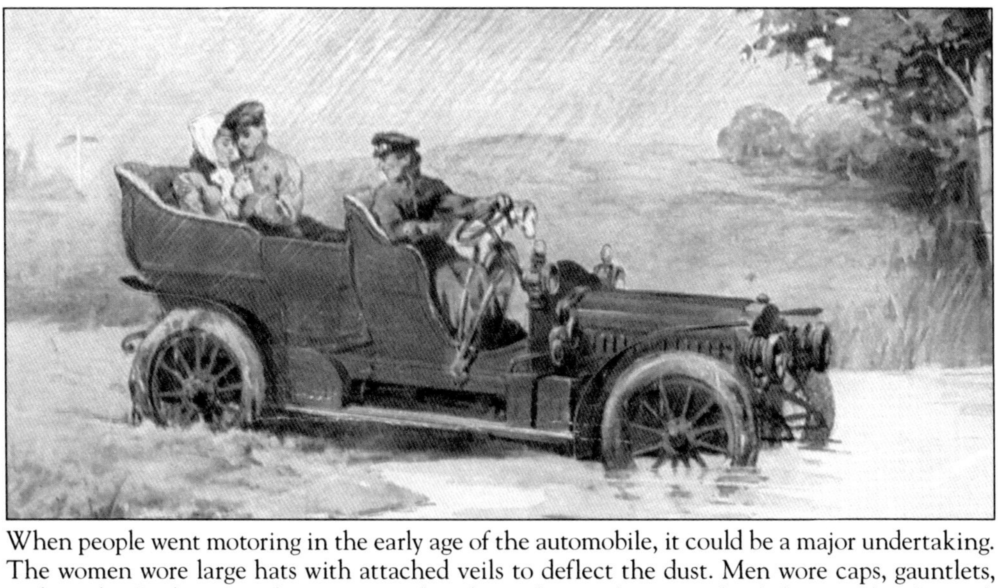

When people went motoring in the early age of the automobile, it could be a major undertaking. The women wore large hats with attached veils to deflect the dust. Men wore caps, gauntlets, and goggles. Both men and women wore long linen dusters that were closely buttoned at the neck and draped down to the ankles. Mud roads could certainly create some interesting situations. This is a c. 1908 postcard.

The outlaw Jesse James visited Cass County on numerous occasions and stopped with his gang at the Watson Trego farm, located northeast of Cumberland, in the 1870s. The men asked for a meal and care for their horses. Following the meal, the men paid generously and left quietly. Later, the Tregos learned that the James gang had committed another robbery in the area and that there was a large reward posted for their capture.

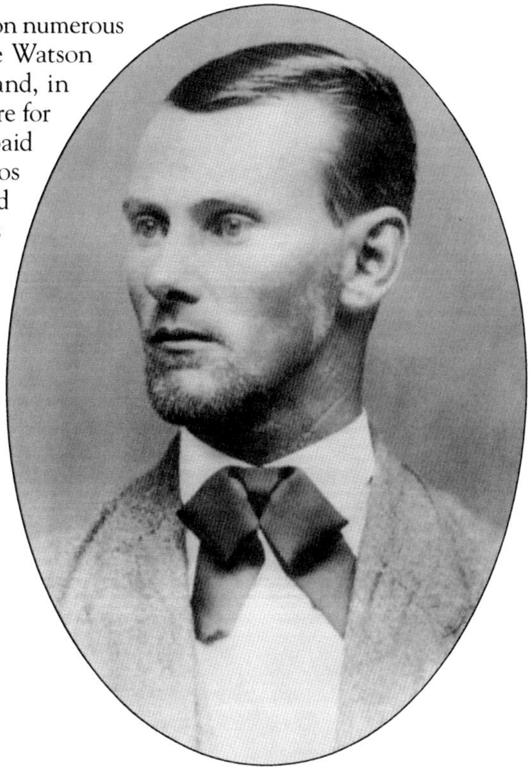

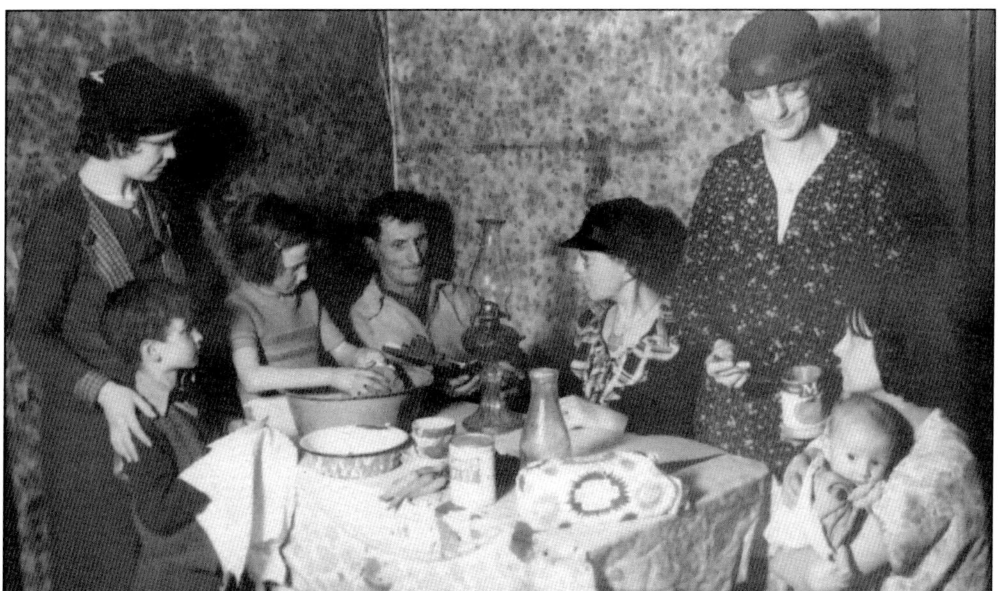

Iowans in the early 1920s were full of optimism. Banks loaned money liberally; people bought goods on the installment plan; life was lived on the principle of "buy today, pay tomorrow." And pay they did; the stock market crashed in October 1929, and life became very difficult. Though money was scarce, farm prices low, and few jobs available, Iowa families worked together to meet the needs of one another and weather the crisis.

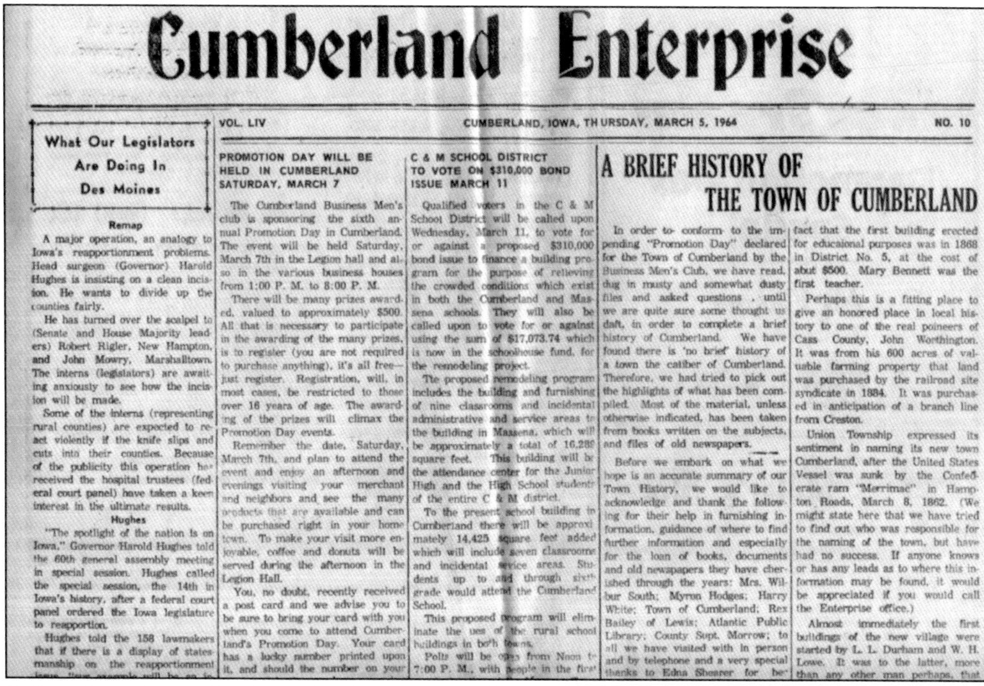

Cumberland Enterprise

VOL. LIV — CUMBERLAND, IOWA, THURSDAY, MARCH 5, 1964 — NO. 10

What Our Legislators Are Doing In Des Moines

Remap

A major operation, an analogy to Iowa's reapportionment problems. Head surgeon (Governor) Harold Hughes is insisting on a clean incision. He wants to divide up the counties fairly.

He has turned over the scalpel to (Senate and House Majority leaders) Robert Rigler, New Hampton, and John Mowry, Marshalltown. The interns (legislators) are awaiting anxiously to see how the incision will be made.

Some of the interns (representing rural counties) are expected to react violently if the knife slips and cuts into their counties. Because of the publicity this operation ha[s] received the hospital trustees (federal court panel) have taken a keen interest in the ultimate results.

Hughes

"The spotlight of the nation is on Iowa." Governor Harold Hughes told the 60th general assembly meeting in special session. Hughes called the special session, the 14th in Iowa's history, after a federal court panel ordered the Iowa legislature to reapportion.

Hughes told the 158 lawmakers that if there is a display of statesmanship on the reapportionment

PROMOTION DAY WILL BE HELD IN CUMBERLAND SATURDAY, MARCH 7

The Cumberland Business Men's club is sponsoring the sixth annual Promotion Day in Cumberland. The event will be held Saturday, March 7th in the Legion hall and also in the various business houses from 1:00 P. M. to 8:00 P. M.

There will be many prizes awarded, valued to approximately $500. All that is necessary to participate in the awarding of the many prizes, is to register (you are not required to purchase anything), it's all free—just register. Registration, will, in most cases, be restricted to those over 16 years of age. The awarding of the prizes will climax the Promotion Day events.

Remember the date, Saturday, March 7th, and plan to attend the event and enjoy an afternoon and evenings visiting your merchant and neighbors and see the many products that are available and can be purchased right in your home town. To make your visit more enjoyable, coffee and donuts will be served during the afternoon in the Legion Hall.

You, no doubt, recently received a post card and we advise you to be sure to bring your card with you when you come to attend Cumberland's Promotion Day. Your card has a lucky number printed upon it, and should the number on your

C & M SCHOOL DISTRICT TO VOTE ON $310,000 BOND ISSUE MARCH 11

Qualified voters in the C & M School District will be called upon Wednesday, March 11, to vote for or against a proposed $310,000 bond issue to finance a building program for the purpose of relieving the crowded conditions which exist in both the Cumberland and Massena schools. They will also be called upon to vote for or against using the sum of $17,073.74 which is now in the schoolhouse fund, for the remodeling project.

The proposed remodeling program includes the building and furnishing of nine classrooms and incidental administrative and service areas to the building in Massena, which will be approximately a total of 16,289 square feet. This building will be the attendance center for the Junior High and the High School students of the entire C & M district.

To the present school building in Cumberland there will be approximately 14,425 square feet added which will include seven classrooms and incidental service areas. Students up to and through sixth grade would attend the Cumberland School.

This proposed program will eliminate the use of the rural school buildings in both towns.

Polls will be open from Noon to 7:00 P. M., with people in the first

A BRIEF HISTORY OF THE TOWN OF CUMBERLAND

In order to conform to the impending "Promotion Day" declared for the Town of Cumberland by the Business Men's Club, we have read, dug in musty and somewhat dusty files and asked questions , until we are quite sure some thought us daft, in order to complete a brief history of Cumberland. We have found there is 'no brief' history of a town the caliber of Cumberland. Therefore, we had tried to pick out the highlights of what has been compiled. Most of the material, unless otherwise indicated, has been taken from books written on the subjects, and files of old newspapers.

Before we embark on what we hope is an accurate summary of our Town History, we would like to acknowledge and thank the following for their help in furnishing information, guidance of where to find further information and especially for the loan of books, documents and old newspapers they have cherished through the years: Mrs. Wilbur South; Myron Hodges; Harry White; Town of Cumberland; Rex Bailey of Lewis; Atlantic Public Library; County Supt. Morrow; to all we have visited with in person and by telephone and a very special thanks to Edna Shearer for her

fact that the first building erected for educaional purposes was in 1868 in District No. 5, at the cost of abut $500. Mary Bennett was the first teacher.

Perhaps this is a fitting place to give an honored place in local history to one of the real poineers of Cass County, John Worthington. It was from his 600 acres of valuable farming property that land was purchased by the railroad site syndicate in 1884. It was purchased in anticipation of a branch line from Creston.

Union Township expressed its sentiment in naming its new town Cumberland, after the United States Vessel was sunk by the Confederate ram "Merrimac" in Hampton Roads, March 8, 1862. (We might state here that we have tried to find out who was responsible for the naming of the town, but have had no success. If anyone knows or has any leads as to where this information may be found, it would be appreciated if you would call the Enterprise office.)

Almost immediately the first buildings of the new village were started by L. L. Durham and W. H. Lowe. It was to the latter, more than any other man perhaps, that

Before the advent of radio and television, small-town newspapers were the only source of news for many people and, as so, were especially appreciated. The *Cumberland Enterprise* was published from 1899 until 1976. An Edna Township reader, referring to a county newspaper, wrote, "It is a regular visitor at our fireside. Gradually it has stole [*sic*] into our graces and affection until now it is . . . one of the family circle as it were."

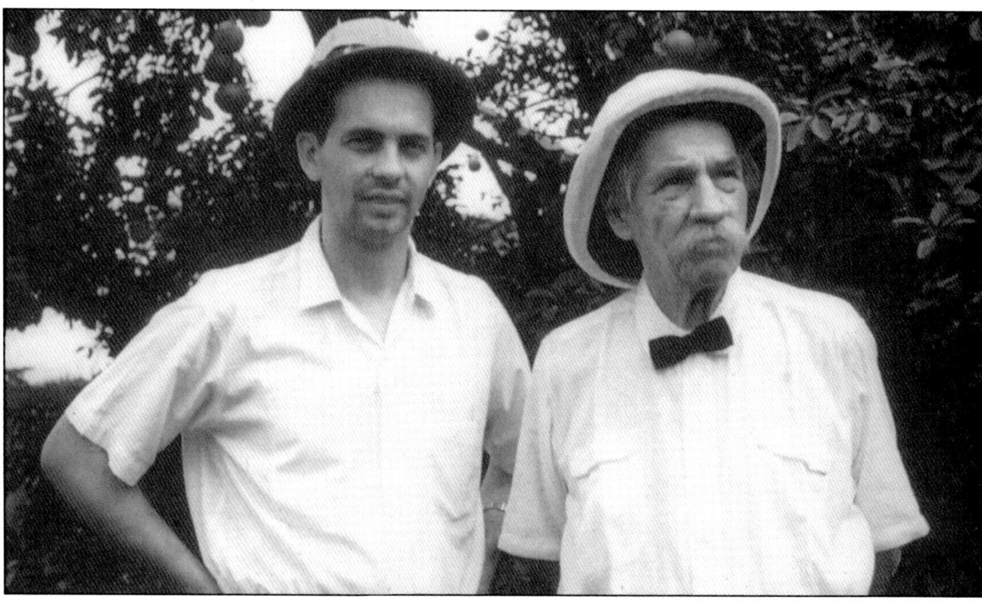

Dr. Dale Weber, on the left, and Dr. Albert Schweitzer are shown in 1964 at Lambaréné, Gabon, in West Africa. Weber was a 1949 graduate of Cumberland High School. When he was a senior medical student at the University of Iowa, he received a Smith, Kline, and French Foreign Fellowship to work with Schweitzer.

Ten

Massena and Victoria Townships

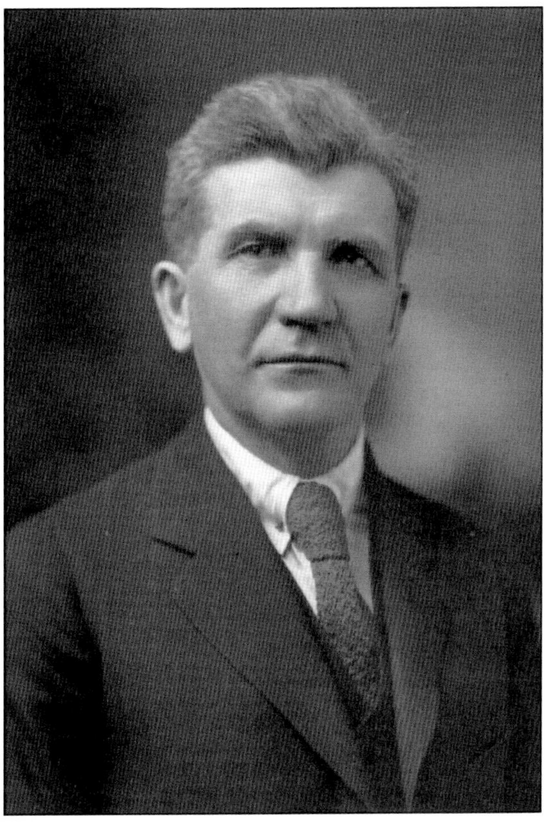

In 1911, D.P. Hogan served as a member of the Iowa House of Representatives and accepted the challenge from Pres. Woodrow Wilson to study the farm credit systems of Europe. Hogan helped plan the Federal Land Bank system and frame the Federal Farm Loan Act in 1916. When the first Federal Land Bank was established in Omaha in 1917, Hogan was selected as the first president and served in this capacity for 17 years.

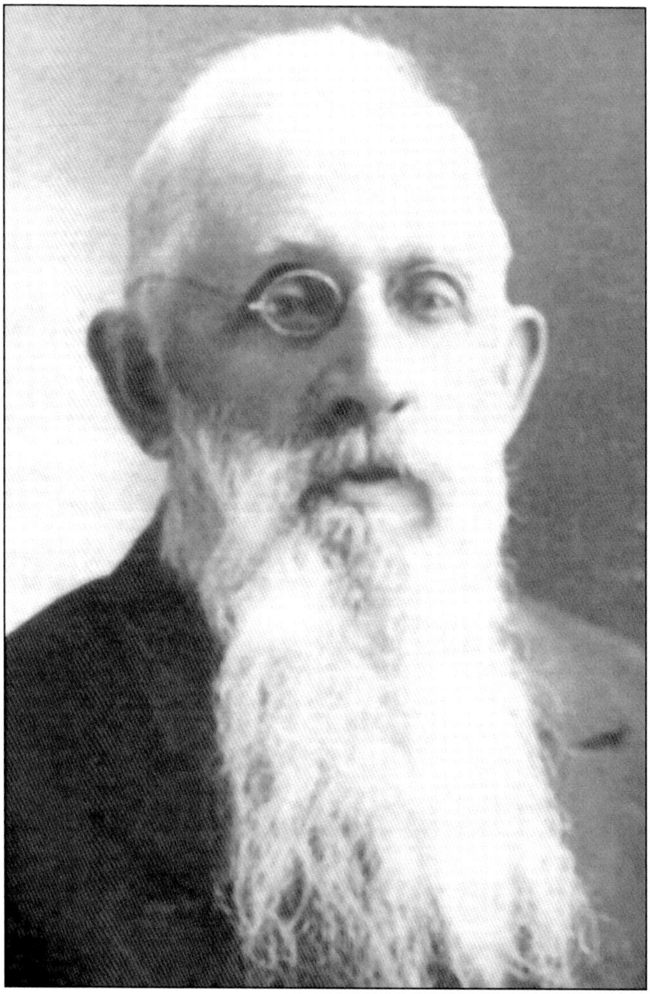

In 1858, Franklin Whitney claimed land along the newly opened Western Stage Line. Whitney, quick to realize a good business opportunity, opened a stage stop. Being a surveyor, he plotted the town of Whitneyville. His cousin Eseck Whitney, shown at left, soon arrived from Oswego County, New York, and purchased land. By this time, Franklin had moved to Lewis. Eseck continued to buy land, operate the stage station at Whitneyville, and run the post office. In 1861, Eseck rented out his land and moved to Colorado to look for gold. Life in Colorado was lonely for his wife, Nancy, and they lived in constant fear of the Ute Indians. Three years later, the family moved back to Massena with enough gold to stock the existing farm and add to its business interests. The 1898 photograph below shows teacher Elvira Whitney with her students at the Whitneyville School.

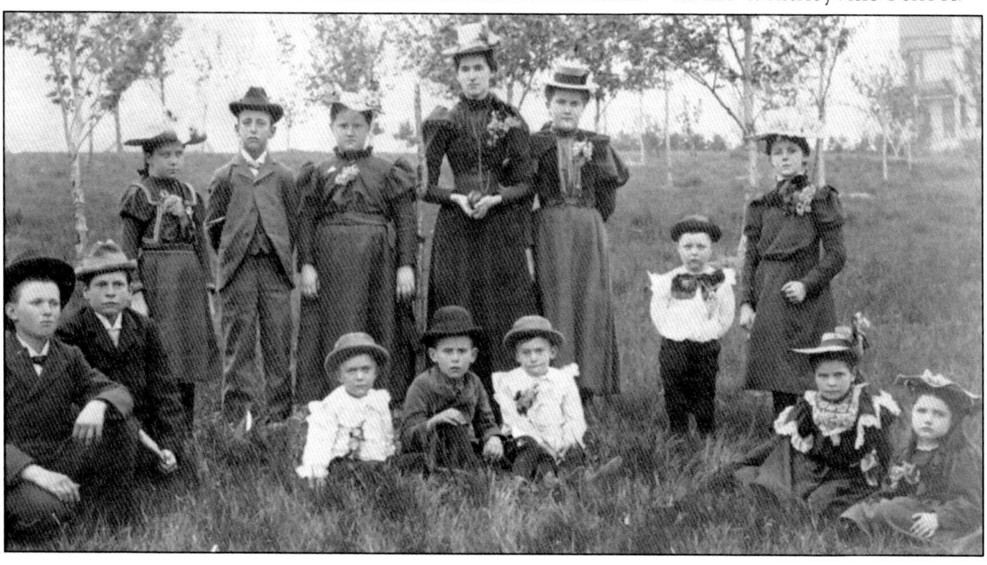

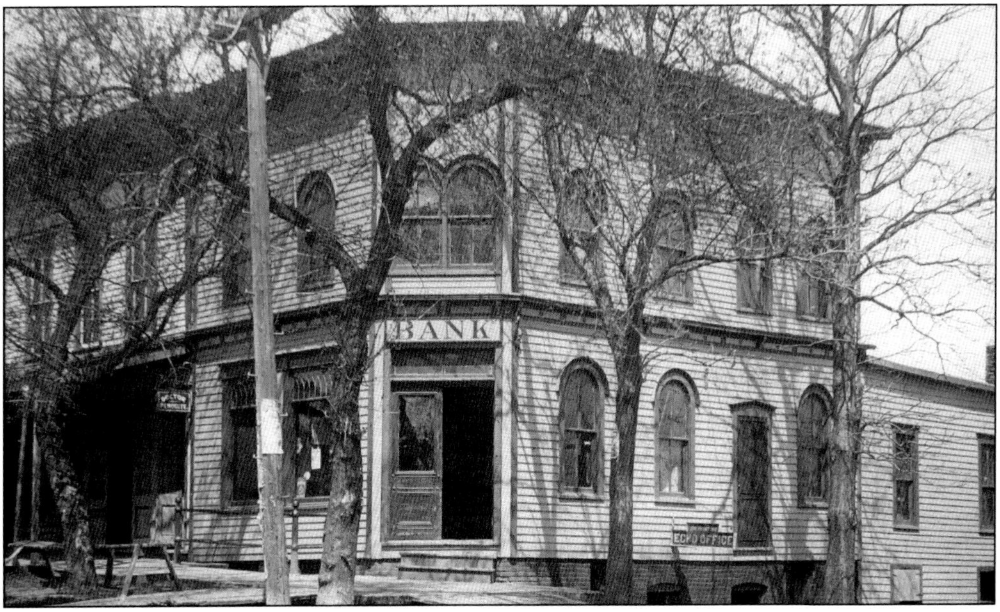

D.P. Hogan and his partner A.F. Okey opened the Farmers Savings Bank of Massena on February 8, 1897. The bank was highly successful, and in 1907, Hogan bought out Okey. Hogan was a true friend of the farmer and was instrumental in advancing pride in the ownership of land. At one time, when the price of land was declining, he wrote, "In these days when some thoughtless people have but little regard for their land, let us not forget that we live by the land, that it sustains our life, that it is the source of all wealth; that the land in our district is the best in all the world, and that it will again be highly prized." The photograph below shows an engraved invitation to the 25th anniversary of the opening of the bank.

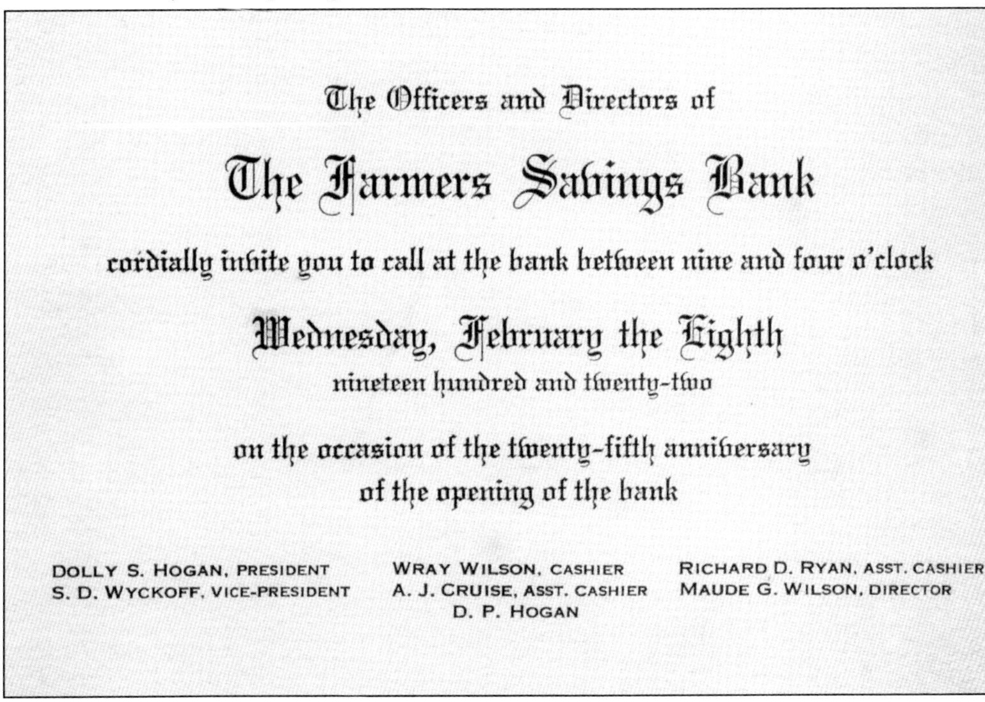

The Officers and Directors of

The Farmers Savings Bank

cordially invite you to call at the bank between nine and four o'clock

Wednesday, February the Eighth

nineteen hundred and twenty-two

on the occasion of the twenty-fifth anniversary

of the opening of the bank

DOLLY S. HOGAN, PRESIDENT
S. D. WYCKOFF, VICE-PRESIDENT

WRAY WILSON, CASHIER
A. J. CRUISE, ASST. CASHIER
D. P. HOGAN

RICHARD D. RYAN, ASST. CASHIER
MAUDE G. WILSON, DIRECTOR

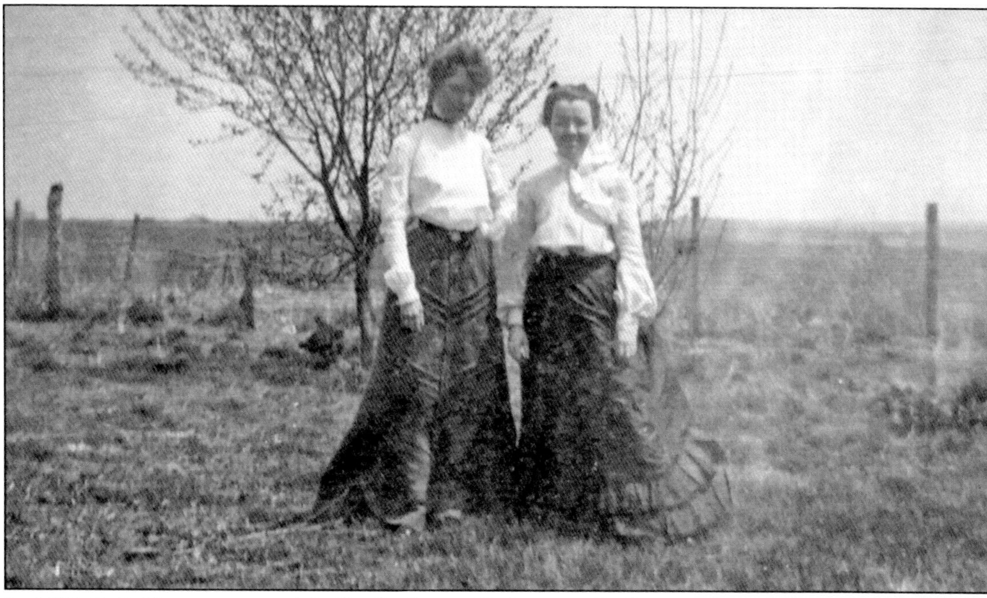

In 1901, D.P. Hogan married Dolly Snelson of Massena. Dolly was the daughter of Dr. William and Mathilda Snelson. William was the local physician and druggist. Dolly was a fine match for the successful Hogan. She was the first woman to graduate from Iowa State Teachers College in Ames. When her husband was working for the federal government in various places around the world, she took his place as president of the Farmers Savings Bank of Massena that they owned. The Hogans traveled extensively overseas in line with his government work. The above photograph shows Emma Spinney Herring, the wife of Iowa governor Clyde Herring of Atlantic, on the right and Dolly Snelson Hogan. The photograph below shows the Hogans in Ireland.

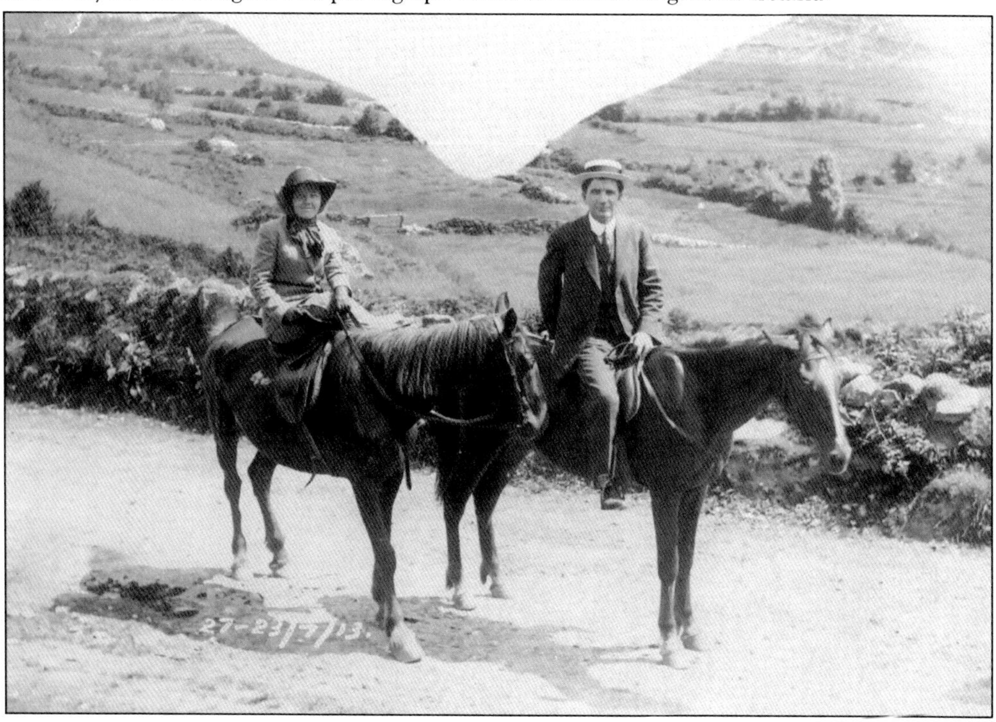

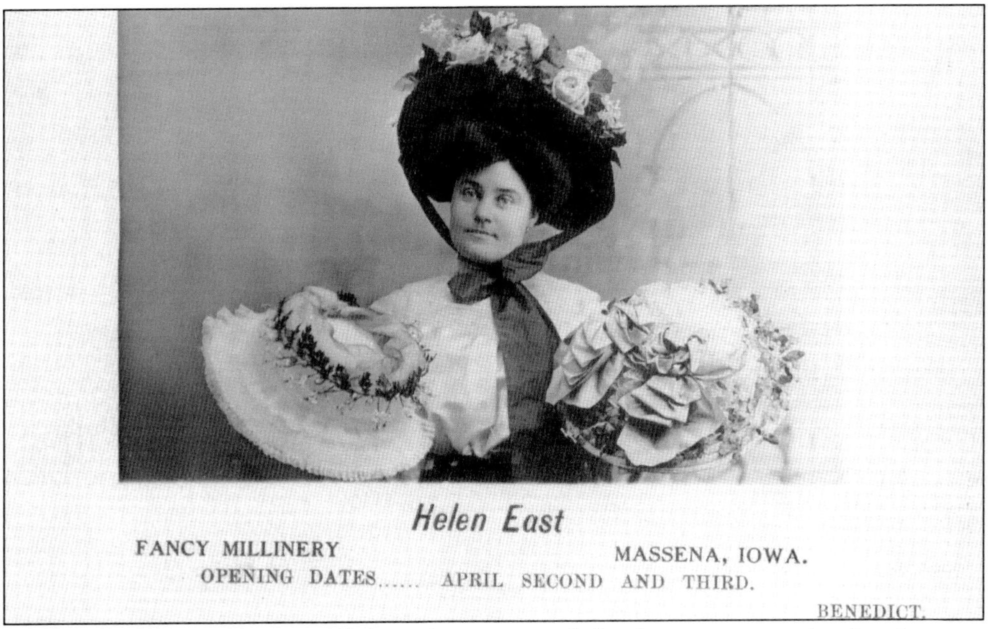

At the turn of the century, a well-dressed woman needed to have an appropriate hat for every occasion. Talented ladies opened up millinery shops and sold finished hats as well as ribbons, feathers, hat forms, net, silk flowers, and trims so a lady could make her own creation if she so desired. On this postcard, Helen East shows examples of her wares and advertises the opening of her shop in Massena.

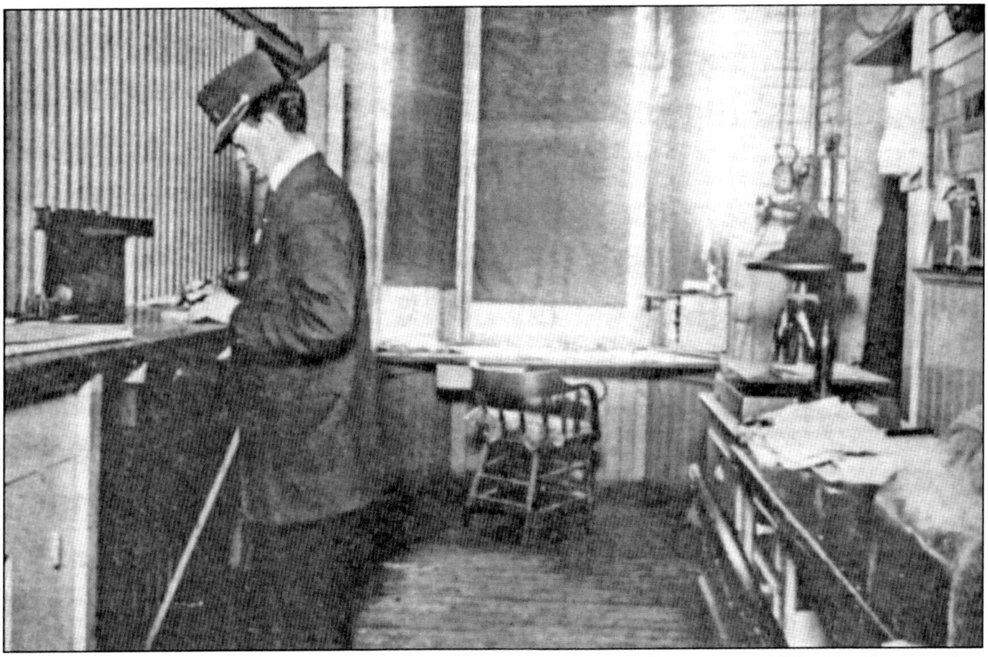

This photograph was taken inside the Massena Depot and shows Donald B. Hopkins in his official railroad attire. At the age of 12, he started working for the Chicago, Burlington & Quincy Railroad. He learned telegraphy and was eventually offered the position of depot agent that he held for several years.

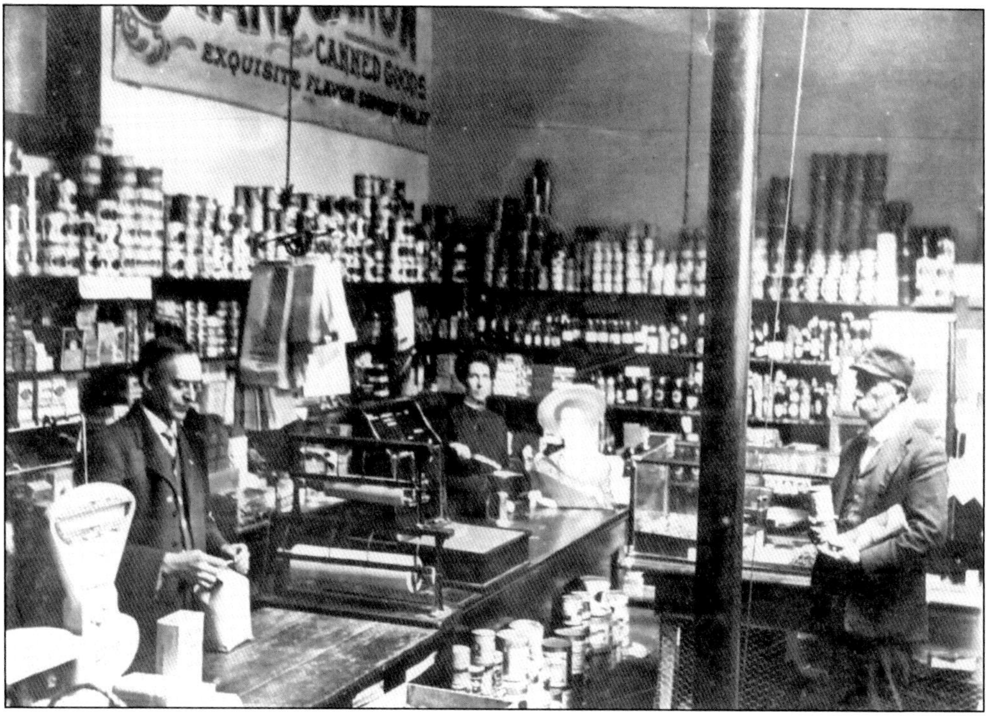

In 1905, Walter Slocum, the man behind the counter, established a general store in Massena. Since it was said to carry almost everything, it was called the "Ideal Store." Slocum was born February 24, 1874. As a young man, he entered into business with his father and, in 1905, moved his family to Massena. He was a progressive and tireless civic leader, enriching his community in numerous ways. He served on the school board and was president when the old wooden building was razed and a modern brick school constructed. He helped organize the annual semiprofessional baseball tournament and served on the homecoming and Chautauqua committees. Slocum also served on the local fair board. He enjoyed young people and helped organize summer recreational activities. The photograph below of Main Street in Massena shows Slocum's Ideal Store located in the center of the block.

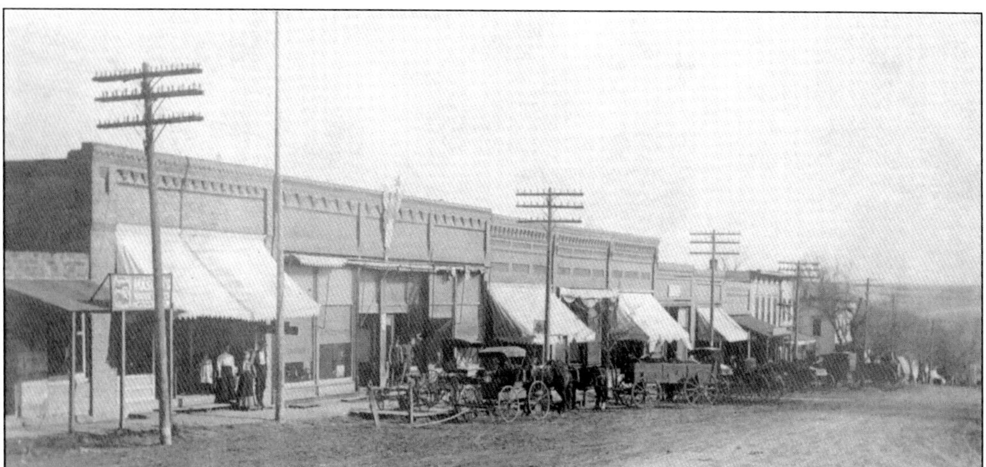

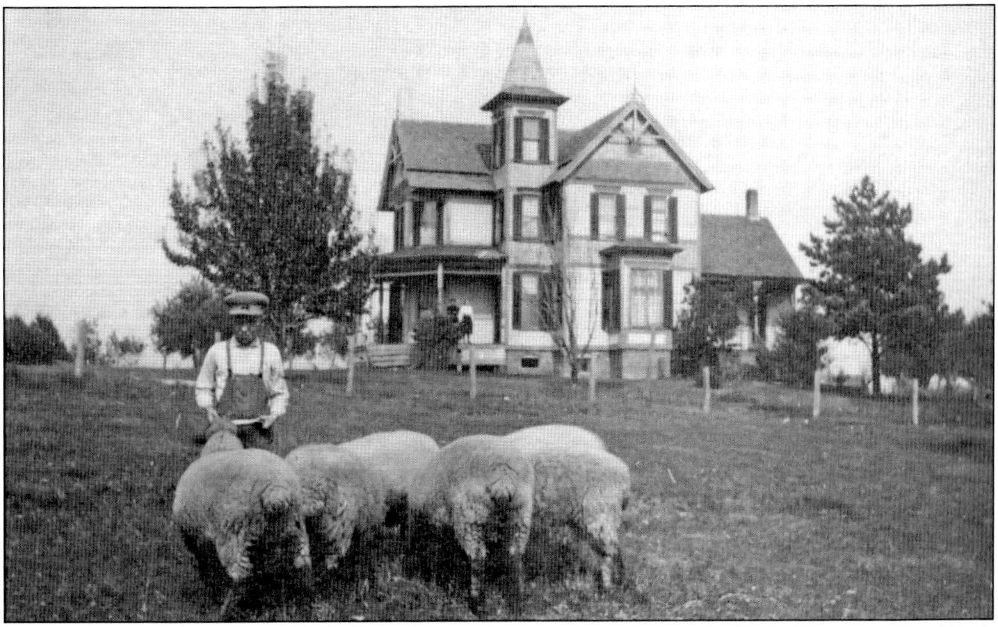

The photograph above shows the Slocum mansion. Walter Slocum purchased an entire city block that included a large house. There, he set up tennis and croquet courts where the youngsters of the town were always welcome. Slocum was a man of many interests and talents. He studied birds and flowers and had an extensive flower garden where he raised many irises and cared for 100 rosebushes. He was an avid collector of Native American artifacts. The photograph below shows Slocum holding a rare Indian fire pit. The collection can be seen in the Cass County Museum in Griswold, where many visitors now enjoy it. In keeping with his love of nature, Slocum requested that his tombstone be a large boulder. His request was honored, and the marker can be found at the Massena Township Cemetery.

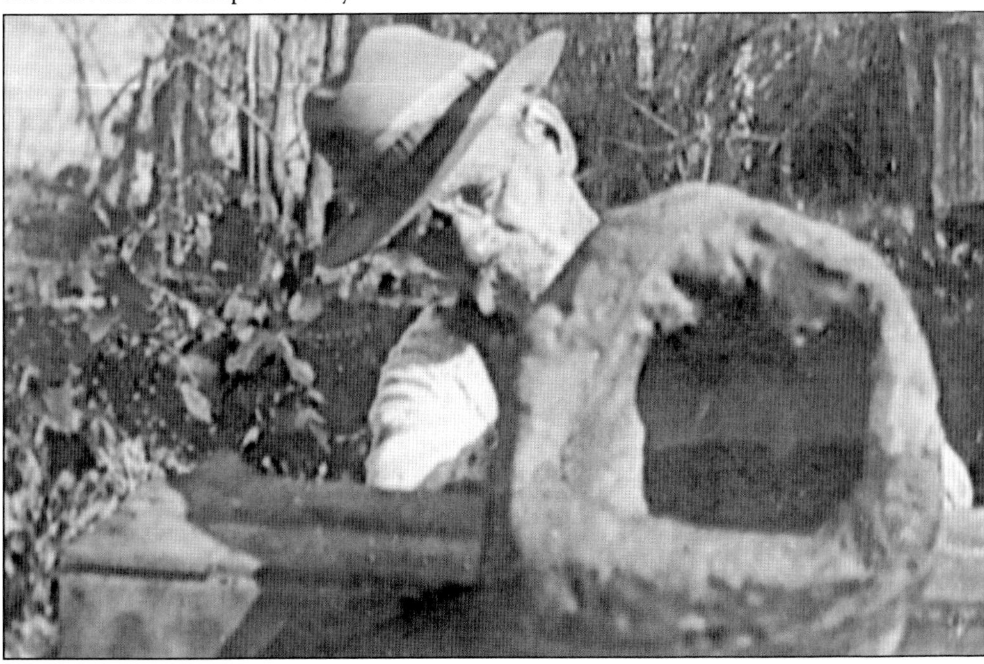

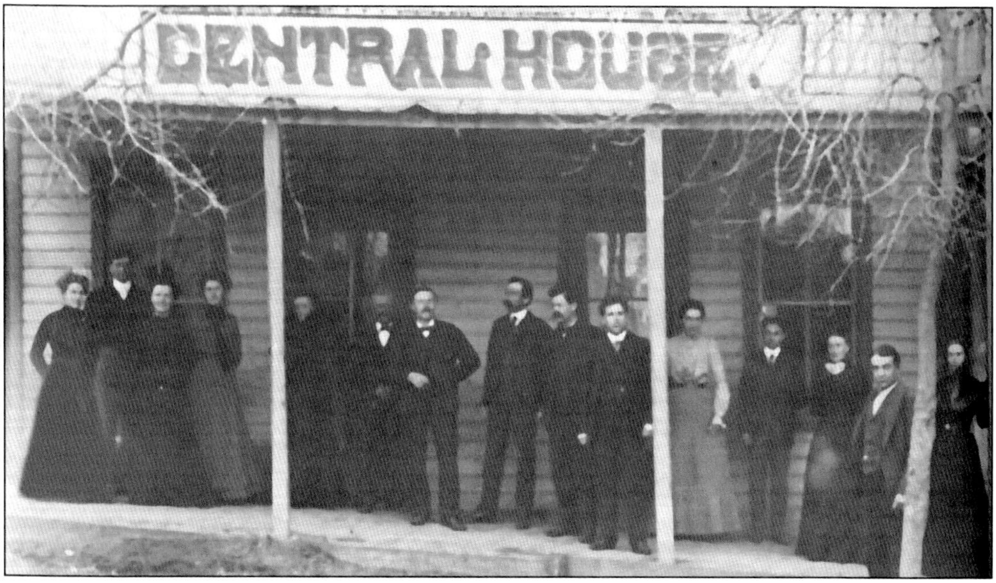

In 1887, William Holste erected this building in Massena, known later as the Bristow Hotel. Mabel Bristow operated the lodging for 47 years. She converted the first floor into a maternity ward and assisted in delivering 200 plus babies during the baby boom of the 1940s and did not lose one child or mother. Bristow did the chores, including meals and laundry. The mothers would stay six or seven days at a cost of $5 per day.

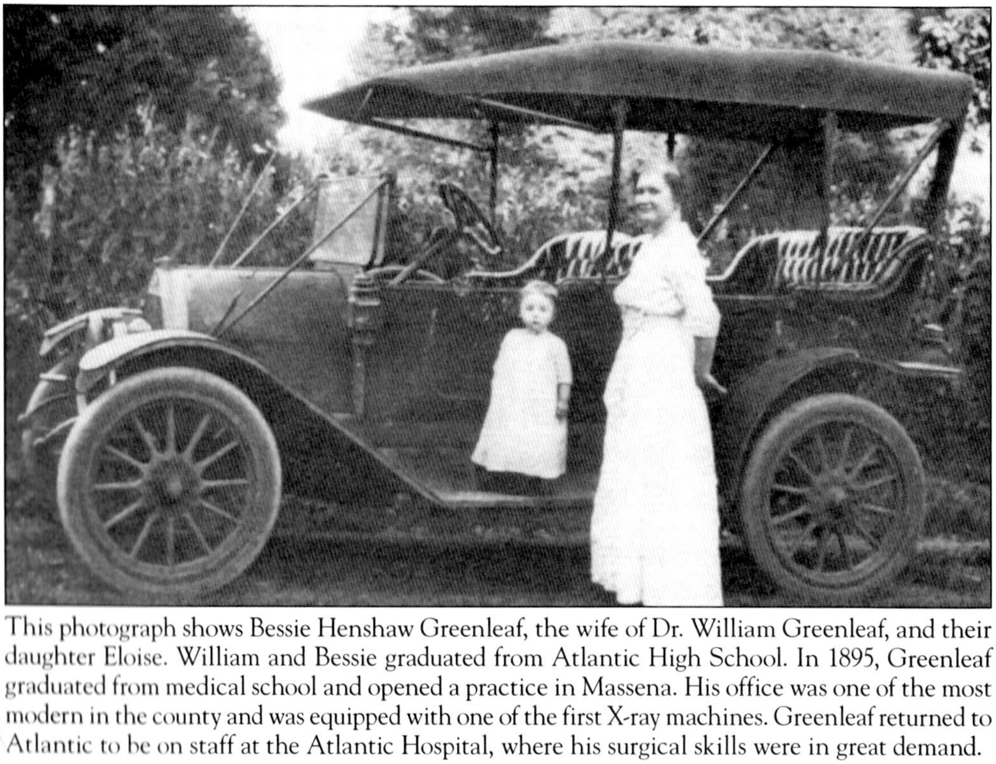

This photograph shows Bessie Henshaw Greenleaf, the wife of Dr. William Greenleaf, and their daughter Eloise. William and Bessie graduated from Atlantic High School. In 1895, Greenleaf graduated from medical school and opened a practice in Massena. His office was one of the most modern in the county and was equipped with one of the first X-ray machines. Greenleaf returned to Atlantic to be on staff at the Atlantic Hospital, where his surgical skills were in great demand.

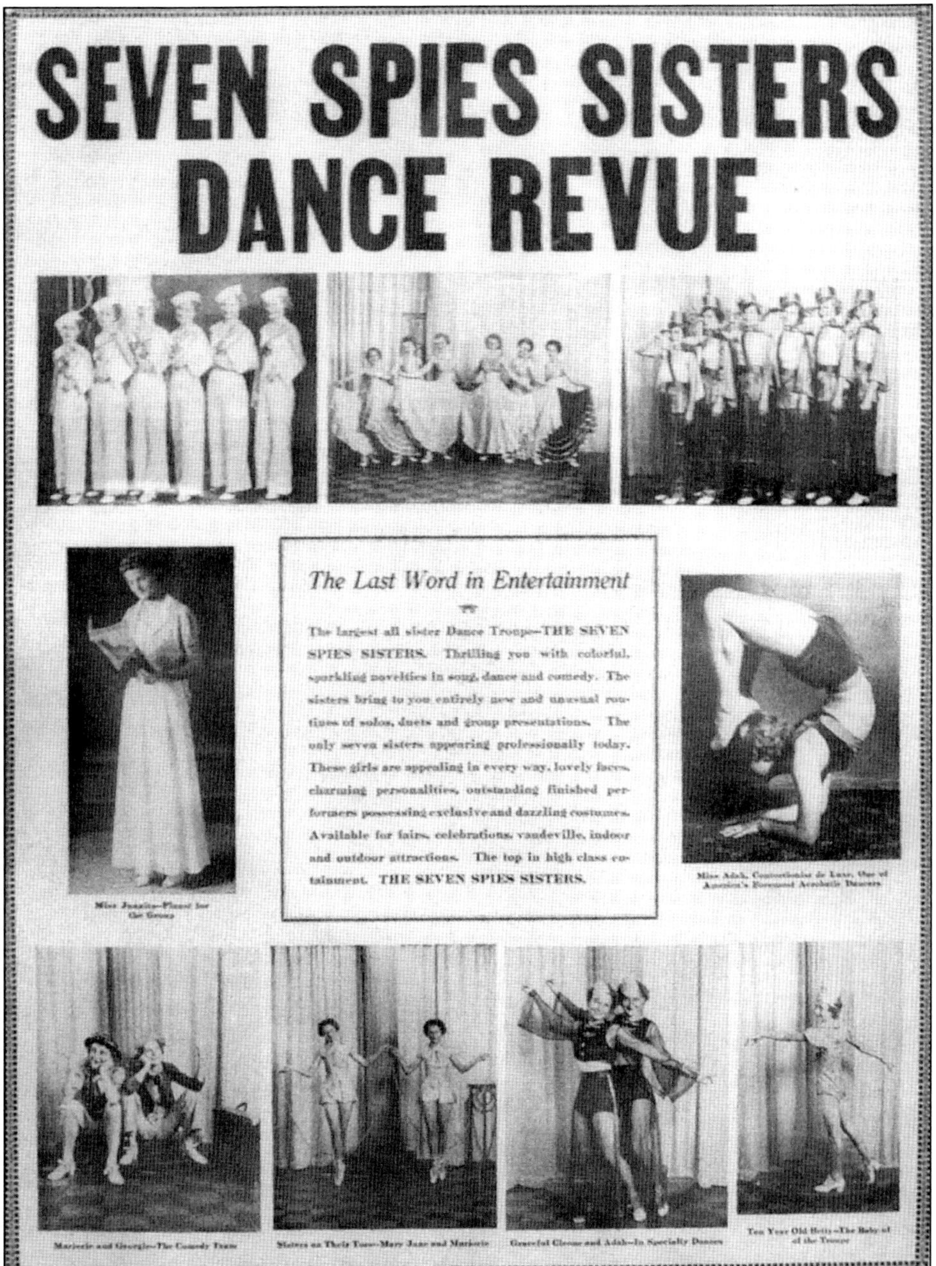

The Spies sisters grew up on a farm east of Massena in the 1930s. The seven sisters were known as the Spies's Dance Revue. The troupe included Cleone, Juanita, Ada, Mary Jane, Marjorie, Georgia, and Betty. Their first teacher was Eleanor Herbert of Atlantic, and they studied in Des Moines, under Rose Adler Pearlman, and in Chicago. With costumes designed and made by Louise Murray Bell of Atlantic, they were the largest all-sister dance revue in the country. They had top billing at county fairs, nightclubs, theaters, and state conventions and performed a variety of unusual acts, including rhythmical tap, soft-shoe, shawl, fan, and Oriental dances as well as acrobatic and comedy routines. In 1938, Florence Spies traveled to New York City to appear on the *We the People* radio show, where she told the story of her energetic and successful daughters.

Consistent with our mission to preserve history on a local level, this book was printed in South Carolina on American-made paper and manufactured entirely in the United States. Products carrying the accredited Forest Stewardship Council (FSC) label are printed on 100 percent FSC-certified paper.

MADE IN THE USA